FOR WORSE NEVER BETTER:

Diary of An Abused Wife and Escape to Freedom

By

Penelope Van Buskirk

NEW REVISIED EDITION

Dedication

To AVB and IVB, my exceptional daughters
who have emerged as successful young women.

Disclaimer

This book is a true story. All names have been
changed except mine to protect the innocent.

PROLOGUE

$\mathcal{I}$ believe an individual's life is like a honeycomb. Each relationship, each experience is analogous to a chamber in that comb. As we age, we build up more and more chambers. The hive gets larger. As changes overcome us and time passes, certain experiences, friendships, memories and relationships go dormant or die. It is only by examining the chambers of our honeycombs that we begin to understand ourselves.

FOR WORSE NEVER BETTER represents a personal honeycomb. Each page fills a psychological chamber. In order to move forward and build new chambers, I had to resurrect and examine those that had gone dormant, stagnant. Although scars will always remain, I had to acknowledge them to overcome the emotional toxicity.

To the millions of women trapped in similar situations, may you find the strength through your experiences, perhaps mirrored in this book, to examine your own chambers and in so doing, create a path for your escape to the peace and freedom you deserve.

CHAPTER I

September 1975
Manassas, VA

$\mathcal{D}$on's hand shot out and struck my face with such brutal force, I tumbled down the stairs like a rag doll, landing in the foyer in a heap. On the edge of consciousness, I could hear little voices calling out, filtering through the air like backyard wind chimes. "Mommy! Mommy!"

Those were the last words I heard before passing out.

When I opened my eyes, streams of morning light were filtering through the beveled glass in the front door, falling in splintered beams across the foyer. A pillow had been placed under my head and I was covered with an afghan. Don sat on the bottom step, crying.

"I'm sorry, Pen," he sniffled, stroking my forehead. "I didn't mean for this to happen. You must have lost your balance."

I stared at him in disbelief. His freshly shaven face glowed with a just washed blush. Dressed for work in a navy blue suit, this handsome six foot man with a Wall Street face, blond hair and piercing blue eyes bore little resemblance to the tyrant the night before.

He stood up and extended his hand. "Here sweetheart," he whispered. "Let me help you up."

As I struggled to a sitting position, pain forged through my left arm that had swelled through the night like rising dough, filling the once loose sleeve of my robe with tie-dyed looking flesh. Bruises covered both arms and every muscle in my body seemed to be on strike.

I awkwardly climbed to my feet. "Don't touch me," I hissed

His crying reached a sobbing stage as he put his arm around my waist and gently touched the injured arm. "I'm so sorry. I never meant to hurt you." He shook his head in shock as if he was touring a war zone. "God that looks bad. Our tempers will kill us both." He tried to guide me toward the living room. "Let's get you to the couch and I'll get an icepack. We've got to get you to a doctor."

Our tempers, I thought and pulled away from him, walked down the hall to the half bath and closed the door. The mirror reflected a pretty, petite face, now marred by large bruises on the forehead and left cheek. The once wispy bangs of frosted hair were matted in dried blood from a cut above the brow. I looked hollow, boneless, like I was wearing some grotesque Halloween mask.

He knocked on the bathroom door. "You okay, honey?"

Please God, I thought, make him leave like he always does. I flushed the toilet feeling like I had to justify what I had been doing and opened the door. The hall was empty. I walked into the kitchen, stood by the bay window and stared.

It was only September yet the leaves on the trees had started to turn gold and orange like miniature sunsets on branches, seasonably uncommon for Virginia. I gazed across the street at the Olympic sized community pool, now closed for the season, the decking stripped of the colorful tables, umbrellas and bikini clad mothers which had given it such life just the week before. The scene seemed to reflect the desolation and emptiness shrouding my soul. Silently stepping up behind me, Don rested his chin on my shoulder and nuzzled his face gently into my neck. His touch felt warm and I struggled to ignore the attentiveness I normally craved. "I promise Pen," he whispered, "this will never happen again."

I kept my back to him. "I want to believe you Don but. . ."

"But what?" his voice began to change from remorse to irritability.

I pivoted slowly and faced him. "I can't."

He turned away in silence. When again he faced me, his tears had vanished. Dr. Jekyll? Mr. Hyde? "It's over," he said too bluntly. "Let's just bury this and go on. And I promise on my dead father's grave this will never happen again."

This was such redundant, pitiable drama. *Bury this? Why? So he could bury ME next time?* I kept my back to him. "Just leave," I mumbled. "Just leave me alone."

Anxious to escape, he grabbed his briefcase from the hall just outside the kitchen. "Handle that arm," he ordered and slammed the front door.

The arm I could handle, I thought silently. *What I couldn't handle was him.*

Seconds later I heard the sound of relief as I heard him pull out of the drive. Anger and sadness nested side by side in my head like eggs in a crate as I forced myself to start breakfast. Seven years of marriage should have taught me never to argue with him when he was drinking. But I had done it again and the pain of humiliation now stung as viciously as if this had happened for the first time. I leaned against the refrigerator door and closed my eyes trying to reconstruct the events of last night. Too fresh to be forgotten, the ugly scene reeled forward without pause like the six o'clock news.

He had been sitting at his desk vacantly flicking a cigarette lighter when I walked into the bedroom. The scowl that distorted his face had been a warning; a facial lighthouse which signaled trouble in marital waters. But I had ignored it.

"Get over here," he shouted.

As angry with him as he was with me, I had dismissed his demand as the post drinking bullying it was, walked over to the closet, took off my uniform and grabbed my robe. I could feel him watching me, a glare which penetrated my mind, firing up disgust and fury I struggled to control.

"Did you hear me, bitch?" he yelled, his voice escalating in volume, his fingertips strumming the desk top.

I had heard that voice for years, a Commander in Chief of the Six Pack. "A deaf person could hear you," I said. "Quiet down. You'll wake the girls."

But his voice grew louder. "Get the hell over here, bitch!"

My back had stiffened in revulsion. "What is your big problem? It's after midnight, I just finished an eight hour shift playing ward secretary to a bunch of demanding doctors and I don't have the energy to fight."

"Fight?" he said with unwarranted laughter. "There won't be any fight as long as you do as you're told." He had held out the phone as if handing me a grenade. "You're calling the hospital and quitting your job. NOW!"

A knot rose in my throat. "What on earth are you talking about? You got me that job without me asking for it and now you want me to quit? Forget it. I've ruined enough job records at your demand." Breathing rapidly, I folded my arms in front of me, leaned against the wall next to his desk and closed my eyes. I should have anticipated this. All his promises to care for the children while I worked were only statements of convenience so I would take the job. Now, staying with the girls at night was disrupting his social life—the one he called business. Parenting had always been at his leisure and this was a variation of the same disparaging theme.

"I've ruined enough job records. . ." he mimicked in a nasal whine. "You ass, don't blame me for your failures. Hey, I got you that job because you wouldn't do it if your life depended on it, not to mention the fact that you wouldn't have lifted a finger to help with the finances around here—but I didn't plan on you starting up with your doctor friend." He paused, took a drag on a cigarette and jutting his jaw out further said, "If you think I'm going to babysit while my wife screws around at night with some over-educated stud you're dumber that I thought."

I pushed myself away from the wall. Tears spilled down my cheeks. "That's a lie, "I said. "When have I ever fooled around with anyone? You never would have known about my problems with this womanizing doctor if I hadn't told you. . .you who was going to take care of the situation, or don't you remember? A decent husband would have protected his wife against some pervert instead of creating something that isn't there. So knock it off!!!"

The veins in his temples danced like greenish-blue worms as he spoke. "You're quitting. Do you understand me?" Waving the phone in one hand and his lighter in the other he underscored the demand. "Get over here and call or I'll burn this place to the ground with you in it."

Confusing bravery with intolerance, I tested the limits of the inebriated threat with a belligerent silence. Suddenly he whirled around in the chair, flipped back the top of his lighter and held the flame against the sill-length hem of the drape. Within seconds fire began to inch up the old green fabric.

"Are you crazy?" I screamed. Lunging forward, I tried to knock the lighter from his hand. He shoved me back with his elbow.

"Quit or burn!" he yelled, his teeth clenched in a menacing growl. "Your call!"

I ran into the bathroom, filled the baby's potty with water, dashed back and threw it on the drapes while Don just sat there. Back and forth I ran in frenzy like a wind-up toy out of control, dousing the flames. When the fire was extinguished, I slumped down on the bed and peered at the charred window covering, now hanging in ragged points.

"Call and quit, god dam you!"

"No! I yelled. "And this has gone far enough." I grabbed a pillow from the bed and ran toward the bedroom door.

Don tore the phone out of the wall and hurled it across the room. I ducked and ran out of the bedroom. The phone hit the door, the bells ringing on impact.

He stormed after me. At the top of the stairs he grabbed my shoulder, spun me around, clamped one hand around the top of my arm and raised the other ready to strike. "You know better than to defy me. Are you going to quit or do you need more convincing?"

Now in the morning light, I looked down at my arm. *Convincing? Of what? How powerless I was?* I wanted to scream at the top of my lungs. I HATE THIS MAN! Only the sound of Stephanie's footsteps on the stairs made me stop. I wiped my face with my hand, pulled the sleeve of the robe down over my arm and masked the emotional torment with a smile. I couldn't let her see this or hear my voice crack with instability. She was still a baby, a little boat moored to me for security. I didn't want to frighten her. Keeping my back turned, I glanced over my shoulder.

"Good morning, honey. Sleep well?"

Stephie stood in the doorway of the kitchen dressed in a ruffled little nightgown which hung on her thin waifish body, the hem just grazing the tops of her feet. She was a sunny five-year-old with long, light blond hair, a pixie face and crystal blue eyes like her daddy.

Still sleepy-eyed, she walked over to the table and struggled to pull out a kitchen chair in front of the window. "Nope," she said. "I had some real bad dreams, Mommy."

I shuddered inside, poured her a bowl of cereal and, standing behind her chair out of view, nervously set it on the table. "What kind of dreams, sweetie? The dragon kind?"

Taking a bite, she sighed. "Nope, not real dragons. I dreamed 'bout you and daddy."

Her words detonated inside me. She didn't deserve this. Naiveté protected her for now but what about next time? Eventually she would come to know the difference between a bad dream and a violent father.

I stood behind her and kissed the top of her head, groping for words to allay her fears. "Isn't it wonderful that bad dreams seem to go away when the sun comes up?"

"Guess so," she answered, swallowing my answer and some cereal in the same gulp.

"Now, why don't you finish your breakfast while I go upstairs and get your sister out of bed. Okay?"

She stood up in her chair for our ritual morning hug. I quaked inside because she had not seen my face. Affection was necessary. She needed reassurance. As she turned around the corners of her mouth curled downward if pulled by gravity.

"Mommy," she said in a voice of shock. "You have boo-boo's all over, lots of them."

I held her tightly. What could I tell her? How would I explain? My voice trembled as I spoke.

"Mommy tripped and fell down the stairs, honey." While I stood there floundering, she pulled away from me. Her eyes widened in alarm.

"Did you forget to hold onto the banister?" she asked.

The simplicity of childhood thinking was a gift given at the right time. "You're right." I giggled. "Now can you be a big girl and help me?"

Her eyes sparkled like blue glass in sunlight. "Big girl?" The term delighted her. "Sure," she said. "Can I do dishes?"

I smiled. "We'll see, honey." Her idea of dishes was playing in soap and water in the sink, baptizing counters and floors in a sudsy mess. "But for now, finish your breakfast so you won't be late for school while I get Bridget up. Okay?"

Climbing the stairs was as emotionally draining as it was physical. Movement of my arm sent pain spiking through my body. But when I reached the top landing and heard Bridget playing in her crib I was rewarded.

"Good morning baby doll," I said opening the door. She looked up at me with chocolate brown eyes. Curly light brown hair hung in disturbed little ringlets around her face like she has spent the night tumbling in a clothes dryer. Unlike her sister, Bridget was a chubby baby with engaging dimples framing each smile like quotation marks. And smile she did.

I strained to lift her out of the crib with my right arm. Luckily she had learned to walk at eighteen months but still needed diapers at night. Cooperative by nature, she laid down on the floor while I cleaned her up. Such a small, helpless little person, I thought, and then remembered this little being last night, who through parental neglect, had fallen asleep in the foyer while her father sat drinking and laughing in the living room with some man I'd never met before. His answer to my complaint had been stiff. "Don't lecture me on parenting, Penelope. Let them stay. Maybe backaches will teach them not to climb out of bed."

Raising his beer can he had toasted his already-toasted friend. "Here's to parenting."

The sound of the doorbell jarred me back to the present. I heard the shuffle of little feet as Stephie raced to answer it. "Mom," she called up the stairs. "It's Mrs. G."

My heart beat rapidly. Fears swirled like a kaleidoscope in my head. *No one could know about this. . .what could I say. . .this is a good neighborhood. . .expensive townhouses. . .things like this didn't happen here. . .they liked me. . .they liked Don. . .I could never stay here if anyone found out.*

My teeth chattered as I took Bridget's hand and raced into my bathroom. I dabbed some makeup on the facial marks but they still showed. Dear God, I whispered, help me. I tugged the sleeve of my robe down as far as it would go, took a deep breath and started down the stairs, allowing Bridget's chubby little legs to cope with each step and delay the confrontation.

"Late start today," I said, stepping into the foyer. "We had a bit of an accident." *Yes, that's good. Accident, we all have them.*

Ruthie's normally radiant smile was quickly eclipsed by a frown. A slight woman, she was about fifteen years my senior with a plain Midwestern face that harvested honesty and warmth. Her clothes bore the mark of a perfectionist; creased slacks, starched blouse. Her innocent light brown hair curled under ever so slightly just below her cheeks. She was the ideal next door neighbor, always there when I needed her and graciously stayed away when I didn't. This morning she was given visual reason to stay.

"How did you get those bruises on your face?" she asked in almost a whisper, her eyes fixed in a stare.

Be casual, I told myself. *Aloof*. "Oh, you know me, Ruthie. Clumsy. I tripped on the top step this morning and pulled a Scarlet O'Hara into the foyer." I followed her eyes as she stared at my arm. Acknowledging her visual interest, I calmly said, "I think it's broken."

I watched her face, her mouth drawn into an O. "What a mess," she said shaking her head in a manner that suggested she was questioning my veracity.

"Mommy didn't hold on to the banister," Stephie blurted out.

Ruthie forced a smile and put her arm around Stephanie in a motherly hug. "She sure didn't princess."

Her voice was strained. We were both uncomfortable. She was married to a caring man who loved her unconditionally. I knew I could never make her understand how trapped I was by the love I have for my husband, how I craved his love and kindness, afraid to walk out for fear of losing the good man he could be and hating him all at the same time.

Ruthie directed her attention to the children. "Can 'Aunt' Ruthie get you dressed?"

They welcomed the idea and followed her up the stairs. In the two years we had lived in our adjoining townhomes, Ruthie had always come to the rescue for the predictable assortment of domestic happenstances. With her children away at college, she had time to rock my children to sleep when they were ill and played with them for hours when I needed a break. But she had never seen anything like this. Then again, the punches suffered in the past were on parts of the body no one could see.

I watched her walk up the stairs, a woman driven by love. *She won't understand,* I thought to myself. *No one will.*

She dressed them, drove Stephie to kindergarten as she did each morning, then returned, and offered to take me to the emergency room.

As we waited for the doctor, awkward silence gave way to apprehension as Ruthie reached over a sleeping Bridget in her arms, and took my hand in hers. "I know it is none of my business," she whispered, "but did you really trip down the stairs?"

This was a nightmare. "Of course I did," I said too defensively.

She lowered her head so all I could see was the top of her shiny brown hair. "Ross and I heard screaming last night," she said. She raised her head slowly and looked me straight in the eye. "And we heard thumping noises and screams coming from your house."

The terror of truth seeped through me as I struggled to keep my voice calm. "Oh," I said, flipping through a stale magazine. "Don and his loud television. I worked last night so I wasn't around to police the volume. Must have been one of those terrible murder mysteries he watches."

I turned my head just enough to watch her out of the corner of my eye. Ruthie's face, though barren of makeup, had a natural, pure beauty. Heat rose in my cheeks. Her look said, *I know what happened to you. Why won't you tell me the truth?*

In the examining room a young doctor pulled back the cubicle curtain and popped the X-ray up on a lighted panel. "Two bad breaks here," he said.

I was losing my mind. Why did I suddenly feel such a macabre sense of exhilaration?

"How did this happen?" he asked. I stared at his face and was relieved I had never seen him before during my shifts at the hospital. I felt transparent as glass but had rehearsed my no-fault version of the accident so much in my head, the delivery was nonchalant.

"I'm clumsy. Tripped on my robe last night and went flying." I inhaled deeply and ended my explanation with a sigh of boredom. Lurking behind my acting, the other part of me wanted to *scream HE DID IT, my egregiously abusive husband.* But a breastplate of pride kept me quiet as I massaged my conscience with self-protecting thoughts. Don did not really mean to hurt me. He had cried this morning. He offered to help me. The anger just got out of hand because I encouraged a drunken man. This would be the last time. He promised.

When the cast was applied I was almost jubilant. Such a perfect pity prop. Guaranteed Don would cry, feel like the brut he could be. He would wait on me as a servant and bestow unequaled kindness. And in all the confusion I would forgive him and believe his promises.

I walked through the hospital corridors carefully trying to avoid seeing anyone I worked with and found Ruthie sitting on the floor in the waiting room, building blocks with Bridget. Wordlessly, she stood, gave me a quick hug, patted my cheek and we walked to her car in silence.

Ruthie put the key in the ignition then paused. "Could we pray for a moment?"

Belief in God was important to me but I couldn't pretend to be observant of the rules of Christianity, especially in public. Although silently rebellious, I was too weak to deny her request and awkwardly bowed my head.

"Dear God, please give Penne the strength to handle what she must and face the truth of her situation. And let her feel your love."

Her words triggered an avalanche of tears in us both. Emotions always betrayed me. "I'm your friend," she said softly. "I'll help you in any way I can."

I felt worthless. A liar exposed. I didn't want her to hate Don, or think that I was a fool or that I really didn't have any place to go but home to my parents. I hung my head. My bravado was gone. "You won't understand," I said.

She squeezed my hand. "Just let me try," she answered.

Later that afternoon I called my mother and made arrangements, ignoring her questions with I'll-tell-you-later responses, sparing us both the contemptible details. Her voice betrayed the strength she was trying to show. I felt her anger, fear. Once again, I was putting her through hell.

As I closed the trunk of my car, a new resentment crept over me, a resentment borne more of my own weakness than Don's brutality. My only option was to return to my parents; parents who despite their love for their five children had criticized most everything I had ever done. I spent seven years defending my choice of a husband, and now, by my return, I was admitting they were right.

My last call was to the hospital. I couldn't leave Virginia with my job hanging. I needed people to like me, to know I was loyal and responsible. I requested a leave of absence from the Nursing Supervisor who quipped, "Understand you had quite a fall."

Bad news traveled too fast. "I've always been accident prone," I said, keeping my voice light. "Guess I better consider moving to a single story house."

"Moving wouldn't be a bad idea," she said softly. "Neither would single."

My stomach flipped and I issued a hasty farewell knowing I had sealed all avenues of backing down.

By four o'clock I was ready to leave. Suddenly the door bell and the phone rang at the same time. Ruthie had not left my side all afternoon.

"Could you get the door, Ruthie? I'll get the phone." I knew it was Don and couldn't let her know how much I really wanted to talk to him, craving his "poor baby" response when I told him the damage. But I also knew just hearing his voice would weaken my determination. With Ruthie out of range, I answered the phone in the most cowardly way possible.

I unplugged it.

Ruthie walked back into the kitchen peering from behind a large bouquet of roses. "Beautiful, aren't they?"

The sweet I'm-sorry-fragrance quickly permeated the room. I could feel Ruthie's eyes on me as I removed the card and was torn between irritability that she was hovering over me yet thankful for her presence.

Forgive me Penne-Roo. They were the same words, different day. Should I also forgive the fact that he had spent fifty dollars we didn't have to waste?

Money! Seized by yet a new panic, I turned my purse upside down and rummaged through the contents.

"What are you looking for?" Ruthie asked.

"My checkbook. I just had it last night. It's gone!"

Ruthie pressed bills in my hand. "This looks like a lot "she said. "But it's not. You'll need to buy gas and food. This should cover it."

I kissed her cheek and she put her arm around my shoulder. "I know you're scared," she whispered. "But you have to do this. Focus on your needs for a change. Marriage does not grant him a license for abuse."

There it was—a word as unbidden as it is unwanted. Abuse. It sounded so criminal. Don? Was he really a criminal? The police didn't think so the only time I called them several years before. Even though blood was pouring out of my nose, the officer said he could do nothing unless he actually saw it happen.

A forked feeling washed over me as I got behind the wheel. It was the first time I had ever shared such secrets and the sharing had helped keep me level. But now someone knew what went on in our house, and if he *ever found out?????* I could never return.

"Where are we going Mommy?" whined Stephie.

"We're going to see Grandpa Whiskers and Grandma! Isn't that exciting?"

"Yes. But will I be back for school tomorrow?"

Tears welled up in my eyes as I pulled away. My heart was pounding like an aortic migraine. Damn that man. Why did he have to punish his children this way? Choices. I was straddling the fence of indecision rocking precariously from one side to the other until I turned around and looked at my children. The decision was made. He didn't deserve a family. Maybe an empty house would force him to change, make him miss us and resurrect the kind man I know he could be. He would be shocked. I had never left before. But it was worth a try. He would know now. I would never tolerate his abuse again.

I had scribbled a note on the back of the "I'm sorry" floral card: *"The children and I have gone to stay with my parents. When and if you feel you can control your temper, call me. Until then, I leave you with your conscience. Only YOU can change what is wrong."*

My old black Chrysler lumbered along rural route 15 at a steady pace, its elephant size and impoverished appearance hidden from view by night. It said *used forever* as it groaned and I alternated my focus between the ribbon of white highway line in my headlights to the rearview mirror, feeling edgy, wondering if escaped convicts felt such fear. I glanced at my watch. Eight-fifteen and we still had hours to go. I could hear sniffling from the backseat and knew Stephie was crying.

"What's wrong honey?"

"I don't want to go away," she sniffled. "I want to stay home and go to school with my friends."

"We aren't going away forever, sweetie. Just for a little while. And I have lots of school work for you from Mrs. Grant so you will not miss any of that. Besides, don't you want to see Grandpa and Grandma? They sure want to see you."

"Yes, but I want them to come to my house."

I knew what she meant. Grandma's house meant no snacks between meals, strict bedtimes and no television. They adored their grandchildren but loved them all with a suffocating rigidity.

"Try and sleep, sweetheart. It will be way past your bedtime before we get there."

Suddenly blinding headlights poured through the rear window. I strained to see what make car was riding my bumper but couldn't. A horn blared behind me. Beads of perspiration oozed off my forehead as if I'd sprung a leak. It was a dark stretch of highway; a two lane road as empty as a cemetery and it was not safe to pull off the road.

The obnoxious flashing of high beams, low beams, further eroded my concentration. I accelerated. Sixty-five, then seventy. But the old car rattled in protest while the car behind me kept pace. I knew there was an exit within the next few miles. There was a truck stop. I'd seen it before.

I approached the exit without slowing down or signaling but the car stayed on my bumper. I parked between two eighteen wheelers under a lighted canopy by the cashier's booth, turned off the ignition and locked the doors.

Within minutes Don was tapping on my window. His face was red, eyes puffy. He didn't smile nor frown but stared. Impatient, he unlocked the door with his key. "Can we talk?" he whispered?" His enervating calm was chilling, like a prelude to detonation.

I climbed out of the car, gently closed the door and faced him with a scowl. He was disheveled and wreaked of alcohol. "Why are you doing this?" His eyes dropped to the cast. "God, Pen, I didn't mean to hurt you. But nothing can be solved by running away." He nervously shifted his weight from left foot to right then back. "So I made a mistake. But I don't want to live without you." He raised his hand in a mock Boy Scout salute. "I'll make it up to you, promise. Just come home."

I stared into his bloodshot eyes and watched his hands tremble as he reached inside his suit coat for a cigarette. Leaning against the car in silence, I willed myself to be strong and folded my arms in defiance. "Are you really sorry Don or are you just trying to save face as usual?"

Tears roll unabated down his cheeks. He reached for my arm. "What will it take for you to come back?" he whined in a slurred speech. "You name it, I'll do it."

"What will it take?" I quizzed. I gazed beyond him searching for courage. "There was a time when you really loved me. You were the first person in my life who ever gave me credit for being intelligent. We complimented each other and laughed. Affection glued us to each other and you were my hero."

Hero. My mental projector jammed on the word as the past collided with the present, and like oil and vinegar refused to mix. Did heroes hurt their wives?

He plunged his hands deep into his pockets. "So I'm not your hero anymore, is that it? What do you want me to do? Wear my old Army uniform or my bronze star?"

"That bond we had has shifted. I have become your enemy, an albatross to your lifestyle. You've sapped my ambition and will and. . ."

"And I love you, Pen," he said softly. "We can't resolve this by separating. Besides, you are injured. You shouldn't be driving. You belong with me where I can take care of you. Not with your parents. Staying with those self-righteous bible bores is not going to improve the situation." He cleared his throat and a new attitude surfaced. "So stop this foolishness and go home. Now." He took a step closer, shaking his finger in my face. "Who's been talking to you? Someone is poisoning your mind. You aren't blameless. You create the anger. But I haven't run away from you now, have I? Climb out of your sandbox and try being an adult."

I turned and looked into the car. My babies were still sleeping. They were such beautiful little girls. I then faced him and held up the casted arm. "Adults don't settle differences by breaking bones. They don't burn drapes and subject innocent children to abuse. Do you realize in the few minutes we've been standing here, you've never once apologized for last night?"

He dropped his cigarette on the asphalt and stomped on it like he was trying to kill a roach. "Quit being so melodramatic. I said I was sorry this morning. How many times do you need to hear it?"

I inhaled deeply. "Hear it? I want to SEE IT. I want to believe it and trust you again. But I won't compromise myself or the children anymore."

He swaggered back to his car and then paused. "You'll come back," he said in a menacing voice. "I rescued you from that stifling Baptist prison seven years ago. You'll be back. I'll damn well make sure of it!"

CHAPTER 2

Easton, Pennsylvania

*a*fter hours of driving, I could see my parent's monolithic home rising out of a rural valley on a street named Mud Run. The white house seemed to erupt from the valley floor. Nestled amid a landscape of mammoth pine trees, the six stories jutted out at peculiar angles as if the architect had developed Alzheimer's during construction. Exterior lights flooded the grounds as I turned off the main road, drove down the graveled drive, crossed over the small bridge spanning a tributary stream to a pond on the other side and parked. There was no need to signal my arrival.

My parents immediately emerged through the ground floor doors which lead to a guest apartment at the base of the house. I could see the torment on mothers' face as my six foot father loomed behind her, his perfectly trimmed white beard framing an imperious face.

Their expressions alone made me want to turn around and go anywhere but here.

Dressed in a flannel shirt and jeans, Dad opened my door. "Well, Penny cat," he whispered. "You have fled from harm." Bile flooded my stomach as he glanced into the back seat where the children were sleeping soundly. "Your mom and I will carry the little ones into the house and I'll come back to unload the rest."

I slowly got out of the car and put my good arm around his neck. He returned my affection with a warm but controlled hug. My stout little mother had worry engraved on her face but she was more lovable as she embraced me with a gentle sincerity. "Hello honey," she said softly. "So relieved you are here."

The children easily fell asleep in the second story nursery. Mom was in the kitchen, her favorite nitch. The galley kitchen was an odd design for such a large house but tastefully appointed with Ethan Allen furnishings. She had brewed a pot of tea and fresh cookies graced the center of the small table. And where was my father? He was probably in his library on the sixth floor or the large master bedroom on the third floor? He had disappeared for the moment.

I had never lived in this house. They had sold our home in New Jersey shortly after I was married and moved to the country for the sake of my younger brothers' love of nature. Daniel Boone would have been envious of the fifteen acres of lush forest surrounding the house.

"Sit down, honey." Mom stared at me through teary eyes. "So tell me what happened." I gazed at her soft face, framed by white lightly permed hair. A soft bang covered her widow's peak. And large, light framed glasses completed her classic grandmother image.

I recited the terror in Virginia and watched her eyes tear. "That's it in the proverbial nutshell. Now, and I know you disapprove, I need to go outside and have a cigarette."

I heard footsteps behind me. "You need to stop, now." a holier-than-thou voice said. "It will kill you and then your children will be parentless asthmatics."

Dad. I pushed my chair back and stood. "You're right, but not now. I've given up enough for one day. So if you'll excuse me, I'll be right back."

As I moved toward the back door he added, "Do not expect me to pay for that addiction while you are under my roof. Have I made myself clear?"

'*I, I, Captain,*' was on the tip of my tongue but I swallowed the thought. His roof. Don's roof. Would I ever live under my OWN ROOF with my own rules? I resisted the urge to slam the door behind me, walked outside, inhaled the aroma of the brisk autumn air, and lit up.

The walls were thin. I could hear my father sternly preaching to my mother. "Mildred, before we do anything, I am calling Don. All stories have two sides. I will need to hear his."

Mom was uncommonly bold. Both parents were born in the south, where a wife was expected to be subservient to her spouse. But this night she took a stand.

"No, Nathan, not yet. Penne (I spell it with an e at the end so I wouldn't feel like the lowest denomination of coin). She needs peace. The children must be comforted and protected from any conversations about this. And you need to prepare for your business trip."

My father was a world renowned engineer in the lighting industry. His picture was in my science book in seventh grade; articles appeared in the *New York Times.* And as I continued to eavesdrop, I was elated to hear that he was scheduled to leave in two days! A minor serenity smoothed the edges of my emotional fragility. With the paternal Moses away from the mount, Mom and I might reach some resolve to my marital holocaust.

Sleep was impossible that night. I had the room next to the nursery and could hear the gentle breathing of my children and rustling of leaves outside my window. It was almost four in the morning before I dozed off and after nine when my throbbing arm robbed me of further rest. Momentary disorientation had me scanning the unfamiliar room before I remembered where I was. Digging through my suitcase I found a robe and socks and quickly headed downstairs with a bottle of pain killers and pack of cigarettes tucked in my pocket. I could hear the children's laughter and was relieved they were bonding with their grandparents.

"Grandpa Whiskers?" It was Stephie's voice. I stood out of view of the kitchen door to enjoy the banter.

"Yes, wee one?" His voice was so soft and engaging I felt relieved.

"Why do you let that snowy hair grow on your face?"

Dad and Mom giggled. "Oh, little granddaughter, don't you like my beard?"

I heard Stephie slurping her cereal. "Nope," she said. "It scratches my face when you hug me. It could make me bleed like mommy's face so could you cut it off until I go back to my house tomorrow?"

That was my cue to make an appearance before Grandpa forgot she was a little girl who had no concept of time.

"Good morning everyone," I said as I bent down, kissed Stephie and walked around to Bridget who was in the high chair, covered with bits of oatmeal. She reached up for a hug and we nuzzled each other. I kissed Mom and Dad and sat down.

"Thanks for taking care of the girls. What time did they get up?"

Mom rose from her chair. "About seven, but we wanted you to sleep in. How's the arm?"

"Painful. After I eat something I can take the pain pills." Seated to my left, Dad patted my hand. "Which bones are broken?"

"I don't remember, Dad. I was too frazzled and embarrassed. I know that there are two breaks. Cast will be on for six weeks. But the ER papers are in my purse. I'll look it up later."

As Dad started to respond, Stephie chirped, "Mommy didn't hold on to the banister, and Daddy yelled at her at night. I heard him. He woke me up." Biting my bottom lip, I patted her hand. "If you're finished eating sweetheart, why don't you go up to the bedroom and put on some warm clothes. Bridget and I will be up in just a minute. Okay?"

"Can grandma help me?" The twinkle in Mom's eyes was heartwarming. Delighted to be alone with her grandmother, Stephie climbed off her chair, held Mom's hand and skipped out of the kitchen chattering about anything and everything.

Bridget squirmed in her highchair, arms stretched over her head, signaling her wish to follow Stephie. I held her chubby little hands. "You finished baby girl? Want to get dressed?" I washed her face and hands, unfastened the highchair tray and was about to lift her out when Dad offered.

"Let me get her," he said. "You shouldn't be lifting the children with that arm." Warmed by his concern, I acquiesced. He gently picked her up, held her in his arms and smiled. Fixated with his face, she stared with total concentration then cautiously touched his beard. "Ow!" she said, and pulled her hand back.

Dad laughed and began chanting a rhyme I remembered from childhood. "*Fuzzy, Wuzzy was a bear but Fuzzy Wuzzy had no hair. So Fuzzy Wuzzy wasn't fuzzy, was he?*" Bridget cocked her head in confusion spawning another laugh from Dad. The heartwarming exchange was a salve for my charred self-esteem.

The phone rang just as they were leaving the kitchen. Dad picked up on the second ring. "Hello? Well good morning, Don. Thanks for returning my call. I have your sweet little Bridget in my arms and we are on our way up to the nursery. Can I call you right back? Are you at home? Okay, give me a few minutes." Deliberately avoiding me, he walked out.

I froze. Anger. Panic. I wanted a cigarette but headed up to the nursery where I hoped I could overhear Dad's conversation.

Mom was just finishing with Bridget. She turned around and read my expression. "Honey," she whispered. "I can see the panic on your face. Your father is only trying to help. Take deep breaths."

"Help? I can't believe he called him," I snapped. "Who in the hell does he think he is? Cavorting with the enemy? He never even listened to your advice not to call. Arrogant man!"

"Don't talk like that, especially in front of the babies."

"It's better than the alternative. I could slap him for consorting with the enemy."

"Penne!" she cautioned in a stern whisper. "Stop talking like that. He is your father."

Father? I silently seethed. *Could he be Himmler's cousin?*

Stephie tugged on my robe. "Mommy, don't be mean to my Grandma."

I hugged her, ashamed of what I was putting them through. Again. "I'm sorry, baby. I love Grandma too."

"Mom, can I impose on you again for about thirty minutes? I want to go upstairs and hear about the conversation Dad had with Don."

"Of course. But try to maintain your cool."

The door to Dads' office was closed. I knocked gently.

"Come in," he said, his voice sounding a bit strained.

He was seated at his island of a desk, his back turned toward the door. Every wall was a bookcase---

with almost seventy-five percent of his volumes on Theology-----the rest, technical journals. Several over-stuffed leather chairs dominated one corner of the room as if he was planning a Summit conference between world powers. Strains of Bach's Brandenburg Concerto played softly in the background.

He slowly swiveled his chair around, looked up and invited me to be seated as if I were being interviewed for a job.

I waited for him to speak, but his silence made me uneasy so I started. "Well, what did that abusive man I call a husband have to say?"

He cleared his throat. "We have much to discuss before addressing the alleged abuse," he said sternly.

I squirmed in the chair then pushed my casted arm toward him. "Alleged abuse? Like what?" I snapped.

"We can begin with your fondness for other men." His eyes were piercing, unrelenting.

I quivered inside. "Excuse me? Where is this coming from?"

He rested his elbows on the desk. "Let's begin with fraternizing with doctors. Sound familiar?"

I exploded. "That bastard! I begged him to intervene in a problem I was having at work with a skirt-chasing doctor and he accused me of fraternizing?
"

Dad rose to his feet. "You will not speak like some harlot, is that understood? And if this cannot be discussed in a civil manner, I will not continue. Don was polite, professional. I expect the same from you."

Tears of anger trickled down my cheeks. I pushed my body forward. "I am YOUR daughter, yet you sit there accusing me of something I have NEVER DONE. How am I supposed to behave? Sit with my hands folded in reverence while you spew accusations founded on the words of a lying wife beater who could charm Satan and win an Academy Award for his performance?"

Dad stood and stretched his back. "Your sarcasm will not resolve anything."

I stood and faced him with blatant disgust. "Neither will your parenting."

I left the room, never bothering to close the door to his self-imposed chamber of judgment.

The kids were outside playing in the leaves with Mom. Dancing and stomping, they tossed brightly colored foliage into the air then tried to catch them as if they were butterflies.

"Well?" she asked. "How did it go?"

Tears flooded my face. "Dad believes Don. In his eyes, I am the evil catalyst in this marital nightmare. Don, the lying abusive womanizer, wears a crown while I wear a cast. I'm done here. I'm going back to Virginia."

Mom wrapped her arms around me. "No, honey, not yet. I'll talk to your father. For now I think it is best that you spend time with the babies. Help yourself to anything you need and try to avoid your father. He needs to be reminded of the numerous times this has happened. I will take care of that." She kissed my cheek and disappeared into the house.

The children and I were in the nursery playing when Mom called us for dinner. I did not see my father all day and little of my mother. Just the idea of sitting at the dinner table with him created knots in my stomach. I tied my hair back, washed my face, took a pain pill and prepared to meet my makers over what smelled like spaghetti & meatballs.

Stephie raced into the dining room, spied my father and bubbled. "Grandpa Whiskers? Where were you today?"

He picked her up, nuzzled her neck and placed her in the chair next to his. "I've been busy little granddaughter. And where have you been all day?"

"Cleaning up your leaves," she smiled. "Lots of them, more than we have at our house". I watched from the doorway as she examined the table. "Company napkins," she says, picking up hers. "So who's coming for dinner? My Dad?"

"Not tonight, sweetheart. So, are you hungry?"

"Yup," she smiled.

Mom carried a large platter of spaghetti and meatballs to the table. She had made a fresh garden salad and what I knew would be the best garlic bread in town.

Bridget clapped her little hands, evoking smiles from her grandparents. Mom had conveniently placed one child on either side of her, carefully preparing their plates. Dad offered the evening prayer, shorter than usual out of respect for the little ones but ended by saying, "And Lord we ask that you will bless Don and Penne with the ability and intelligence to work out their differences. Amen."

Differences? I took two bites of food before leaving the table. "Mom, will you be kind enough to bring the children upstairs after dinner?"

She nodded her head, the sadness in her eyes overwhelming. "Of course, honey. Where are you going?"

I looked straight at my father. "I'm going outside for some fresher air and a cigarette."

Relief. At six o'clock the next morning, I woke up refreshed, knowing Dad had left for the airport. I got out of bed, tossed on some warm clothes and went downstairs. The children were still asleep and I could hear Mom's distinctive footsteps upstairs. Slipping out the back door, I began a long walk through the woods to clear my head. My father and I did not speak again beyond required courtesies. And mother had not had an opportunity to tell me if she was able to penetrate any of the barriers which seemed almost surreal. My hatred level had become toxic. Don. Dad. Life. My walk turned into a run. Branches and leaves cracked under my sneakers as I picked up the pace. Could I ever trust any man again? Could I trust myself? Panting after just ten minutes, I slowed the pace and stopped against the trunk of a large tree and slumped to the ground. Lighting a cigarette, I watched the smoke spew from my mouth like some Disney dragon. Trapped? Bitterness was eroding the modicum of common sense I had left. And then I remembered Ruthie's parting words. "*Marriage does not grant him a license for* abuse." Shouldn't that apply to fathers' as well? Hell, yes.

I jumped up and ran back to the house. The kitchen lights were on. Mom was sitting at the table, staring at a cup of coffee when I came through the door. "I wondered where you were," she said, keeping her back to me.

I quickly pulled off my jacket and sat across from her. "Well? Did you talk to him?"

She got up from the table. "Would you like some coffee, honey?"

"Yes, please. So can we talk before the kids wake?"

She silently sipped coffee before speaking. "I know how angry you are with your father but he was only trying to gather the facts. . ."

"Facts my foot! He acted like I was some lying, bed hopping wife, who deserved to be thrown down the stairs. Don't cover for him Mom, like you always do. I won't listen to such crap."

Her face was etched in worry. "I'm not trying to cover for him. He is a stickler for honesty. You know that. He was just trying to get to the truth."

"The truth?" I shouted. "So Dons' version is honest and I am a liar. Is that it? If so, I'm leaving here before that self-righteous man who has the audacity to call himself father returns. What's the difference between a verbal fist and human fist? Both inflict unbearable pain."

Mother's face abruptly turned from worry to anger. "Do not talk about your father like that. He has provided well for this family. Yes, he is stern. But he loves you all more than you will ever understand."

"Stern? Just give thought to how he has treated my twin and rethink the word stern. Did he think she ordered polio from a mail order house when she was two? No, cruel is more accurate."

Visibly shaken, she started to leave the table. "This is not about Patty. This is about you and your marriage. Your father knows Don abused you. He simply wanted to understand what triggered the attack."

And I would like to know what triggered Dad's attack on me. I left the kitchen deflated.

CHAPTER 3

October, 1975
Easton, Pennsylvania

*S*tephie raced into the laundry room crying. "Honey, what's wrong?"

"Grandma wants me to go to school here. But I want to go home to my school." She wrapped her arms around my waist and sobbed. "You promised. I want to see Daddy. He said he missed us when I talked to him on the phone. And I miss him and my friends. Please Mommy? Please take us home."

"It's going to be okay, Stephie. Daddy and I are talking, trying to work things out. And I'll speak to your grandmother. Okay?"

"Can you do it now? She's in the kitchen."

"Sure."

We walked downstairs hand in hand. Bridget was still in her highchair eating breakfast. Mom was outfitted in her traditional turtleneck and slacks, her squat chubby frame engulfed in an apron with a little red hen crocheted on the bib.

"Hi Mom. Do you have a minute?"

She dried her hands. "Sure, honey. Want some tea?"

"Not right now, thanks. Let me take the kids up to the nursery to play. Be back in a second."

When I returned she was settled in a plush rocker in the cozy living room. The crackle of burning logs in the large fireplace offered a soothing ambience. Lush plants thrived by the ten double hung windows around the room. I took a seat on the couch facing her.

"So tell me about your talk with Don last night," she said.

"Pleasant. An abundance of apologies, assurances it will never happen again."

She swiveled in her rocker and stared at the fireplace. "And you believed him?"

"I have to, Mom," I interrupted. He does miss us."

"I'm sure he does. You also know he needs to save face." Her face contorted in worry. "But, given his violent temper, and the abuse you have taken in the past, your chances of this happening again is almost a given. I suspect his father was the same."

Without prelude, she steered the conversation into an uneasy arena. "You and the children will be safer here. I have already talked to the kindergarten teacher. I want you and Stephie to go with me to the school tomorrow to meet her. She is a kind woman, a member of our church, so I'm certain Stephie will really like her."

Enraged that she had made arrangements for my daughter's life without ever discussing it with me, I struggled to keep silent rather than spew words I would regret. Knowing she was right did not change my mind. And although Dad and I were cordial, I couldn't involve him anymore. Strange, I thought that I could forgive my husband for extreme violence through his withering apologies, but couldn't begin to embrace any forgiveness for my father's actions. He had never apologized. How can one forgive another if that person takes no blame for their actions?

I shifted uncomfortably on the couch. "Mom, I appreciate what you are trying to do, but I need to make my marriage, our lives, work. In spite of everything, I still love the man and he is the father of our children."

I left the room without further comment, lacking the intestinal fortitude to tell her how trapped I felt between two prisons and silently decided to take my chances of marital incarceration in Virginia.

Several days later I was in the nursery packing suitcases when Dad appeared in the doorway. "*Pennycat*? Can we talk?" It had been over three weeks since we had muttered more than essential greetings.

Promising start, I thought. At least I had been reinstated as *Pennycat*. "Sure, but I need to finish packing."

He caressed his beard as he spoke. "You know your mother and I are against you returning. Don's abuse may only continue if you go back without a mutual resolve and we are obviously concerned about your safety and the safety of our grandchildren."

I stopped packing and faced him. "You need to have a little faith in me, Dad. I know that is hard for you, given the fact that you think I behave like some raucous call girl, but I'm not. I am a good wife and mother and my priorities have always been grounded in the care of my family."

Silence and then his arms were around me. "I know you are not a loose woman, but you have always been the wild pony. Of my five children you are the most outspoken."

I stared into his piercing eyes. "From a genetic standpoint, where do you think that came from?"

He laughed. "So you consider me outspoken?"

"Look up outspoken in the dictionary, Dad. I wouldn't be surprised to see your name as part of the definition."

"Truce," he said with a grin. "I shall absorb that insult in silence."

I watched my parents' wave as we pulled out of the drive. Their facial expressions exuded the sadness of loved ones saying goodbye forever to someone they knew was now on the endangered species list. I had to ignore what they thought. It was almost November and we needed to get home. Don had sounded so jubilant last night on the phone. I was excited to return and felt no fear. I knew with the cast still on my arm he would be visually reminded of what could never happen again.

I was also certain he would never visit my parents.

"Mom," Stephie called from the backseat. "Daddy has surprises for us! He wouldn't tell me on the phone but he said we are all going to be very excited."

"Wonderful," I said. "What do you think they are?"

"New toys," she shouted. "Daddy loves to buy us toys!"

The children were asleep when I pulled into our drive and within seconds Don came running out the front door, his arms flailing, and a huge smile on his face.

"Baby," he shouted, opening my door. "My God how I have missed you all. He hugged me with such intense passion it was as if we were embracing for the first time in our lives.

"I missed you too, sweetheart. You look good and relaxed." I glanced at his face and saw spots of paint. "And the paint on your face doesn't look too bad either!"

He kissed me hard. "I'll carry the kids in and everything else. But first, surprises."

By now the girls were awake. Stephie quickly got out of her car seat and opened the door. "Daddy"! Daddy!" she shouted. He picked her up, swung her around then picked her up again for more hugs. "Hi baby girl! Daddy missed you so much!"

"Do you have new stuff for us? Can we have them now, please?"

He laughed. "Just hold on little pumpkin while I get Bridget. Then we can all see them together!"

With Bridget in his arms, we followed him to the front door. "Presenting the first surprise," he announced like an emcee.

We stepped into a newly refurbished foyer. The ratty carpeting we had tolerated had been replaced with ecru colored tile which flowed from the entry, down the hall to the living room. Where the tile stopped, plush rust colored carpeting took over. The once anemic walls were wallpapered in a designer striped print. "Oh my God, Don! This is just gorgeous," I said, anxiously repressing the urge to ask what bank he robbed, or who the decorator was. His taste in interior design had always reflected the absence of any semblance of color coordination and an exaggerated love for Early American faux trash. But this? Our house looked like a model home.

Stephie pulled on his shirt. "It's pretty, Daddy, but how 'bout *our* surprises?"

He stooped down to her level. "Hey, pumpkin. Would I forget my favorite girls? Why don't you walk over to the patio door?" He stood Bridget next to her. "Both of you cover your eyes until I tell you to open them. Okay?"

He slowly opened new, tailored drapes. "You ready?" he said excitedly. "Okay, open your eyes."

A shiny new swing set painted in primary colors looked like something from The Magic Kingdom. To the right, nestled in the ivy bed, was an enchanted playhouse complete with a functioning cottage door, two shuttered windows, and small flower boxes which showcased freshly planted orange & yellow mums. Squealing with delight, the kids raced toward their dream yard holding hands.

I wrapped my arms around Don's waist. "You're amazing. Thank you so much for all of this." Although haunted by the source of funds for the makeover, I pledged to enjoy this yellow brick road. They all led to something, didn't they?

"It's the very least I could do after what I put you through." His hug meant everything. I needed to trust in him again.

That night, we cuddled up in bed together like newlyweds, under a new richly patterned comforter. The burned drapes had been discarded replaced with wooden, louvered shutters. Embraced in relief, we spoke little. As we succumbed to the restoration of sleep, Don gently reminded me that he had scheduled a doctor's appointment the following day to remove the cast.

Thanksgiving Day
November 1975

"I'm learning to read, Grandma Alice" Stephie announced.

She kissed her softly on the cheek. "I'm so proud of you pretty baby," she said. "Smells mighty good in this kitchen, doesn't it?"

Stephie jumped down from the table. "Yup, it's Turkey Day. You like turkey, Grandma?"

She hugged her and smiled. "You bet!"

Don's mom had flown in from California for Thanksgiving and Don's birthday. Her presence was instantly magical. She had never met Bridget and immediately picked her up. Always smiling, especially around her first born son---the favorite of a family of five-- this handsome woman never showed any signs of the grief she had to be feeling as her husband had committed suicide three years before, two days before Thanksgiving.

The heavenly aroma of roasting turkey permeated the house. Fresh pies were on the kitchen counter and the table was set.

"Mommy," Stephie shouted from the dining room. You didn't put napkins on the table. Can I do it?"

"Sure. Do you know where they are?"

"Yup," she yelled climbing the stairs. "I can read now."

Read? I thought. *Why would she need to read to find the linens?*

Minutes later I heard Alice laughing from the dining room. "Stephie, honey, I don't think your mom meant these kind of napkins." I took a quick peak at the table and stifled my laughter. On each plate was a Kotex napkin.

Thanksgiving was an occasion that would have made Hallmark jealous. The dinner turned out perfectly (rare for someone like me who had the cooking skills of a three-year old). Alice left the table after dessert and came back to the table with stacks of beautifully wrapped gifts. Some were for her grandbabies, others were for Don's birthday, exquisite ties and shirts and a gift certificate for Brooks Brothers. And the ultimate surprise? An early Christmas card, with a check for five thousand dollars! Don and I were overwhelmed, grateful.

He stood up, kissed his mom and went to fetch some champagne glasses.

"A birthday toast," his mother began. "May you be blessed with love and success."

Don stood. "One of those blessings has already come true. Are you ready for this one? I have been promoted to manager!"

Alice jumped to her feet. "Oh, my dear son. Congratulations. Just what will you be manager of?"

He blushed. "Officially, the manager of our Worchester office."

"Worchester?' she queried. "Where is that?"

He could not make eye contact with me. "Massachusetts," he said.

I suddenly spit champagne on the tablecloth, excused myself, and raced upstairs. He was still the General in a domestic army. Surprise had always been his control.

CHAPTER 4

January, 1976
Boston, Massachusetts

*W*e sat in a small cocktail lounge in a lavish Boston hotel, trying to relax after three grueling days of house hunting. It was an affluent night spot, with glass top tables, chairs upholstered in a burgundy stripe and ivory basket weave. Dimly lit crystal chandeliers floated from the ceiling like ornate spaceships, their attachment hidden in the dark. A pianist played softly at a baby grand piano in front of a large arched window, framing the musician in a painting of serenity. Conversations hummed around us, the words bleeding into the air. I was enamored by the atmosphere; it spoke of the way I loved to live. But I was in agony about the move.

"I don't think I can live here," I told him as calmly as possible.

He gulped down his drink. "You'll do just fine. You need to understand that to be successful, I can't stay in one place. And this is the region I have been given."

I avoided eye contact by playing leapfrog with cocktail stirs. My anger had been kept at bay since his announcement. "Why didn't you discuss this with me before accepting it?"

"Discuss what?" He threw his head back and laughed. "You mean the new salary, a bigger house and some pretty impressive trips? What's to discuss?" He paused, lit another cigarette and folded his arms on the table. "This is my job," he said softly, "the job which puts food on the table and sexy black dresses on your back." He raised his eyebrows. "And you do look sexy. My sexy, beautiful wife."

Flattery got him everywhere. Nourish my weakness and I was all his. I couldn't get beyond wanting him, being with him and craving his approval. I looked up and smiled. He had been so caring on this trip, warm, provocative, and dressed like the executive he had become, thanks to his mothers' generous gift. His expensive blue blazer, pinned stripped shirt and coordinating ascot produced a Hollywood image. And that smile. It was not just his charm-the-world-smile tonight. This one was real, sincere and would make most people want the name of his dentist. I stared at him and knew I wanted a future with this man. But I needed him to love and respect me as I did him.

"Have another drink," he said. "You're too uptight. You need to relax, have some fun." He winked. "My little girl. Don't worry. You will love Massachusetts. It's a brand new start in a brand new place." He raised an almost empty glass. "Here's to a lifetime of happiness and the appearance of our waiter."

I stared out the window at a city I had only read about. Light snow was falling and the flakes seemed to swirl around aimlessly as if undecided where to land. *Like me. Who needed a brand new place?* The thought of leaving Virginia, of having Stephie change schools, of making new friends fogged my brain. I had finally found a friend to confide in, someone to help me and now that support and my sanity were about to be severed by my own weakness.

"Hon?" Don's voice was soft. "I know what you're thinking. And I know how afraid you are. But don't be. We're a team, you and I. And I will always be there for you."

A team? Yes, we were a team. But only he was the captain.

We left the lounge holding hands to the elevator. As the doors closed, he slipped his arm around me and kissed me deeply. And the fear I had had all evening began to dissipate when we opened the door to a lavish room overlooking the city. We turned off the lights and stood in front of the window watching the snow sparkle under the street lamps. He put his hands on my shoulders and I shivered convulsively as the passion returned to our lives. He was gentle, the Don I had always loved and I earnestly strived to enjoy the present without thought to the past.

The following morning we signed the final escrow documents for a split ranch house on a large lot bordering a golf course in a small town west of Boston. Our borrowing capacity had not allowed us to purchase something new as usual, so we had to settle for a home riddled in the previous owner's neglect. The neighborhood was nice, upscale. And the house had the potential to be a showplace—but only with money. When escrow closed, we would own over two thousand square feet of repairs and only enough money to replace washers in the faucets. The exterior of the house looked as uncared for as the inside and I harbored that sinking feeling of again moving backwards by leaving a newly redecorated home.

I left the realtor's office with a buyer's hangover, second guessing the purchase. In reviewing the papers, I had discovered that our home in Virginia, which had already sold, had two mortgages---the original mortgage and an equity line of credit he had taken out in October to refurbish the Virginia home. When the escrow officer left the desk to make some copies, I stared at the signature page. The captain had mastered my signature. I looked at Don, and pointed to the signature. "Forget it," he whispered and I stared at him in silence. *Had I just signed for an apocalyptic future?*

You guys are about to go on a fun filled adventure," Don told the children the day after our return. I watched unobserved from the kitchen as he got down on all fours and the children climbed on his back like floppy little jockeys. He whinnied and galloped his way down the hall into the living room, then reared like a stallion. The girls slid to the carpet, giggling. He stood up, lifted each one and popped them on the couch. He wiped his forehead with the back of his hand then snuggled between them.

"Where are we going, Daddy?" Stephie asked.

Don was at his best role playing. "Well, it's a very famous place called Massachusetts. Daddy has a new job there." He paused. "And you know what?" He encouraged unison, raising his hands like a conductor.

"What?" they chorused.

"Your mom and I bought you a big new house with a huge playroom." He stretched his arms out for emphasis.

"Does it have lots of toys, Daddy?" Stephanie asked.

Don wrapped his arm around her shoulder. "It will, Pumpkin."

Stephie was quiet for a moment and her face slowly melted into a frown. "Can I still go to my school?" She looked up at him for reassurance.

"That is the best part!" Don threaded his voice with excitement and ran his hand through her soft blond hair. Bridget sat, hands in her lap, an untrained musician in her father's orchestra of excitement, then smiled, the only level of understanding this three year old had.

"You're going to go to a new exciting school. You'll have the chance to meet new and exciting friends. Won't that be great?"

I stayed out of sight, watching Stephanie, knowing what she must be thinking. Another school? Another change? Suddenly I saw myself as a child and realized I had instilled my own fear of change into this little girl.

"But I like my old school," she said, her emphasis on the word old.

Don hugged her. "I know you do, honey, but you'll like this one even more." He paused for emphasis then blurted out, "And you know what?"

"What?" Bridget parroted.

"Your new house has a huge back yard. And do you know what Daddy is going to buy to put in that back yard?"

"A pool?" Stephie shouted.

"Something better than a pool," he said.

Stephie's face contorted. In her world a pool ranked number one with no rival. "Then what?" she said with mild disgust.

"A brand new puppy!"

The girls clapped their hands and squealed. Suddenly, Stephie jumped off the couch and Bridget scrambled to play follow the sister. "Wait a second," Don said. "Where are you guys going?

Stephie stopped running and gave Don a look of boy-are-you-stupid. "To the pet store," she said. "And we want a white one!"

March, 1976
Manassas, VA

Don was in New England leaving me to plod through the task of boxing up our lives. The house had sold too quickly and I found myself grieving over the impending loss. Ruthie and I spent as much time as we could together but there was little she could say to cheer me. I had no sense of adventure. Don was scheduled to return in two days for his farewell party in Washington

D.C. and we were moving the following weekend. The physical move did not require my elbow grease as the company had hired packers who would pack everything but my bad attitude. I functioned in a melancholy stupor, accomplishing what I could with the least possible effort. And then the mail arrived and I lost what little reserve I had.

There was a small envelope addressed to '*Dommie*', a nickname his baby sister Victoria had given him years before. The postmark was Baltimore, Maryland. My pulse began to hammer. Victoria lived in California.

"You received something strange in the mail," I told Don when he called.

"How strange?" he asked. "Not from the IRS I hope."

I sighed loudly. "Not unless they know you by Dommie."

He laughed. "Good old Victoria. Open it."

I had waited for those words all day. I tore open the envelope and pulled out a card. "It's a greeting card," I snapped. "There is a picture of a gorilla on the front wearing tacky boxer shorts. Printed on the waist band is '*HE MAN*'. Your sister certainly could use some guidance choosing cards."

"Well?" he asked. "What did she say?"

She. I swallowed hard and tried to read without emotion. "*Dearest Dommie: Thanks for all your help and understanding. What am I going to do without you? The flowers were beautiful. Love, Diane.*"

There was a pause on the other end of the line. "That was thoughtful," Don said casually.

I was seething. There was safety in distance. "Sure was," I squawked. "Leave it to you to find a home wrecker with manners!"

Don laughed. "Will you relax? She's just a little old secretary the company has had in the Baltimore office since the Civil War."

"Which Civil War?" I said. "Ours or the one between the North and the South?"

There was silence at the other end. "By the way Pen, did you find a dress for the party? If not, don't forget. My new bosses from Boston will be there. So will Philadelphia. We need to look our best."

"Which would you prefer?" I snapped. "Tramp or empress?"

"Just make me proud," he said," "the way you always have."

Click.

I stood in front of a full length mirror checking every inch of me before we left for the last company party we would attend in Washington. Always using looks to mask my fears, I accelerated the glam for this occasion. Instead of having my brunette hair highlighted as I had for years, I became a blond. The smooth lines of the sleek floor length black gown showed enough cleavage to make me appreciate the magic of an underwire bra. Without it, the only cleavage I would ever have was in my butt. The gown had a tailored slit down the front, which parted slightly when I walked, revealing just enough leg to be elegant, not cheap. Don was standing in the foyer as I carefully walked downstairs. He was awestruck and I was ready to take on any clerical help from Baltimore.

In the car, Don took his right hand off the steering wheel and touched my knee while we drove. "You're breathtaking," he said. "I don't think you looked this gorgeous on our wedding day."

Wedding day, an emotional petroglyph for most women, never to be erased. As cars whizzed by us on the freeway, I leaned my head back, closed my eyes and began wallowing in the now comical memories of that optimistic ritual nine years before. *Had it been that long?*

Most of the congregation knew I had changed grooms at the last minute, an action which seemed to bother my family more than me until I saw the rejected fiancé in the last pew and wondered if I had been stupid enough to send him an invitation. Worse, he was smiling.

From the large old pipe organ in Don's church, music surged from a soothing cadence to the strains of the processional as my bridesmaids walked like a parade of metronome-timed Barbie dolls. There was a shuffling of feet which filtered through the church like falling dominos as the congregation rose for our entrance; and then the hush of embarrassment, a temporary glitch in feeling like royalty, when my father and I had to stop abruptly in the aisle because my eight foot train had caught under the door leading to the sanctuary. The not-so-whispered demands of my six-year-old-brother could be heard as he demanded I pay him fifty cents to free the frock. *What bride carried change down the aisle?* I thought. Then a jingle of pocket change announced my father's willingness to produce the bridal train ransom.

The aisle seemed endless that day, a path from one world to another, strewn with rose petals. As Dad and I continued our walk, I focused ahead on the ushers who emerged in front of the altar, lined up like pallbearers, their hands folded in traditional reverence.

A chill ran through me now as I remembered counting the heads and coming up short. The ushers were all there. The groom was missing.

As the musical crescendo swelled in volume, so had the door leading from the pastor's study to the altar; a wooden edema provoked by June humidity. Imprisoned behind the stuck door, Don had pounded on it from the inside. The efforts of ushers to free him sounded like a SWAT team. Finally freed, Don raced to take his place beside me, his face glistening in sweat, the pleats of his tux shirt wilting. And I remember thinking, *what else will go wrong* when it did.

"The rings, please," the minister intoned as the ceremony neared its end.

My brother untied the gold from his pillow. With a devious grin, he lifted his hand in a mock pitching mode. Don and I stood frozen, unable to improvise this script change while the best man earned Most Valuable Player by snapping the rings out of the child's hand before the brat had a chance to pitch a no nuptial.

A hand on my arm pulled me back to the present. "You awake?" Don asked. "We're almost there."

I stared at him as he drove, so handsome, his expensive cologne permeating the car like it had on our first date. The journey back in time had not relaxed me, but intensified my resolve to keep my husband for myself. . .

I stepped out on an emotional plank. "Will your Baltimore flower girl be at this party?" I asked.

He laughed. "Is that still bothering you? Rest assured, Washington does not include Baltimore's clerical staff in social functions. And even if they did, a fifty-five year-old woman is no threat to you."

Waiters moved effortlessly through the bubbly crowd in the ballroom of the Shoreham Hotel, skillfully balancing silver trays laden with glasses of champagne. A receiving line of company dignitaries formed to the left of the double doors, their corporate pecking order defined by their place in line. The Vice President of the region was first, followed by the general manager and his wife. I scanned the faces. All were familiar but one. A lone but dazzling woman stood shaking hands at the end of the line, her shoulder length raven hair touching a piece of a navy blue, off the shoulder sheath which must have had reinforcement built into the bodice to support her Grand Canyon cleavage.

The Senior Vice President made the introduction. "Penne, I'd like you to meet Diane." Her name roared through me like a funnel cloud. "Diane works in our Baltimore office," he said, "and she organized this grand affair."

Organizing affairs must be your specialty, I thought as I shook her hand, which was limp.

"Amazing," I said, offering a nefarious grin. "You don't look a day over fifty-five."

She frowned and I knew my name would never be on her Christmas card list. I turned my head slightly to see a red-faced Don behind me and wondered, *which list are you on?*

With all eyes on us, I flashed the expected smiles using a generator of courtesy to fuel the look and phoniness as a temporary shield for fractured feelings.

Don was a natural politician. His rehearsed smile looked real. It was imperative he perform as a happily married man and offered silver--tongued conversation sprinkled with recurrent signs of affection toward me as we made our way to the bar. His drink was served first; straight vodka was not exactly a bartender's challenge. As I waited for mine, Don gave me a husbandly peck on the cheek. "I'll be over there," he said, and disappeared into the crowd. My eyes followed him as I tried to sort anger from desire.

I felt a gentle tap on my shoulder. I turned to see Kevin, the Vice President of the region.

"Good to see you again," he said. A stout man in his early fifties, Kevin was dressed in a caramel colored suit, off white shirt and brown tie, looking more like a polyester candy bar than an executive. His white teeth glistened and his tanned face suggested he conducted more business on a golf course than in an office.

"I just wanted to thank you," he said, "for being such an open-minded woman. Don is proud of you, as he should be."

It was a confusing statement. "Open minded?" I asked. "Is that meant to be air-headed or flexibility?" I took a sip of my drink and waited for the cocktail coziness to free my inhibitions.

He chuckled. "Adaptability is more like it. Thank you for allowing Don to take Diane to that dinner."

Dinner? What was he talking about? I didn't interrupt him "Not many wives would have been as objective. But like Don explained, you didn't want him to compromise business while you were away caring for your father after his heart attack." He shook his head, like I was some miracle woman he couldn't begin to understand. "Every man needs a strong, bright woman behind him if he is going to succeed in the corporate world. You have obviously been just that."

I grew increasingly more uncomfortable as Kevin continued to feed me compliments like he was throwing bread crumbs to a duck. "Do you know he credits you for his drive and that you are his business confidant?"

Words backed up in my throat like paper towels in a toilet. I couldn't speak. He took a gulp of his drink, offered me a cigarette and stared at my face. "You look surprised," he said, flicking his lighter, "like you were hearing this for the first time."

I inhaled deeply, turned my head, and blew a jet stream of smoke into the air. "Shock is more accurate," I said. "But I suppose this is typical in any marriage, isn't it? Or do you always tell your wife what an asset she is to you?" The liquor was working. My hurt didn't show.

He thought for a moment, sipped his drink, his eyebrows knitting in concentration. "I'm divorced," he said, his voice almost apologetic. "But I did pay all her credit card bills when we were together. It was my way of saying thanks."

I laughed. "Would you like to say thanks to American Express for me this month?"

He tossed his head back and laughed. His smile was flirtatious. "According to Don, you are a frugal being, keeping him in line."

A blush inched up my cheeks. "I couldn't keep a ruler in line," I responded.

Kevin put his hand on my shoulder, like I was one of the good old boys. "I wish you and Don all the best in New England." That said, he walked away to join the other suits.

Several hours later I was aware of Diane watching Don and I as we left the hotel. I slipped my arm around his neck, kissed him, then turned my head, and winked at Diane.

We were almost home before either Don or I spoke. "Sure was magnanimous of me to condone Diane accompanying you to corporate dinners while I was caring for my ill father, wasn't it?" The anger I had held in abeyance all night was unleashed.

Don struggled to maintain his composure. "It was one dinner, not dinners and it was business. Pure business," he said harshly. "Telling Kevin you supported it didn't make the idea seem inappropriate or scandalous." His face was hidden in a wastrel cloud of cigarette smoke. "Besides, didn't he praise you? I mean you are the envy of every guy in my region!"

He knew I craved flattery. "Yes, so it seemed," I said. "You've given me credit for all sorts of things I knew nothing about."

Don laughed. "You loved it and you know it."

"Inebriated praise?" I snapped. "Like your bottled explanation of a fifty-five going on twenty-five woman sending you love notes?"

He reached over and patted my thigh. "You're making something out of nothing. We had a dinner meeting with a client, who, at the last minute, decided to bring his wife. We needed another woman at the table. You weren't around. It was a corporate decision."

Corporate decision, I thought. Was this the new category to justify another woman? Was it also a corporate courtesy to send her flowers? Or was it just a coincidence that she called him *Dommie*? "Oh yes," I said in a steely voice. "I almost forgot. I was up to my mitral valve playing nursemaid to an exceptionally fit father." I paused, lit a cigarette and rolled my window down half way.

Don let out a deep sigh. "Why must you read adulterous thoughts into every association I have with a woman? Creating your own soap operas for amusement?"

I quickly got out of the car when we got home, furiously wiping away tears. Don followed, paid the babysitter, locked the door behind her, and then threw his car keys at me. I ducked and he grabbed my arm and slapped my face. "Stop your damn melodrama. You create our problems, not me." He stormed up the stairs and slammed the bedroom door.

In retaliation, he returned to Boston a day early. As I worked through the monotony of moving I couldn't help wondering if his flight had included a layover in Baltimore. Literally.

Two days passed before he called. Employing the safety of distance, he sounded confident. "I just needed to reassure you that there was nothing between Diane and I beyond business." He paused then said, "Pen, as usual, you are imagining things."

"Did I imagine you told me she was fifty-five, Don?" My words were clipped and I made no effort to sound pleasant."

He sighed loudly into the phone. "You would have automatically assumed something was going on if I had been honest," he said, resting his defense on my potential childlike behavior.

I fought to stay moored in reality. But because we were moving, beginning a new life in a new town, I knew I couldn't risk our future together by drowning in it while living in a sold house.

"I truly love you, Pen," he said. "I've made a lot of mistakes. I'm sorry I slapped you. But I'll try harder to keep my temper in check. I can't do any of this without you behind me."

CHAPTER 5

April, 1976
Auburn, Massachusetts

*a*s the cold bleak days of March chilled April's arrival, I was convinced Paul Revere's ride had had more to do with keeping warm than announcing the advance of the Redcoats. What little I saw of Massachusetts the first month spawned possibility. I knew when the daffodils mustered sufficient strength to puncture the frozen ground the state would be glorious and hoped this same strength would be realized by humans as well because the people were as cold as the weather. Not one neighbor had ventured to our front door to welcome us, although there was a casual wave here and there acknowledging our existence.

After living in the cozy cordiality of Virginia, this state had all the appeal of a prison; the people apparently trained at birth to be withdrawn and indifferent. It was a safe bet that if I said hello to any stranger, the person would either grunt like a warthog in acknowledgment or, worse, stare at me as if hair was growing in long tendrils out my nostrils. If by chance the stranger was congenial, I had to decide whether they were vote-hungry politicians or transplants from some distant land like Connecticut or Rhode Island. It was the mind-your-own-business state and the absence of any welcome made me edgy.

I began to envy Bridget whose life went on uninterrupted in her little room where stuffed animals and dolls continued to be her best friends. For Stephanie, daily chants of *I hate it here* escalated the erosion of my sanity.

"She's getting that from you," Don insisted.

"No she is not. Contrary to your opinion, I don't mope around here talking about how much I despise this place. I just think it." I paused for a moment to see if he was listening. He wasn't. "Don, it's that school she is in. Kindergarten is so regimented and stiff, her teacher sounds like Attila the Hun's mother."

He laughed. "Kids embellish things, Pen. Just give it time. If this teacher is as bad as you say, I'll take care of it."

A week passed and the problem worsened. Stephie fought me daily to stay home from school. Treated by her classmates as an outsider, this once outgoing child had become withdrawn. Her eyes had lost their sparkle. I struggled to encourage a positive environment.

"Want to go on a picnic? I asked one morning, adding "after school?"

"Sure," she said. "But I want to go on the picnic instead of school."

"Honey, we can't do it that way. So does the picnic sound good for this afternoon?"

Without answering, she left the room, ran down the hall to her bedroom and slammed the door. The walls were never too thick for a mother to hear her child sobbing. I couldn't wait for Don to take care of it. I paced in front of the phone trying to decide what to do and finally decided to be an adult, her mother. I snapped the phone off the hook, called the school and asked to schedule an appointment with her teacher.

"She is quite busy," the receptionist said. "The best I can do is fifteen minutes, at three-thirty this afternoon."

"That will be fine," I said, silently thinking, *I'll only need two minutes if this woman is as bad as I think.*

"Before you hang up," she said, "I see your daughter's name on the absentee list. Is she ill?" *With terminal unhappiness I wanted to say.* "Very," I answered crisply, "and she is getting worse by the day."

The receptionist treated me like I was an idiot. "Have you taken her to the doctor?"

I didn't need to sound irresponsible. "Of course," I lied. I didn't know a doctor, dentist or a friend. But it was only after I hung up that I realized how alone we really were. So alone I had to take Bridget and Stephie to the teacher's conference.

We were getting dressed when Don walked in early and eyed me cautiously. It was rare that I dressed like a real adult in the middle of the week. "And just where are you going?" he asked.

"I am going to the school to meet Stephanie's teacher. We can't go on like this."

He put his briefcase on the kitchen table. "I think I better handle this," he said.

I grabbed my purse. "No, I am. You stay with the girls until I get back."

He ran his fingers through his hair. "I don't like this. Just how long will you be gone?"

I hated accounting for my time; he never accounted for his. "Two weeks, maybe three," I said in my best Alice-in-Wonderland voice and walked out the door.

Young yet crackly-voiced, Ms. Papp was cold, bitter. Dressed in a long black pleated skirt and a yellowed blouse buttoned to the neck to avoid any suggestion she might be female, this woman did not smile. Her detestable demeanor made me wonder if she had completed her student teaching in a juvenile detention center.

"Hard to believe this is the same child," she said, staring at a report in her lap. Seated in front of her desk, I could see the name of Stephanie's school in Virginia at the top of the page and knew the contents. It was a glowing account about a happy, intelligent child who lived to excel.

Hard to believe you call yourself a teacher, I thought. "What makes you say that?" I asked.

Straightening her posture from a question mark to a yard stick, she glared at me. "She's too quiet," Papp said, her New England accent compounding the insensitivity. "Stephanie just sits there and says nothing, nor does she voluntarily participate in any activity."

I seethed inside thinking, *if the kids decide to hang you I'll buy the rope* and swallowed a wad of hostility. "Ms. Papp. Have you given any consideration to the fact that Stephanie just turned six last week and needs time to adjust to her new environment?"

She wrinkled her lips. "Are you telling me how to teach?" she asked.

This was incredible. A kindergarten teacher behaving like she had been assigned to a group of misfits. "No," I said firmly. "I'm not telling you how to teach. I am merely suggesting you try and analyze this situation from a child's perspective."

She sighed in disgust. "I'm a teacher," she said, rising to her feet. "Not a psychologist. If your daughter needs professional help, I suggest you speak to the principal."

I stood abruptly. No wonder Stephie was terrified. "There is a need for professional help," I said tersely. "But it has nothing to do with Stephanie." Controlling the urge to wipe the blackboard with her face, I left in a huff, proud of myself for not being a wimp.

"Psychologist?" Don yelled. "My daughter? We'll just see who needs a shrink. I'll take care of this first thing in the morning. If there isn't another teacher, there is always another school."

Hot tempered parents, I thought. What an abysmal environment for our children. We needed to grow up if we expected our children to.

"But I don't want to go," Stephanie cried the next morning. "I hate her."

Don bent down to her height. "It's okay, Stephie. Daddy's going to take you to school and you and I are going to make everything okay."

Three hours later I paced the sidewalk waiting for Stephanie's bus. It had been such an anxious morning. I had expected Don to call. He didn't. When I called his office, he was in a meeting and could not be interrupted.

The yellow bus appeared at the top of the street. I struggled to erase the anxiety as the bus pulled up and stopped. When the doors opened, Stephie bounded down the steps, SMILING.

"Mommy, Mommy," she called, running down the sidewalk, papers clutched in her hand. "Guess what?"

Her smile was so invigorating. "What, sweetie?"

"Daddy got me a new teacher." Her eyes were dancing, her face animated. "And you know what? She likes me."

"How wonderful," I said. Taking her hand in mine, we skipped back to the house, swinging our arms as she chatted on endlessly about her morning.

"Can Bridget and me have a tea party for lunch?" she asked.

"Bridget and I, "I corrected her. "Sure, as soon as she gets up from her nap."

The brown lawns of winter had finally turned to thick blankets of movable green that gave our barn red house a warmer, glad-we're-here ambiance. Stately pine trees lined the perimeter of the back yard and on a clear day we had a panoramic view of Holy Cross College and the moss-covered city of Worcester, which spread like crumpled green paper in the valley below.

But it was a lonely view, a desolation heightened by Don's frequent business trips and life in a town that did not encourage the presence of outsiders. Each day I woke and the bitterness was still there, like dried egg yolks on a plate. On several occasions, I drove Stephie to school instead of her taking the bus, hoping to meet other mothers. I was the only parent at the bus stop in the morning and was so desperate to find playmates for her; I considered tripping some mom at the school to get her attention. A few would return my smile, but after a simple exchange of *Good morning*, they would move on. Hanging on to what remained of my self esteem, I kissed my daughter good-bye each morning and prayed she would not become as meek and spineless as her mother.

Bridget and I would return from school to a house which needed so much I never knew where to begin. Money was tighter than an "A" cup on Dolly Parton, so household improvements could only be made through recycling the old. It was difficult to remind myself of the beautiful home we left in Virginia. But I did. Curtains were made from elderly sheets and throw pillows for the couch from used clothing. I scrubbed what could be cleaned and tried to cover what could not then waited with expectation for Don to come home. I filled the house with cooking aromas of his favorite foods and hoped he would notice my efforts.

He didn't so I feigned cheerfulness and begrudgingly participated in his new passion of gardening (a welcome relief from the cultivation of Diane blossoms). Gardening was a somber word for body numbing yard work. Weekends were spent replacing winter-withered shrubs when we could afford them or raking away the mounds of leaves and debris which had rotted in piles under the trees for years. It was only by participating that we spent any time together at all.

I was bored with myself, annoyed by a fear that kept me from knocking on neighbors' doors like some migrant Welcome Wagon hostess. Worse, I knew he was bored with me. As dust began to disguise most of our possessions, I ignored the cleaning ritual. While Bridget napped one morning, I plopped down in a shabby chair in the den and began reading some old magazines.

Business? I thought. The only business I was in was feeling sorry for me. I rolled the magazine up and started to toss it away when a small banner on the cover caught my eye. 'What have you done for yourself lately?' *Nothing*, I thought, and read on.

Two paragraphs into the article and I felt the author was talking to me. She fluidly described the voids in life. Yes, the voids had always deflated my spirit and consistently contributed to my misery. I needed to do something for myself, to venture out on that proverbial limb and try something I had fantasized about for years. Expanding my horizons beyond the narrow world of marriage was important. But expanding those horizons beyond the limitations I had imposed on myself was now mandatory. Suddenly I felt an untapped energy within me.

"Do you want to change?" the author asked. "Improve your life?" *Yes*! I said out loud but fear of failure quickly dragged my yes to the ground like a fallen kite. I envied people who were challenged by change and motivated to seek new paths. Why was I living my life, longing for love, acceptance and respect from a man who only provided enough to make me crave more?

Suddenly I sat up and willed myself to face a frequently discarded fantasy. I had wanted to write for years; first for myself and later for publication. I majored in English in college, and loved to write. It was if a genie was suddenly spinning some unexplainable magic. I mentally leaped from what I had become—a lazy, depressed, housewife—into a fairytale limelight. *Wouldn't I be proud of myself? Wouldn't Don and my parents be proud of me? Success would feel wonderful. An Oscar for best screenplay?*

As usual, I had overstepped the bounds of daydreaming.

The next morning I was surprised that the excitement was still there. I avoided the usual route of '*dread dreaming*', dropping into some black, negative hole in my brain.

Where could I begin? After I dropped Stephie off at school, I went to the library. The building was so old, it had probably been visited by Nathaniel Hawthorne.

Mrs. Griffin, the children's librarian, was a friendly little grandmother type who fawned over Bridget when we stepped inside. I quickly revealed my newcomer status and she warmly offered to show us around.

"If you would like to look for books for yourself," she said, "I'm not busy this morning." She looked down at Bridget and smiled at this little girl who made my heart dance. Her long, curly pigtails had an extra bounce this morning. Yellow ribbons floated in her hair like sunbeams. Dressed in a blue and yellow dress with white ruffles, Bridget looked like she belonged in an expensive toy store, standing on a highly polished glass shelf. She smiled at Mrs. Griffin, who promptly took her hand. "Bridget and I can have so much fun in the children's library," she said.

The bleakness that was Massachusetts faded as I plumbed the shelves for information on the publishing industry. In thirty minutes, I had stacked ten books on the check-out counter. Bridget appeared from around the corner, struggling with books she had gathered with Mrs. Griffin's help.

"You a writer?" she asked, as she checked out my stack of books.

"Someday, perhaps."

She held up my new library card. "Well, Penne," she said. "I'll keep watching for your books."

I smiled. "The ones I just borrowed or the ones I hope to write?"

She laughed. "Both."

A fire roared in the den fireplace and spread warmth through the cold downstairs. It was June but the nights ignored the calendar. The children were asleep, Don was on another trip and I was elated to discover how refreshing it was not to sit and brood or worry where he was. How cleansing it was not be so tied to his life that I had to lengthen my emotional umbilical cord to thoughts of what he was doing.

I quickly lost myself in words, sentences and plots, creating recipes of expression. It was exciting as I skipped from reading to writing, especially for someone who never liked being a student. Hidden from the real world behind a typewriter, I began to unlock surprising paper courage. I flourished, easily sounding like the President of General Motors if I wanted to, or some daring young woman looking for love in places most would never consider. The escapism was intoxicating and released me from the jaws of self-pity.

Each morning I woke with a renewed spirit and littered the den floor with crinkled attempts. I didn't give up and only stopped to provide the bare essentials of keeping a household running, the tedium of chores now minimized by a new directive. Unwilling to risk criticism I

Knew Don would levy, I hid my new world when he was around, storing everything out of sight before he returned.

"I need help with the yard," he said one morning. "And since you are home all day, I don't think it would kill you to trim some of the shrubs and weed the flower beds."

My hatred of yard work had never been a secret. "If I have time," I answered.

He was on his way out the door. "Not if, Pen. Make time, like you really have anything important to do." He shook his head in disgust and left.

I waited until late afternoon. As the children played, I began trimming bushes that were ugly to begin with, making vicious cuts with the hedge trimmers. I began in the front, making myself visible to a neighborhood which seemed to have houses without people.

Today, however, I was given reason to recover dormant social graces.

"Welcome to Massachusetts," a white-bearded man shouted from the street. "Where are you from?"

A beat up gray Volvo was parked in front of our drive so I walked down to greet him. Dressed in black slacks, a crisp blue shirt and patterned tie, he had the girth of a man who probably made a career out of eating.

"Virginia," I said. "Are you from around here?"

He chuckled. "In the present tense, I live right down the street." He pointed to a beige home four doors down. He had a unique spark of gaiety about him and as he talked I was thinking he would make a terrific Santa Claus. "As far as my background," he said, "I used to have lunch with the Puritans."

I laughed. "Then I'll bet you've met my parents." I extended my hand and introduced myself.

"Tom Hanson," he replied. His handshake was warm but firm. Pensive and unrushed, he was very easy to talk to.

"You picked a beautiful day to take the afternoon off, Tom."

He groaned. "Especially when you've worked all night," he said.

My eyes widened. "All night? Are you an obstetrician?"

"Don't I wish," he said with a wink. "No, Assistant D.A." He watched my face. "But don't be impressed."

"Too late for that," I said.

He studied me for a moment. "Well nice to have you here. Sure beats the swamp puppies who owned this place before." He began to walk toward his car then stopped. "I'll ask my wife to stop by. She's unmistakable; red hair, grass green eyes and talks too much." His laugh said he was amused by her talk. "But," he continued, sticking his hand in the air. "She's one brilliant lady. Just ask her."

I stood in the drive envying a woman I had never met. How wonderful it must feel to have a husband who thought you were brilliant. That was my definition of a marital utopia.

Clouds rolled in the next afternoon and colored the atmosphere in a desire to write. Reluctantly I turned off the typewriter and promised myself I could finish later. Don had left a list of things for me to do and most of it concerned the stupid yard.

I was mowing the grass, a wicked sweat rolling down my face when silver Audi pulled into the drive. I turned off the mower, wiped my hands on my jeans and walked down the drive.

"Real friendly street isn't it," she said, walking up to me. I faced a vibrant head of red hair, a guarded smile and plain face.

"If you change the definition of friendly," I said. Her handshake was as firm as her husband's.

"I don't mean to take you away from what you are doing," she said.

I smiled. "Not a problem. And you're right about the street. Friendly is not the word I would use to describe it. I think my neighbors want to pretend I'm not here."

She laughed. It was a hearty laugh which seemed to come deep from within, a natural zest. "Don't feel slighted. Once you get to know them, you'll wish you didn't."

Laughter felt like a pep pill. Looking at her, I was suddenly embarrassed by my hobo attire. Although she stood about five feet tall, Kathleen's six foot ambiance was defined by her rich, brown suit that confirmed she was nothing close to a homebody type. I didn't ask her what she did because I would not have known what to say if she asked me the same.

"So you're the gardener," she said. "Do you do it because you want to or because you have to?"

It hit me as a strange question. "Personally, I detest it. If it were up to me I'd fill the entire yard with concrete and paint it green. And you?"

"Just the results," she said. "But I pay dearly for that pleasure."

She could probably afford a gardener. "So Tom doesn't like to do that male thing of trying to control Mother Nature?"

She let out another hearty laugh. "Tom? He wouldn't care if our yard looked like some forest in the Amazon. He's a lawyer. All he has ever done was present arguments of why he couldn't do it."

I giggled. "Remind me to ask him for a copy of those arguments," I said; not *that I could get away with it,* I thought.

Kathleen smiled. "You can make it easier than that. Do what men do when they don't want to do laundry or dishes? Tell him its men's work."

I could suddenly hear Don's voice in my head. "Men's work?" he would snap. "Have you forgotten that I work all day? The very least you can do is help with the yard."

A chill rushed through me as I stared at her. I could never imagine ever having the freedom to say that, or worse, ever having her in the same room with Don.

"I'm having a neighborhood get together next week," she said. "Just two other women. I'd love for you to come. We could use a new face, new opinions."

Frightened yet enlightened by the invitation, I accepted. "I do have two little girls and no sitter. Will that be a problem?"

"Of course not," she said. "My daughter is fifteen and loves little kids. Bring them along and Dana will have a ball."

"Thanks," I said. "I'm looking forward to it."

As she pulled down the drive I looked at my watch. I hadn't finished Don's damn list and it was after five. I hadn't thought about dinner. Beds weren't made. And his desk was flooded in my stuff. There was a blizzard of wadded up paper in the room and my books were lying around open, on the floor, the couch, the coffee table, as if someone had it in for their hard covered souls and shot them in place.

I tried to start the lawnmower again. It wouldn't even burp much less roar. I kicked it as hard as I could and pulled my foot back to try and destroy it completely when Don's car pulled up the drive.

He got out of the car, tossed his suit coat over his shoulder, grabbed his briefcase and crossed the lawn. "I saw you kicking that," he said sharply. "What is your problem?"

I wiped the sweat off my forehead. "My problem? Your lawnmower won't start. So that makes it your problem."

He sighed. "Push it back into the garage. I'll look at it this weekend." He started for the front door then turned and yelled, "What's for dinner? I'm starving!"

"Your choice," I shouted. "McDonald's or cream of trimmed shrub soup!"

CHAPTER 6

*K*athleen's house was a pearl among pop beads in the necklace of houses which comprised the neighborhood. The yard was a botanical wonderland. Ornately trimmed shrubs kissed the foundation of the house and a plethora of spring flowers formed a floral rainbow border along the drive. The thick green lawn was so flawlessly trimmed it looked like she had hired some horticultural hairdresser to perfect the appearance.

The expensive siding looked new, the beige color free of chipped paint that bubbled all over my house. Wide wooden shutters, painted a deeper shade of beige, framed each window. Beveled glass in the intricately carved oak front door defined elegance.

Intimidated by the opulence, I walked up to the front door with the children and prepared myself to appear confident, casual and likable. "What a palace," I said as Kathleen opened the front door. "It's like visiting Versailles in New England."

"A palace in the making," she grinned. "I'm not finished yet."

I couldn't even afford to start, I thought, as Bridget tried to pull her hand out of mine.

"Dana?" Kathleen called and turned to me. "She has been looking forward to this all day. She loves little people."

Her daughter responded quickly and bounced into the living room. A petite teenager, Dana's long, luxurious red hair was neatly tied in a long wavy ponytail and her sparkling green eyes reflected an immediate fondness for my children.

She bent down to their level. "Hi," she said, clapping her hands. "Would you like to come and play with me downstairs?" She extended a hand to each and they went skipping away.

When they left, my eyes roamed around the living room and into the dining room which looked like an expensive show room. Rich, vibrant fabrics on sofas and chairs enhanced the Early American motif. Deep reds, subtle blues and whites were so carefully camouflaged in intricate prints it took me a minute to realize the patriotic color scheme existed.

Furnishings in the dining room were a high gloss oak. The table she had set continued the impeccable taste. Lenox china, finely crafted silverware and Waterford crystal gleamed on the deep plaid of the tablecloth.

Two women were already seated at the table. A thin, regal woman with almost white hair, older than the rest of us but not old enough for her hair to have lost its color was dressed in a summer cotton blue print skirt, long sleeved man-tailored blouse and lightweight blue blazer. Horn rimmed glasses sat perched on a delicate nose. The other woman was frail, probably in her early forties. She had salt and pepper hair and skin so white it looked as bleached as the ruffled blouse she wore. Small pearl earrings dotted her lobes and accentuated her look of fragility bordering on nervous exhaustion.

Kathleen made the introductions. "This is my sister, Carol Murrow," she said and the white haired woman offered a business wattage smile.

I extended my hand in a firm shake. "Hello Carol, very nice to meet you."

Pointing to the frail soul, Kathleen introduced Patricia Bentley. "Hello," I said kindly. Patricia nodded her head and instantly stretched her mouth into an anemic imitation of Mona Lisa.

I felt a bit awkward as I took my seat, out of place in such a refined setting. Unsure of where to put my eyes, I stared at the crystal.

Carol picked up a goblet by the stem. "Beautiful, isn't it?"

"Without question," I replied. *And so are you.* She was the epitome of sophistication as she gently twirled the glass in the sunlight.

I picked up the empty glass in front of me. "Quite a contrast to what my husband and I have," I said. "Most of our glasses came from a special Texaco offer and silently asked the question, how could these people eat so much grape jelly?"

There was a chorus of laughter and the relief in their acceptance relaxed me. Kathleen filled the water goblets, poured coffee, placed an ornate platter of finger sandwiches and fruit in the center of the table and took her seat. She was a natural leader and in minutes we were sharing the basics of our lives, laying the bricks of familiarity on which to structure friendships: Number of kids, ages, and finally husband's occupations.

Carol's husband was a dentist. 'Decay Jay' she called him. Priscilla's husband was a high school English teacher. She never gave his name. Asked if she had a nickname for him, she simply smiled and shook her head no.

"And Tom," I asked Kathleen. "Do you have any nickname for him?"

She laughed. "I have a few but most of them have four letters."

"So," Carol said, helping herself to a pastry. "Now that we've zoomed through the hubby bios, what do you do?"

Beside toil and whine, I thought? The truth would have bored anyone and I sensed that these were not Betty Crocker women. "I'm trying to establish myself as a freelance writer," I said. "But so far I would have to write a short autobiography titled, 'Failing Is as Easy as One-Two-Three.'"

There was a buzz of electricity in their laughter. "What was your major in college?" Carol asked.

I stirred some cream in my coffee. "According to my parents, it was partying with English as an afterthought."

Their laughter was spontaneous. "And you?" I asked Carol.

She looked at Kathleen. "I was a business major at the University of Mass but never finished. I quit, got married, popped out a few tax deductions and am now partners with Kathleen. She's the CPA, the one with the brains. I just handle little things."

Kathleen laughed. "Little things? Come on now. Being the President does not classify you as a person who does little things."

I tried to hide my awe. "What kind of a company?"

"Ryder Trucks," Kathleen answered, as she refilled my cup. "We rent them, to others, of course."

"And," added Carol, "we always make sure there are several in stock for personal weekend use. Potential 'D-Days'. She turned and winked at her sister.

"D-days? Don't tell me you guys moonlight as drivers?"

"Only for us," Kathleen said. "Our husbands are home on weekends." She grimaced at the statement and shared a knowing look with Carol. "Friday's we can handle. By Saturday we've usually decided to divorce them and by Sunday morning we have trucks in reserve to haul laundry and dirty dishes to the dump." Carol looked at Kathleen as she finished and they broke into hysterical laughter.

I looked over at Patricia. Her weak smile was only a social offering, not one of agreement. She had an air of refinement that said she was never called Pat; a woman whose hen-heartedness was out of place at that table. As much as I was enjoying the husband putdowns, I could feel her discomfort and needed to be coerced into the conversation. "So where did you go to school, Patricia?" I asked.

She fumbled with her silverware. "I went to secretarial school," she said in a meek voice, "until I found the perfect husband."

"Perfect husband?" Carol said laughing. "You must have the only one in captivity."

"Then lucky you," I joined in. "I couldn't put the word perfect and my husband's name in the same paragraph."

Patricia was trying to laugh but wasn't the actress she needed to be at that table. Careful, I told myself. You've just had more experience, in acting, that is.

"I didn't know there was such a creature," Kathleen added, "unless Sears really does have everything."

The laughter was such an emotional surprise, something I had not heard in a long time. And the subject matter was tantamount to having a conversation with Joan Rivers.

Patricia offered a feeble smile and finished her coffee in an awkward gulp.

"You'll have to see Patricia's house," Kathleen said, "especially her collection of decorator pillows. They are handmade." I felt the mockery in her voice and was suddenly uncomfortable for Patricia.

"I'd love to." I turned to Patricia. "So you must be an interior designer."

Patricia's mouth twitched. "Oh no. Just a housewife. Kathleen talks about the pillows because of the stuffing, not the exteriors."

I slowly sipped my coffee. "Are they needle-point bank accounts?" I asked.

Kathleen answered. "She defined economy. Every pillow is stuffed with cotton from vitamin and aspirin bottles!"

Patricia blushed. The color looked good on her pale cheeks, but humiliation was the wrong shade. I felt sorry for her and tried to soften her discomfort. "You and me both," I said. "Trying to fix up that rat trap we just bought without any money has me using anything I can find in the house." Patricia smiled and I continued. "You want to talk economical? I just wallpapered the bathroom in cancelled checks!" It was true.

"You did what?" Kathleen asked her laughter almost uncontrollable.

"Hey, they matched the flooring. And it gives you something to read on constipated days."

The CPA in Kathleen surfaced. "And if you're audited by the IRS next year? Then what?"

I thought for a moment. "The toilet seat cover is plush. I'll just hire you, have the agent come to the house and pop some Ex-Lax in his coffee."

Patricia was finally laughing with the rest of us so we spent the next hour entertaining each other with outrageous decorating ideas.

"Whoever lived in that house before we bought it must have had a lobotomy when it came to taste because it sure isn't there," I said.

A frown suddenly enveloped Kathleen's face and I knew I'd said something stupid.

"She wasn't allowed to decorate," Kathleen said dourly. "Her husband was transferred to Texas. She refused to follow, but with five children, she couldn't afford to keep the house either. She moved back to New Jersey with her parents." Kathleen struck the table with her fist. "He was such an ass; a bully. If I had had the money, I would have purchased the house for her so she could stay here." She picked at invisible crumbs on the tablecloth as everyone grew silent as if we were enacting a moment of mourning.

"I'm so sorry," I said. I didn't need to borrow any of Patricia's sheepishness. "I had no idea your friend lived there."

Kathleen lifted her head. This time she was smiling. "No need to apologize," she said softly. You're right. The house was uncared for. Her husband controlled all the money. He wouldn't allow her to buy an egg without his approval. He didn't give a lick about anything but himself, a demigod of the engineering world." She tilted her head to one side and gave Carol a small shrug. "We're glad someone bought it. That house has been sitting there like a tombstone for almost a year." She paused, then added, "knowing her husband made me a man hater. The biggest egotist I have ever met in my entire life."

Thoughts of Don hammered at my confidence. I glanced over at Patricia. She was looking at her watch and began to gather her things. "I really must get home," she said.

Two hours had passed quickly. "Me too," I parroted, glad for the escape. "It's the maids' day off," I said, pushing my chair back from the table. "Actually, she's off seven days a week. *And the truth I thought to myself?* Don was angry enough last night with the war zone of a den, unfinished yard work; so angry he had shoved me against the refrigerator door. He would be more than irritable tonight if the same thing happened. I knew what could follow irritable. Medical bills. Mine.

Dana brought the children upstairs. "Can they stay?" she pleaded.

"Me stay wiff her," Bridget said and Dana hugged her for the unsolicited comment.

I looked at Kathleen. "It's fine with me," she said. "Such darling little girls. Let them stay and we will bring them back in a few hours."

Carol began clearing the table. "Nice to meet you," she said. "Let's do this again."

I nodded my head, wishing I had the freedom to offer my house as the next gathering place. But I couldn't. The interior decay was bad but this group could never see the domestic decay. Patricia, Kathleen and I walked to the door together. "Hope you write like you speak," Kathleen said. "You could have a seismic effect on the publishing industry."

I walked outside wishing I actually lived as I had talked. "Cross your fingers," I said, "and thanks for the coffee and encouragement."

Patricia was anxious to get home as well, and walked briskly ahead of me. The homes were all built on large lots, each just a half acre. Her house was three doors down from mine on the opposite side of the street and looked almost as neglected. She seemed so delicate, like a cricket trying to survive on a toad's lily pad and was as out of place with Kathleen and Carol as I was in New England.

"Hope to see you again," I said as I caught up to her. I looked up her walk. A short, balding man, dressed in a short sleeved shirt and tie, loomed in the doorway.

"You're late," he shouted. "I have to get back to work."

She smiled briefly. "A pleasure meeting you," she whispered, then skittered up her walk like a sandpiper.

"Sorry" she said to him, her voice chirpy. She scurried up the stairs and vanished into her house like an apparition.

I was still playing the role of a confident woman thinking *that poor woman is married to such a jerk*, when I approached our drive and remembered *so are you*.

The house was empty and I was anxious to put my newfound inspiration to use. I hurried to the den to finish a piece I had been working on for weeks. The flow of words came quickly I couldn't type fast enough. Within a few hours I was typing the last page when I saw Don standing in the doorway of the den and froze.

"What the hell are you doing down here?" he said. "And where are the kids?"

I pushed my chair away from the desk and realized I had never changed clothes. I was still dressed in a skirt, tailored blouse, pantyhose and heels, I stood up. "Just fooling with something," I said. "The girls are at a neighbor's house playing. They'll be home soon."

His eyes roamed the den and then back to me. "What's with the dress up clothes?"

"A neighborhood luncheon," I said. "I met some lovely, professional women."

He laughed. "Professional women? Hope you don't mean hookers."

Anger rose in my throat but I let it pass. "Hookers? One is a CPA; the other is the President of their company."

"Company?" he laughed. "You mean a little craft shop or something?"

I was thrilled at the thought of telling him. "No, as a matter of fact, they own a Ryder Truck Enterprise. They have over fifty trucks so far and doing very well."

"Really?" He looked perplexed. "Do their husbands actually own it?"

"No." I walked past him. "They do."

He followed me upstairs. It was almost six o'clock and I hadn't started dinner. "Don't make me anything," he said as he walked down the hall to the bedroom. "I had a late lunch."

The front door was open and a fresh breeze drifted through the screen door and up the stairs into the kitchen. Kathleen was about to ring the doorbell when she saw me at the top of the stairs and I waved her in. Bridget and Stephie raced up the stairs ahead of her and threw their arms around my waist. "Me home, mommy," Bridget said.

Kathleen stood in the kitchen and laughed. "They are angels," she said. "Dana wanted to keep them forever."

"Thanks. I think they needed to be away from me for a while. Can I pay Dana for her services?"

"Oh no," Kathleen said. "Dana loved it as much as the girls did."

As she turned to leave, Don shouted down the hall. "Where the hell are my jeans? Didn't anything get done around here today?"

I could feel my face flush. "In the closet," I shouted back.

"Such helpless babies, aren't they?" Kathleen said.

"Not really", a deep voice said curtly. A cigarette dangled out of his mouth as he rolled up the sleeves of his shirt.

My stomach knotted as I made the introductions hoping she would leave.

Kathleen frowned. "Then you're one of the rare ones," she said, punctuating the sentence with a laugh. "Most men are."

Don flashed his I'm-tolerating-you-look-smile. "Well, as long as they make enough money for you girls to spend, it doesn't really matter if they take rattles to work, does it?"

Kathleen wanted to say more but had the good sense not to. "Nice to meet you," she said, extending her hand. Reluctantly, Don shook it and she left.

Embarrassed, I closed the front door. My heart raced as I walked back to the kitchen to start dinner.

"Where did she come from?" he asked.

I kept my back to him. "A neighbor. She has one with the nicest house on the street. Her husband is the Assistant District Attorney. Why?"

"She's not your type. If you're going to waste away the day with catty women, get a part time job." He snapped the newspaper off the kitchen counter and strolled into the living room.

Oh yes she is but the subject wasn't worth an argument. I smiled to myself, proud I could control my tongue this time; prouder still that no matter what he said, I intended to do what I wanted to.

Stephie ran in the back door which led off the kitchen onto a deck. "Is dinner ready?"

"In a minute, sweetie. Go wash your hands and round up Bridget."

She stood in the kitchen looking at the front and back of her fingers. "But they aren't dirty," she whined.

"Mind your mother!" Don's voice boomed from the living room which was separated from the kitchen by a pony wall. "And stop whining or I'll give you something to cry about!"

Stephie rolled her eyes in disgust. "Why is Daddy so mad?" she whispered.

I bend down and whispered in her ear. "He had a bad day at the office, honey."

I was glad she was too young to understand it was only a bad day at the office because he had to come home.

Then I heard her tell her sister, "Dad doesn't like it here anymore."

●   * *

CHAPTER 7

October 1976

*T*he mail truck was in our drive. When the doorbell rang my heart jumped. <u>Redbook Magazine</u> *liked my article;* Positive thinking. *They must have sent the acceptance certified mail.* I'd been waiting months for this. "You've made it, Penelope," I told myself out loud. I raced down the stairs, jumped from the middle step into the foyer and pulled the door open.

My mouth dropped as dreams slammed into reality like bird poo on a windshield.

"Damn it," I snapped.

"Hello would have been nice," Don said. "Why is the door locked anyway?"

He walked past me carrying the mail, smelling like leaves and sweat. With the promise of a turkey dinner, I had escaped the dead leaf drudgery as the promised aroma filled the house.

"Smells great in here," he said sorting through the mail. He stopped at a manila envelope?

"What's this?" he said, holding it up. "Looks like your handwriting."

My return envelope. I stared at it, and the arrow of rejection penetrated my fledgling ego. Before tears could surface, I took it out of his hand and raced to the bathroom. Ten minutes later he knocked on the door.

"Leave me alone," I shouted. Never one to wait, he walked in on my disappointment.

"Why are you crying? It's just another silly contest, isn't it?"

I handed him the envelope and walked out to the kitchen. He followed and wrapped his arms around my waist. "So that's what you have been doing in the den; playing author. Why didn't you tell me? I'm proud of you for trying." He nibbled my neck. "And this isn't bad."

He turned me around to face him, placed his finger under my chin and gently lifted my face to his. "You're competing in a ruthless industry. Only the very best stand a chance, Pen. It's a good hobby, but I doubt you will earn any money doing it."

Money was the yardstick by which he assessed value in anything. "Why not look for a little part time job. You'll be less frustrated."

Only the best didn't include me in his eyes. Playing author? I couldn't speak and hated myself for my own inadequacies, and hated him for having so little confidence in me. *Get a little part time job?* Would he be happy with a little part time job when he was setting his sights on becoming president of his company in the future?

Then I remembered Kathleen's comment: 'Write like you talk.' And only I could decide if there would be a next time.

November 1976

It was another Saturday and I hated Saturdays. I wanted it to snow, do something, so we wouldn't have to contend with the mess of Mother Nature. Lawn mowing was over until spring and I had watched with pleasure when the first frost murdered the mums and weeds in one icy blow. But Don could always find something living out there he needed me to tend to.

He was sitting at the kitchen table drinking coffee when I stumbled down the hall. Hoping he would be swallowed up in the newspaper for at least an hour, I poured a cup of coffee and headed for the den. The cold November morning had triggered a few ideas I needed to put on paper before they were lost.

I started for the door. Suddenly Don reached out and grabbed my hand. "No time to play Hemingway today," he said. "We have more important things to do."

I frowned. "Like what? You can't mow frost."

"Sit down for a second," he said, folding up the paper. He had a strange smile on his face; one I thought he would use as tender to get me involved in something I didn't want to do.

"I will when I get downstairs." I made another attempt to leave when he got up for coffee, then pulled out a kitchen chair and pointed. "Like I just said, we have things to do and not much time to complete them."

I slumped in the chair like a brat and tapped a bare, cold foot on the ugly gold linoleum. "What's this 'we' stuff, big guy?"

He looked across the table and smiled. "We are going to host a Christmas cocktail party for the region."

I gazed around the kitchen thinking he was forfeiting good judgment in the name of management. "Here?" I said. "You know this place isn't company ready. The house either needs more work than you and I have time to do, or a match. You choose." I reached over and grabbed his lighter. "Since we don't have matches, this should do." I clicked the lighter and a small flame shot up.

He laughed, grabbed a piece of paper off the counter and started writing.

"What are you doing?" I asked. "Sending me some corporate do-it-or-else memo?"

He didn't look up. "Making a list of to-do's, what-if's and maybe's for this house."

I grimaced, pulled a thick tablet out of the kitchen drawer and popped it down on the table. "When you're finished with volume one—which will be the kitchen—I'll be in the den."

He looked up, a mischievous grin on his face. "Stay put." He looked around the room and jotted something down. "Now, I figure with a bit of effort, this room could look like a quaint country kitchen."

I laughed. "Really? And just which country were you referring to?"

"Come on, Pen. Work with me."

Ego entertaining made him lighthearted, whimsical and warm so I easily conceded. "Okay. I could make new curtains, blacken a few pots and stop polishing the faucet in the sink so it will look like pewter. Is that quaint enough for you?"

"That's my girl," he said. Now I knew he was serious and gave the kitchen another look. It was a large room, centrally located between the dining room and the living room and not such a bad place as long as you didn't look at the floor. The cabinets were scratch-free knotty pine and the new appliances did add a bit of polish. Maybe he was right, I thought.

"Come on. Let's take a tour, honeybunches." He hadn't called me that in years. He draped his arm around my shoulder and we walked into the living room.

"This place could double as a morgue," I said. Wallpapered in cheap, tasteless, white butcher-like paper, the room had little appeal with the exception of a large, rock fireplace and the new couch he had purchased in his remodel for the Virginia home.

"Look." His voice was optimistic. "All we need to spice up this room is drapes to soften the government white look. You are a master at that. If anyone can make something out of nothing, you can."

I sneered. There were four double hung windows and an Arcadia door leading to the back deck, which translated into miles of drapes. "Aren't you confusing me with that chick that spun straw into gold?" I let out a long sigh. "I'll give it a try if you do your part."

He stared at the bare wood floors which was his part. "These hardwood floors need a bit of varnish and the fireplace should be cleaned out." He kicked the fringe of a wannabe Persian rug. "We'll get this cleaned. I'll take care of that after you make the drapes."

The idea of having a glittery Christmas party was beginning to sound appealing. "Okay", I said. "Maybe with a large Christmas tree, evergreen boughs and red velvet bows, we could have sufficient Band-Aids to keep the snowstorm on the outside where it belongs."

His eyebrows arched. "You mean put the tree up before Christmas Eve?" His tradition had been rigid.

"Or pretend you're Jewish," I answered. "It's up to you."

He shrugged his shoulders. "You win, in the name of corporate necessity." He checked his list. "Okay, let's move on to the next eyesore."

Eyesore, I thought. Why, with all the money he was earning and driving a company car, were we still struggling financially? I never saw the checkbook so I had no idea. At that moment I decided: *Next week* I will find the checkbook.

"Pen?" he snapped his fingers. "Stay with me here. We need to finish this list."

I looked down at my tired blue robe. "Okay, as long as you are not referring to me as the 'next eyesore'. He smiled and I followed him down the hall to the bedrooms. They were all on the same floor, to the left of the kitchen and could be easily viewed by any guest who wanted to use the bathroom. He quietly opened Bridget's door. She was asleep, her wavy hair spread out on the pillow like a Christmas angel.

"This room is so small," I whispered, "she probably feels like she never left the womb." Collectively we scanned the room. Walls were papered in faded neglect; an off white paper which had a white background with faded little grandma flowers every few inches in varying shades of pathetic pink. "What do you think?" I said.

He pulled the door shut. "That's what I think."

Stephie's room and the master bedroom were directly across from the bathroom. "We can't close all the doors," I said softly, opening the door to her room. She was buried under the covers. "Maybe you should paint this room."

Don shook his head and closed the door. "We don't need to go that far. Her maple furniture makes the room look rustic which is acceptable for New England."

"Rustic?" There was a squeal in my diction. "Has the word tenement eluded you?"

"No. But the money to fix it up has. Besides, it's just a kid's room. It won't matter."

By the time we finished with our bedroom and got to the bathroom, my level of tolerance was two quarts low. We stood in the doorway. "Well, if cleanliness is really akin to godliness, you should only invite atheists," I said.

He shook his head. "What made you think cancelled checks would make great wallpaper?" he said. "And those signs. Where did you get them?"

A hand carved wooden sign saying *DEPOSITS* hung just above the toilet. Another sign, *WITHDRAWALS* hung on the linen closet door inside the bathroom. "Kathleen's son made them in woodshop."

Just the mention of her name made him frown. He and Tom had become great friends but Kathleen was an unpleasant side effect to the friendship. "I should have guessed," he said. "And before I forget, they are not invited. This is for company people only." He looked down at his list. "Let's finish this up."

The jovial romp ended, his mood easily blackened by the mention of her name. We walked downstairs to the den. "Get that writing mess cleaned up," he said in an agitated voice. Sweeping the air with his hand he added, "And put all your garbage in the closet."

And your stuff? I thought. His debris was labeled important papers, not to be touched by my un-business-like hands. I didn't want to argue and followed him around the room. Knotty pine paneling made this the coziest room in the house. A large stone fireplace offered a bit of Abe Lincoln charm and three small windows at ground level offered more light than view. Built-in shelves were filled with neatly arranged books. An overstuffed blue chair was pulled up by the fireplace. A matching couch, the rips hidden by pillows, nested under the windows. A large television faced the couch, the only new furniture in the room. Old school desks served as end tables, their sloping, antique (scratched) surfaces blending in with the historical feel of the room. We had moved the chair and school desks from Virginia. The rest had been picked up at yard sales. Christmas puffery, I decided, would hide most of the imperfections if they made velvet bows that wide.

We ignored the downstairs bathroom/ laundry room and the children's playroom and walked upstairs. Don started a shopping list while I made breakfast.

"Are Gene and Angelina coming?" I asked. His boss was a wonderful man, conspicuously handsome with the manners of a king. His wife, however, was someone who should be bound, gagged and tossed into Boston Harbor.

"Don't start," he said. "Of course they are both coming. And it doesn't matter what you think of her. You'll just have to tolerate it. I expect you to be gracious. He is my future. She is his wife. Do you understand me?"

Yes, master. In remembrance of her, I cracked an egg so hard on the rim of the frying pan it splattered all over the stove and on the floor.

December 1976

The electricity of Christmas pumped through me as I paused in the doorway of the kitchen where Don was racing to set up the bar.

"My God," he said. "You're exquisite." He looked me up and down. "Good, a long dress. Your varicose veins won't show and you will be more relaxed. So where did you get the dress?"

"You don't want to know."

He braced himself against the kitchen counter, dressed in a new suit. "Yes I do. I didn't give you enough money for a dress like that."

"Of course you didn't. You needed the money for the new suit you have on." I ran my hand over the soft black velvet. "I altered the bodice to a look-at-me-view and tailored the sleeves from court jester to First Lady. Goodwill doesn't have much of a collection for designer gowns."

"You're kidding? My wife shopped at a store for beggars?"

"It's called a thrift store, Don. The money you gave me was just enough for this."

He eyed me with a new thoroughness. "Don't you dare tell anyone, got it? I would be the laughing stock of the region. And don't have more than one drink or you'll start blabbing. Got it?"

What a comment coming from a man who could drink through a distillery in a week.

"If anyone asks where you got that, I want you to say Saks or Filene's. Especially Angelina. She is a walking brand name."

The house gleamed tonight. Electric candles with single white bulbs were centered in each window. There was a roaring fire in each fireplace and the hardwood floors could double as a mirror. The Austrian inspired valances enhanced the floor to ceiling drapes that featured a designer-looking print in deep greens and blues on a white background. I was pleased that they looked professional instead of Penne-made. And who would know they were made from sheets which I had lined with more sheets, or that the rods were actually wooden closet dowels I purchased at a lumber supply yard?

As we stood in the kitchen, Don's mood changed from bad to good. "We did it, honeybunches," he said. "The place looks great." He looked over the chest-high pony wall and stared at the Christmas tree in front of the window. "You'll be rewarded for this, "he said. Just wait until Christmas morning."

"That's two weeks away? At least give me a hint."

He thought for a moment and said, "Crab legs."

I shook my head and walked into the dining room to check the buffet, and stared at a large crystal bowl I had borrowed from Kathleen, filled with crab legs and shrimp laid out on a mountain of crushed ice. *Crab legs for Christmas? Hairy little legs? Surely he wasn't getting me an electric razor?*

The table was laden with every showy delicacy he could think of for me to prepare. Tall red candles stood at attention in the center of fresh evergreen and pine cones. Napkins were tied with red velvet bows and the silverware (a Texaco special, of course) shone like we borrowed it from Buckingham Palace.

"There's the door bell," Don said. "I'll get it. You fill the ice buckets."

"Hope we're not too early," said a strong male voice. I stood in front of the refrigerator and cringed as Gene and Angelina Arigone followed Don into the kitchen.

"Welcome," I said and officially assumed my role as cheery hostess.

Angelina kissed me airily on the cheek and I could smell the alcohol. Her eyes darted from one wall to the next. "Gene told me you bought a fixer-upper," she announced. "Don't mind if I take a little tour, do you? Fixing up old houses like these is my specialty."

Without waiting for a response, she clicked off down the hall in three inch heels like some empress of interior design. The deep green cocktail dress hugged her body like a pea pod. Within minutes she clicked her way back to the kitchen and walked up to me fluffing her long black hair with her fingers. "Now what type of window treatment are you considering for that window over the sink?" she said, pointing. Her nails were wickedly long and painted transfusion red.

I stared at the white Priscilla curtains trimmed in fabric matching the tablecloth. "The coverings are new," I said. I had finished them just the night before in a race against morning. "I like the look and won't be changing them."

She nodded her head from side to side. "Frumpy," she announced. "Shutters would work better. I know a great little shop in Boston. I'll introduce you to the owner."

Why not introduce me to your wealthy parents instead you only child brat? Fuming, I looked over at Don for backup. But he was too engrossed in conversation with Gene to hear the insults.

As our other guests began arriving, Angelina insisted we look at the rest of the house, "I need to attend to my other guests," I said sharply.

She walked over to Don. "Sweetie, could you handle the arriving guests for one moment while Penne and I take a tour of the rest of the house?"

"Of course, Angelina," he said sweetly, kissing her check.

"Okay," she said, "I have a few suggestions.

Steaming inside I followed the domestic diva down the hall to the bathroom which I assumed she had already seen. She flipped on the light and announced, "This room has no character."

Then the room has your name on it, I thought bitterly.

"You need to liven it up. Replace the tile in here with a shower enclosure. And I would get rid of the checks on the wall. They are foolish looking."

Who the hell was this demon? I thought silently. *And why do I have to stand here and listen to her inebriated insults?*

"Not going to happen," I said nastily.

She looked at me as if I was some beggar. I met her cold stare thinking she was the most insensitive, ill-mannered trollop I had ever been around who probably wouldn't offer me a drink of water in the desert if she owned the water company. "Old New England homes are difficult," she lectured, rubbing her lily white hands together as if she was freezing. "You have to know what you're doing. You'll have to see our home and the marvelous changes I've made. You won't find anything like it in New England."

I wish I hadn't found anything like YOU in New England. We walked back into the kitchen where Don was mixing a pitcher of martini's as Gene looked on, his handsome face highlighted by the warm flow of light from the ceiling fixture.

"Would you like a little Smirnoff, Angelina?" Don asked.

She snuggled up against him and put her finger on his chin. "And what else?"

Give her Smirnoff, I want to suggest, with a dash—no—make that a jigger of glue to keep her mouth shut.

Don caught my eye and gave me a slow blue-eyed wink. Putting his finger to his lips, he begged my silence as Angelina prattled on.

"I designed our master bath and created this darling breakfast nook with the architect. You don't buy an old house like this unless you know how to fix it up." She rolled her eyes at the ceiling. "Of course you have to afford it too." She paused and put her drink on the counter. "I need to use your bathroom," she said. "The plumbing does work, doesn't it?"

Gene rolled his eyes in disgust and strolled into the dining room. "Beautiful spread, Penne," he said. "And your home is lovely."

"Thank you," I replied and pulled Don to my side. "About the only thing she hasn't taken credit for tonight is the creation of heaven and earth." I whispered.

"May have slipped her mind," he quipped. "Just be polite no matter what she says."

Guests began arriving in a steady stream and within an hour the house was alive with festive dresses, clinking glasses and laughter. Over forty people circulated through the living room, dining and downstairs in the den. Soft Christmas music played in the background as I moved through the crowd with trays of food, keeping an eye on Angelina, who made herself one drink after the other, vodka straight up. She mingled with a few people who seemed to tolerate her with a 'you-are-the-boss's-wife courtesy' then disappeared downstairs. Finally I could relax.

It was almost eleven-thirty and I was chatting with several couples near the stairs when Angelina walked up from the den. She approached me, staggering. "I told your children to go to bed," she said, her body swaying as she spoke. "It's much too late for them to be up. Children should never be at an adult party."

Fueled by two drinks, I jumped out of my chair. "And just who put your name on my mailbox?" I said too loudly. The room grew silent. "For the record, I am their mother and I want them to join us. I prefer the company of kind little children."

Snickers filtered through the room as Angelina stood there and smiled, as if my words had popped like soap bubbles before reaching her ears.

Don was behind me in a flash. "Penne!" he snapped, then consciously calmed his voice. "Will you watch your mouth?" he whispered.

The anger crawled through me like electricity. Suddenly Gene stepped up between us and put his arm around my waist. "Penne is right, Don," he said calmly. Angelina deserved more than that."

He turned and stared at his wife who had propped her Smirnoff soaked body against the arm of a chair. His face was red with embarrassment as he leaned into me and whispered, "I'm so sorry, Penne. Wish I could blame it on liquor, but I can't. She was born rude."

But you weren't, I thought, and found myself studying this incredible man with dark black hair, perfect complexion and straight nose. The electric look in his green eyes made me think I had come face to face with Sir Galahad.

Suddenly, a hand clamped firmly around my upper arm and Don steered me back to our bedroom away from the guests. "What the hell is the matter with you?" he snarled. Shutting the door, he shook me as he talked. "First you insult his wife and then you stand there like some dopey teenager ogling her husband."

"Get your hands off me," I said, making no attempt to lower my voice.

He put his hand over my mouth. "Will you keep your voice down? You are making a fool of yourself."

I pulled his hand away and opened the door. Gene was standing in the hall. "Ah, sorry to interrupt. I just came back to get our coats."

He stepped between us into the bedroom and pulled their coats off the bed. "Don't let my wife create problems between you two". He put his hand on my shoulder. "You have really tolerated a lot from her tonight, Penne."

He looked at Don. "This woman is a sweetheart," he said. "Hope you know how lucky you are." He patted my shoulder and walked down the hall.

He and Angelina were the first to leave. At the front door, Angelina threw her arms around me in a sloppy hug. "See you in San Francisco," she slurred.

"Angie!" Gene whispered too loud. "Be quiet!"

She giggled and put her index finger up to her mouth. "Uh oh, that was a secret, huh."

I wasn't sure what to expect when I awakened the next morning. Don had fallen asleep five minutes after the last guest disappeared. There had been no aftermath and I shuddered thinking it had just been delayed.

He slept until six o'clock that evening. I heard him trudge down the hall as I stood at the stove stirring beef gravy. He stepped up behind me and I flinched. His lips met my neck in an unexpected kiss and a chill ran through me as I turned around. "What's that for?"

"For the great job you did last night." He took his coffee mug off the rack. "How old is this stuff?"

"Just made it," I said as euphoria floated from my cheeks to my toes, like a prisoner who had just been pardoned. His alcohol consumption had apparently obliterated some of his memory from last night. "Hungry?"

"Sure. Just let me get some coffee and wake up and then we can have dinner."

"Kids," he called out as he sat down at the table. "Come here for a second. Daddy has a surprise for all of you." They scurried to his side as he pulled an envelope out from under the placemat and held it above his head.

"What's that Daddy," Stephie asked.

"An early Christmas present," he said smiling.

She frowned. "In an envelope?"

He reached over and playfully tapped her head. "Big things can come in very small packages, Steph."

Leaning back in his chair he peered inside the envelope. "Wow!" he said, snapping it shut.

"Let me see," Steph said stretching her hand toward the envelope.

He picked up Bridget, put her on his lap and pulled a chair up beside him for Stephie. "Pen, sit down for a second, okay?"

Always the showman, he pulled out a white and blue piece of paper and held it in front of Stephie's face. "Can you read the top pumpkin?"

Stephie had been reading since she was four. "U,ah,n," she struggled.

"Let Daddy help you. The first word is United."

"Oh, I know the second word," she said. "Airline. It was on TV." She turned her head and looked at him in wide eyed wonder. "You bought us a plane?"

We all laughed. "Close," Don said giggling. "I bought you all a ride on a plane all the way across the country to California!"

"Don," I yelled. "Your region qualified?" Corporate Leadership Conferences were the gold rings of any year, all-expense paid trips throughout the country. And we had never been. Angelina's parting slurs now rang with understanding. And so did crab legs. San Francisco! But I never dreamed we could take the children.

"Who wants to see Shamu and Mickey Mouse?" he shouted.

"Me!" the kids yelled in unison.

"Aren't those attractions in Southern California, honey?" I asked.

"Yup, about thirty minutes away from Mom's house. We will all stay with her for a week, and she will care for the kids while we are in San Francisco. Okay?"

Beneath my smile I did my usual thing of worry. We all needed summer clothes. Extra money had already been spent by Santa Don and I knew the company would not pay for new wardrobes to meet an overdressed mouse and a whale.

"I can see the worry on your face, Pen. But don't. First of all, my little girls fly free. And after Christmas, just use American Express and get us all outfitted. Okay?"

"And when the bill comes?" I smiled. "Do we leave home without it?"

He got up from the table and kissed my cheek. "I'm in management now. Don't be cheap, hon. We need to look our best. Let me worry about the money. You worry about looking like a classy wife."

Let him worry about the money? Was this impetuosity without financial foundation? Amex would let us know.

CHAPTER 8

March 1977
San Francisco, CA

*T*hree thousand miles away from Massachusetts, I pressed my nose to the window glass in our hotel suite, enchanted by the sights and sounds of San Francisco. Palm trees (I had never seen one before) poked up where least expected. People dressed in colorful seersucker and cotton ambled amid food and curio stands on Fisherman's Wharf.

My body tingled with the excitement of being in this worldly city and of the elegance that surrounded us. How glorious, I thought, as I walked through our suite, for his company to think he was important enough to be worthy of such accommodations. The sitting room featured plush beige couches, marble top tables and a large oriental vase of exotic flowers on the coffee table. A European ambience flowed through the bedroom with its sunlit oak dressers, designer window coverings and a bed so large it looked like an island in the room.

Don was standing by the window in the bedroom. I approached him in silence, slipped my arms around his waist and looked out across the San Francisco Bay, trying to focus on what he was watching so intently.

"Isn't this magnificent?" he said. "Look over there." He pointed with his index finger as darting seagulls played above the wharf like misguided balsa wood planes. Gray-blue water stretched in choppy wavelets across the horizon and about half a mile away, an island appeared, a foreboding mass, resembling a fort, rose out of the water. "That's Alcatraz, the most notorious maximum security prison ever built," he said.

"The gannet," I said, shaking my head. "It's such a strange name for a place like that."

He looked at me. "What do you mean 'gannet'?

I smiled. "Alcatraz comes from the Spanish word gannet, which is a species of bird."

He looked annoyed. "How did you know that?"

"I learned to read in first grade," I giggled. "And survived Spanish in college. It's one of the ten words I remember." I could tell by his expression I needed to feed his male mentor appetite. He was happiest imparting information to me and not the other way around. "Is it vacant?"

He puffed out his chest. "Sure. It was closed by the Federal Prison System many years ago."

I snuggled against him. "Wouldn't it make a great hotel?"

He looked down at me and laughed. "Hotel? There's nothing around it but water with a treacherous undertow. You can't even swim in it. Why a hotel?"

"It's all about theme. Employees could dress in black and white stripes and guests could never leave the island without paying their bill."

"You're crazy," he laughed. "I'll write Sheraton when we get home, see if they share your vision." He drew me into his arms. I nipped at his lips and felt his shuddered responses.

"How much time do we have before the cocktail party?" I whispered.

His breathing was raspy. "Two hours."

Nips were not enough. We kissed with a pulsating passion. As our words turned into noises, a language without consonants, we grabbed at each other's clothes in a lustful frenzy. Naked on the bed, we lost ourselves in each other's arms the way we used to be.

Don looked like a celebrity tonight. Dressed in black slacks, white shirt and black tweed blazer; he hobnobbed with his sales team, introducing me to managers from around the country. Gathered in a ballroom in the hotel, these company stars were enjoying the celebration and their natural gaiety combined with a never ending liquor supply kept the fun continuous.

He kept me close to his side, his arm forever slipping around my waist. I was sharing his importance, and we lime lighted as a sincere team. Tonight I was not at all bothered by the fact that he was still the captain.

Feeling the buzz of two cocktails, we left the ballroom in an hour to tour the city with two other couples who, after dinner at a lavish restaurant, went their separate ways. Anxious to show me a silent itinerary gleaned through his military assignment at the Defense Language Institute, Don hailed a cab to Lombard Street, purportedly to be the crookedness' street in the world. Giddy, I removed my high heeled shoes and challenged him to a race.

"I think you've had a little too much to drink," he said but removed his shoes.

I kissed his chin. "Actually, I've had way too much. Are you going to take advantage of me?

"Absolutely," he said, and we began our race up the street.

The constant anticipation of loving and of being loved continued for the five days of the conference. And in the fascination for each other, we fell in love all over again.

"I hate to leave this place," I said.

"That's what I love about you, Pen." He smiled, picked up the phone and called the front desk for a bell hop.

"Love what?"

He covered the mouthpiece of the phone. "You'll always be my little girl."

As we drove back to Los Angeles to be reunited with the children, I was at a peace. I felt safe.

I eased back on the couch in his mother's house like a slug, exhausted from two days of wading through duck like throngs of people in Disneyland and Sea World. Mental snapshots of the children kept popping up and I smiled, remembering our sheer joy as we watched the famous attractions take them by surprise.

His mother's house was a warm, inviting atmosphere to unwind. Outside the front window, thick, lush ivy crawled in professionally trained symmetry. Gazing through the living room I could see the back yard through French doors. A large pool surrounded by fruit trees, pines and white rock, dominated the yard. In the distance I could see mountains with peaks of snow I didn't have to shovel.

Inside, the Early American décor offered fodder for silent amusement. Eagles seemed to be the foundation as the symbolic birds stood watch on the tops of lamp harps and held towels in their beaks in the kitchen and baths.

My eyes were drawn to family pictures which sat on every available surface and I lazily began tracing Don's childhood from frame to frame. He sat as a baby on the piano and as a toddler with his baby brother on the end table. On the mantel he glowed in a tuxedo at his Junior Prom, his arm wrapped photographically rather than lovingly around the waist of his date that looked like a twelve-year-old playing dress up. By the time my eyes reached the library table, Don had become a Staff Sergeant in the Army with a smile that suggested he was a self-proclaimed hero long before the Army knew his name. Snuggled close to that silver frame was a small picture of Don the family man—Stephie and Bridget were babies. Our contrived poses and say-cheese-smiles made us look like an ad for the American Dairy Association.

"Bored?" His mother startled me as she appeared in the doorway. Her face was tanned, healthy looking and she challenged aging in a short denim skirt and flowered top.

I looked up at her and smiled. "Bored? Not even close. Content is more accurate."

"Did Don take the girls to Hollywood?"

I laughed. "Oh yes, cameras and everything. He had them thinking they would be having cokes with 'The Fonz' from 'Happy Days.'

Her laughter was like a wind chime. "He's always been optimistic. Could I treat you to a vodka and tonic out by the pool?"

I stretched my arms over my head and stood. "That sounds great."

Birds chirped, a gentle breeze ruffled the blue water in the pool and backyard sprinklers soaked thickets of bone dry pines as we relaxed in plush deck chairs. I laid my head back and caught the warmth of sun on my face. "This is the life I've always dreamed about," I said. "When I was in junior high, my parents bought an above ground pool. At first it was fun. But after one week with four brothers and sisters, it was like trying to swim in a bucket. I sat out there every day, thinking of friends who were going to exotic, splashy places like Florida, California and Hawaii for their summer vacation. I wanted so much to be like them so I tried to get the deepest tan I could. Every day I spent at least two hours in the sun. By September, I had a traveled tan instead of that day-in-the-backyard look. And this was the setting I imagine, a paradise with palm trees."

"You're always welcome to stay," she said. "You sound just like Victor. He really loved this place."

The mention of my father-in-law's name kindled a snug memory and I turned my face toward hers. "I've never known another man who treated me as well as he did. He made me feel like a princess and I adored him."

"Mr. Charm," she said and gulped her drink. "He was good at that. Always made outsiders feel like royalty. He was forever inviting strangers to dinner, offering to put them up when they fell on hard times, spending time and money his own family could have used."

The negativity was a complete surprise and made me flinch, not sure how to react.

"I think it was guilt," she continued and gave me an opaque look. "No, I take that back. I know it was."

Singed by the term outsider, an unwanted pallor now permeated the conversation. I studied her as a breeze caught her hair and blew it back from her face. I expected to see signs of anguish. What I saw was anger.

"I'm over his death," she said, and rattled ice cubes in her glass. "It's his life that still haunts me." She shook her head, pulled herself out of the trance, stood up and raised her empty glass like a parched Statue of Liberty. "Care for another?"

"No thanks. It doesn't take much to make me soar."

She laughed. "Me either, but I like that uninhibited feeling once in a while."

I wanted to get up before she came back but knew I couldn't be rude. Trapped in a dialogue I didn't care to be a party to, my stomach had knotted as I waited for her return.

In seconds she returned to her chair and began speaking like the 'play' button had just been pushed on her emotional recorder. "In death, Victor changed the lives of this family forever. Victoria took it the hardest." She looked up and talked into the sky. "Victoria just disappeared. She stayed with friends. She didn't want to attend the funeral." She turned her head in my direction, her eyes wandered above my head. "Victoria was his favorite." Her tone turned suddenly bitter. "He had taken her to school in the morning. When she came home, he was dead."

I trembled inside. "It must have been awful. I don't know if I could have been as strong as you had to be."

She breathed in audibly and a shadow crossed her face. "Did Don ever show you the suicide note?"

Where was she going with this? "Yes."

She straightened her back against the chair. "Do you remember any of it?"

I looked away for a moment to concentrate then shifted my gaze beyond her as I spoke. "I thought he couldn't stand the back pain anymore."

She stared alternately at the ground and me. Leaning forward, she placed her hand on my arm. "His back was fine," she said, her voice sparked in anger. "But his morals had ruptured a long time ago."

I withdrew momentarily, feeling shame as I recalled how easily I had discarded my mother's assumptions about his family. Now I couldn't discard the truth and feared my ability to handle it.

Her eyes narrowed as she leaned back in the chair. "He wasn't the loving man everyone thought he was. Underneath that gentle exterior was a violent, abusive man." She grew angrier with each word and tears began to trickle down her face. "I never had a broken bone until I married Victor. And his lap had more girlfriends than a napkin." She shook her head wearily and stared up at the sky. "You have no idea what it felt like to be hurt, dehumanized by a man you loved more than life itself. It had to be one of the most humiliating experiences on earth."

Jolted by her confession, I had to put my hands under my legs to quell the tremors. Tears coursed from my eyes as I wrestled with whether or not I could confide in her.

Then she made the decision for me. "I couldn't bear to tell my children so I ask that you not share our talk with Don." She wiped her eyes with a napkin. "He has enough pressure. And he idolized his father. They all did. And I don't want to take that away from them now that he's gone." She reached over and held my hand. "I'm sorry if I upset you, Penne. I just had to get it out. I don't think the pain in my heart will ever go away, even when I die."

Say something, I thought. "You were a good wife, Mom. You didn't make him behave that way. He was sick. You can't blame yourself for that. You had no way of knowing."

She nodded her head. "The signs were always there. I just loved him too much to see it. Thank you, honey, for understanding."

The sun flooded her face and a faint smile formed on her lips. "Donnie is so lucky to have you, and you're so lucky to have my Donnie. Covet his fidelity. Appreciate his gentleness. It has to be the greatest gift in life."

I closed my eyes as the vision of my Utopian family ruptured, exploding my doe-eyed fantasy, and the truth quivered with a grim resonance. I kept my eyes tightly closed and envisioned palm trees snapping off at the top and crashing to the ground. A dense black cloud was shrouding the sun. There was no breeze, no pool. The paradise was gone and all I could think about was getting out of there.

I never wanted to come back.

CHAPTER 9

June 1977
Auburn, Massachusetts

*T*he telephone rang and Don fished in the dark for the receiver. "From whom?" he said, and sat up in bed. "Oh. Sure. I'll accept the charges."

I turned on the light. The look on his face reflected worry blended with intrigue. "Lar, good buddy, how are you doing?" Cradling the receiver between his chin and shoulder, his eyes darted over to the clock. "A little after two," he said, then nodded. "No, it's not a problem. What kind of help?" His eyes narrowed as he listened. "How much do you need?" Sure, I can handle that. I think Western Union would be the fastest."

By the time he hung up I had a dozen questions. "What was that all about?" I asked.

Don yawned. "He's an old friend who needs some help."

I sat up in bed. "What old friend?"

He propped his head up on his arm. "His name is Larry Birkland. I wrote insurance for him in Virginia when he was in the Navy."

"And?"

"And he's living in Utah now. Lost his job. He wants to come to Massachusetts to job hunt and asked if we could put him up for a few weeks."

"What about the Western Union bit?"

Don rubbed his hand over his face. "He needs money."

Now I was irritated. "What does he want money for?" I said in a snippy voice.

He plumped his pillow. "Tires," he said nonchalantly.

I leaned my head back and sighed. "We barely make it from paycheck to paycheck. We can't afford to wire money to a perfect stranger."

He pushed his head into the pillow. "He's not a stranger. He's my friend. Where's that Christian spirit of yours, anyway? Or are you only nice to your fellow man when it's convenient?"

I snapped off the light. "That's not fair. I'm just a bit uneasy about some guy living in our house with you away all the time and I don't think we should be sending money we don't have."

"Oh come on. The guy is harmless." Don rolled over and put his back to me. "And I'll take care of the money."

I pulled the covers up under my chin and stared at the ceiling. "How?"

Don groaned. "Don't worry about it. Goodnight."

Sleep was the last thing I wanted to do. Questions poured through my head. How did this guy find us? And why had I never heard of him until tonight?

One week later, Don walked from bedroom to bedroom clapping his hands like some NFL coach. "Everybody up. I have a big surprise for you but we'll have to hurry."

I looked over at the clock on the night stand. It was almost seven-thirty. But it was Saturday and I didn't want to get up.

"Fill me in, pleasssssssssssse," I begged as he pulled the covers off me.

His eyes twinkled. "Let's just say I'm fulfilling a promise long overdue."

"I know a secret," chanted Stephie in the hall.

I popped up in bed. "You told the children and not me?"

A smile enveloped his face. "Sure, and they won't tell. Right kids?"

"Right Dad," they yelled as they raced down the hall.

We had been riding in the car for an hour and suspense was making me crazy as Don and the girls talked and laughed about what? I didn't know. I cut through the chatter. "Will you guys please let me in on this?"

"You'll see, Mom," Stephie said.

Don pulled the car up to a hanger at an airport in Connecticut which seemed to be miles away from the main terminal.

"Let's go," he shouted, scrambling out of the car. "I know his plane has landed by now."

I tagged behind them through the airport hangar. Don suddenly stopped in front of a door marked 'Shipping Office'. "Wait out here," he said, pointing to a row of chairs. "Be right back." He disappeared into the office, the black office door closing behind him like a shark's fin.

"Come on kids," I whispered. "Can't you at least give me a hint?"

Bridget put her finger to her lips. Her eyes sparkled under light brown bangs. "It's a secret, Mommy."

Minutes later the door opened and Don walked briskly beside a uniformed man to a loading dock, motioning for us to follow. Two large planes sat out on the tarmac, their bay doors open. We walked past the yards of large shipping cartons to the end of the dock then stopped.

"Here he is, folks," the man said, and pointed to a crate as large as a refrigerator. "Hope he survived the flight okay, sir," he said to Don.

"Who is 'HE'? I demanded.

"You'll see Mom," Stephie said, her voice high with excitement. She unfastened the clasp of her purse and pulled out a long, heavy leash. "Here Daddy," she said.

Don squatted in front of a grated opening. "Thanks pumpkin."

"Where did you get that Steph?" I asked.

She looked up, a mischievous grin on her face. "Daddy gave it to me before you got in the car."

Don unlocked the grate on the crate. "Now everyone stand back. He doesn't know us yet and he'll probably be frightened."

"He's frightened?" I said, and moved away from the cage.

An enormous shaggy dog with fluffy white and black fur lumbered out of the cage and stretched. The girls squealed as Don attached the leash to a thick, black collar.

"What kind of a dog is that?" I stammered.

"Old English Sheep pup," Don said. "Remember, I promised the kids a dog when we moved up here. It's about time I fulfilled that promise. Right kids?"

"Right Daddy," they chimed.

"And we wanted a white one, right Daddy? " Stephie said.

"Right pumpkin," Don laughed.

I stared in disbelief. "Pup? A puppy doesn't weigh close to fifty pounds!"

"Can I hold him Daddy?" Bridget asked.

"Not now, honey. He's pretty big and he might drag you. Let's find a place for him to go to the bathroom."

"Bridget bent down and looked inside the cage. "He did poops in here, Daddy."

Don smiled. "He probably needs to go again. Why don't you guys help me hold the leash?" The dog sauntered in front of them like a polar bear.

"What's him name?" Bridget asked.

"His name is Abercrombie Bear, sweetheart. But we'll just call him 'Bear', okay?"

The company car, an Oldsmobile, left little room for such a massive beast so Bear sat in the back seat, half off and half on the children; children who were intimidated by his size yet hesitant to say anything to their happy father who whistled as he drove.

"Who sent that thing?" I asked

"Larry. It was his way of thanking us for our forthcoming hospitality."

"And what do we feed it? Live rabbits?" I turned and looked at Bear. All I could see was a large tongue hanging out of his mouth. His eyes were completely obscured by bangs of fur.

Don patted his shirt pocket. "I have all the directions for care and feeding right here. Don't fuss. We are now the proud owners of a very rare breed of dog, especially in New England."

"Did he also send you the pedigree papers so he can be registered in our name?"

"No, but I'm sure he will bring them when he comes."

Bear was too large to fit in a standard dog house. Actually, Bear was too large to fit into anybody's house. We either needed to build him a condo in the backyard or assign him a guest room.

Finally at home, the dog shuffled through the once clean kitchen, slobbering and sneezing. "This won't work," I said as I watched his spittle drip down the pantry door.

"But Mom," Stephie wailed. "He's ours. Daddy said so."

Don gave me his shut-your-mouth-look. "Mommy's just teasing kids."

After dinner, the girls and Bear curled up on the rug in front of the television and fell asleep. "Now do you want to get rid of him?" Don whispered and winked.

"If he'll sleep twenty-four hours a day, then no. But answer me one thing. Why did this obscure friend of yours have money to ship a dog and no money for tires? In fact, why did he treat the animal to airfare when he is driving out here anyway?"

Don jabbed his cigarette in the ashtray, his eyes hardened. "We've just been given an expensive, beautiful dog which we've never paid a dime for, and all you've done is complained."

Never paid for? I think silently. The Visa bill had arrived the day before but I hadn't shown it to Don. Three hundred dollars had been wired to Larry the day after his phone call. The dog had already cost us plenty and something told me there was more to come.

CHAPTER 10

July 1977
Auburn, Massachusetts

*L*arry Birkland was a surprise. He did not act nor look like the type of person Don usually befriended and I stared at him unflinchingly as he and Don stood in the driveway rekindling their friendship like I was invisible.

Larry was about six feet tall, balding and scarecrow scrawny. Dressed in faded designer jeans and an ivy league shirt, he was unremarkable. A sloppy, used-car salesman mustache covered his upper lip like bangs on a two-year-old. He didn't smile, just smirked which I interpreted as menacing. Leery Larry was my silent name for him.

I waited until Larry walked around to the back of his car to quiz Don. "Isn't that a new car he is driving?" I whispered. "Why would he need tires?"

"Don't be rude," he said sharply. "You don't know that so don't bring it up."

"Look who's talking," I said. "Your friend is about as rude as they come. Did you even notice he didn't even say hello when you introduced us?"

Don pulled me back from the car. "Learn the difference between rude and shy," he said nastily. "And you can be a bit more hospitable. You'll make the man feel uncomfortable."

I stormed back into the house. This jobless soul, who was only going to be with us for a *few* weeks, had not arrived with a *few* suitcases. He was towing a U-Haul trailer packed solid with boxes. No furniture, just boxes and the car he was driving was a brand new Mercury Cougar with the dealer sticker still pasted on an inside window.

Don gave Larry the children's playroom downstairs, which was not exactly a room at the Sheraton; more like a doublewide boxcar with toys. The previous owners had converted one half of the two-car garage into this room with the same abandon for taste as the rest of the house. Aqua indoor-outdoor carpet, thinner than a tortilla, was glued to the cement. Two old day beds formed an L in a corner of the room and poorly installed shelving bowed with the weight of the children's toys. But Birkland made himself at home as if this arrangement was due him.

By the time Larry had unpacked, dinner was ready and the aroma of roast beef permeated the house as I called everyone to the table.

Larry sat down at the table; his hands still dirty from unpacking, surveyed the food with a critical eye and frowned. "Sorry," he said, suddenly pushing his chair back. "I can't eat this stuff. I don't kill animals to survive. I'm a vegetarian."

We watched in shock as he left the dining room, walked through the kitchen, grabbed a few pieces of fruit from the refrigerator like he owned it and disappeared downstairs.

"Mommy," whined Stephie. "I don't want to eat this either."

"Me too," Bridget mimicked.

"Eat your dinner," I said sharply. "You both like roast beef."

"This is ridiculous," I said to Don. "The man is a user, rude and now he's toying with nutrition. I refuse to play any sacrificial games for this lunatic!"

"Will you calm down?" he whispered. He balled up his napkin and tossed it on the table. "He's just different. That doesn't make him a lunatic."

I reached over and grabbed his shoulder. "He's not as generic as different. The man is weird. Charles Manson is probably his best friend!"

Don pushed my hand away. "Quit being so dramatic. And keep your voice down. You'll make the poor man feel unwelcome."

Then get me a bull horn, I thought, as Don flashed me one of his God-are-you-stupid looks and disappeared downstairs.

In the stillness of the night, I laid awake in our bedroom, waiting for Don. The hands of the clock seemed to move in arthritic jumps and minutes felt like hours. At a pinch after one a.m., Don finally walked into the bedroom. "How well do you know this guy?" I asked in punctuated whispers. "You've never talked about him before."

I heard his belt drop to the floor and pocket change being popped on top of the dresser. He got into bed and squirmed. "I thought you were asleep," he said and plumped his pillow. "But to answer your question, I haven't talked about lots of people I know. The only thing you need to know is the he is my friend and I expect you to grant him every courtesy. Understand?"

I hugged my side of the bed knowing there was nothing I could say to change his mind. I wanted to tell him I was afraid of his friend but knew he would respond callously, telling me I was afraid of everything, a statement I couldn't defend. At some point during the night, the quiet gave way to a fitful sleep.

August 1977

Mornings always came too fast. Plagued by sleeplessness for the past three weeks, I rarely wanted to get up. As sunlight streamed through the blinds, I rolled over to see if Don was awake and found he was more than awake. He was gone. Escaping to his office had become a convenient habit to avoid being near Larry, or, more accurately, to avoid my incessant complaints.

I grabbed my robe, walked out to the kitchen and made coffee. Suddenly strong arms wrapped around my waist. I looked down at the big hands in front of me. They weren't Dons'.

I spun myself free of Larry's embrace like a spool of thread. "The room and board around here does not include unsolicited affection," I snapped. "Keep your hands off me!"

Larry stepped back, gave me a sinister look and helped himself to coffee. "Don't try and pretend you didn't like it," he said with a smirk.

"I don't have to pretend, Birkland. I didn't. And don't ever touch me again." I stormed out of the kitchen, threw on some clothes, woke the children, dressed them quickly and told them we were going out for breakfast.

Two hours later I returned, thrilled to see Larry's car was gone. While the kids ran up the steep steps in the backyard to play, I unloaded the groceries. Balancing several bags, I tried to open the front door when I felt someone behind me.

"Looks like you could use some help," he said. Feigning chivalry, he lifted the bags out of my arms, set them on the front porch then turned around and kissed me.

I shoved him away. "You bastard! What the hell are you doing?" I yelled, wiping my mouth with the back of my hand.

He smirked. "All women love my kisses," he said.

My body stiffened in revulsion. "You pervert!" I slapped his face. "I'm not all women. Keep your damn slimy hands away from me!" I took two steps away from him before I thought of it. "Where's your car? I demanded.

Larry smirked. "In the garage, of course. I don't want the sun to destroy the finish."

"Get it out now! It is not your garage and this is not your house. And while you're at it, pack your bags and get the hell out of here!"

Larry's only reaction was to stand there like a telephone pole and smirk.

"What did he do?" Don's voice cut through the dark. He reached over me and turned on the light. Bed was the only place we had left for private conversations.

"Will you please lower your voice?" I whispered. "You'll wake the girls." I tugged at the covers and put my back to him. "You heard me the first time," I said into the pillow.

He laughed much too loudly. "You must be doing something to encourage him." His voice was cool, matter-of-fact. "Just show him your varicose veins. That should stop him cold. I know you don't like him here but making up little soap opera diversions won't work. He stays."

I sat up in bed. "I didn't make up anything, damnit. I'm not a liar and your know that. What happened actually happened. Husbands are supposed to protect their wives, not belittle them or put them in harm's way."

He ignored me. I turned off the light and marinated in hatred over this man who saw me in terms of his own discretions, distorting reality to do it. I was angry at myself. I wanted to slap Don's face and hurl insults at him and began to feel nauseous over my inability to do so. How could he put me in jeopardy and then be able to fall asleep? I decided I would do whatever it took to protect myself and my children, beginning tomorrow.

Don was in the yard mowing the grass when I slipped away from the house.

"Well hi, stranger," Kathleen said as she opened her screen door. "Haven't seen much of you lately. "What's up?"

It was just past nine on Saturday morning. The humidity from yesterday was unabated and helped to fuel a funnel of anger inside me. "Birkland," I snapped.

She patted my back. "Tom and I were just talking about him." Her angry expression gave me relief. I had come to the right place. "Come on out to the porch. What some coffee?"

"Sure." Her cool house was a welcomed respite from the heat and the porch was cooled by overhead fans. Tom sat at the table, surrounded by mounds of newspaper. Seeing me, he folded up his paper and smiled. "Well hey, little lady. How's life?"

I pulled up a chair. "Nothing an overdose wouldn't cure," I said.

He laughed as he stroked his beard. "So where's the hubby this morning?"

"Mowing a dead lawn," I said.

"And your guest?"

I ran my fingers through my hair. "Who knows? Probably robbing some store."

Tom stiffened his back against the chair, a frown forming on his face. "Didn't Don say he came to Massachusetts to job hunt?"

"Yup. But in the few weeks that vagrant has been here, he's only left the house twice, on the weekends when he supposedly has Naval Reserve meetings."

Tom tossed his head back and laughed. "Yes, I know about that. I met him in your drive last weekend dressed in a Navy uniform."

I grimaced. "What's so funny about that?"

"The blouse. It was covered in every medal known to the armed forces."

I struggled to keep my irritation from showing. "So?"

"So?" he patted my hand. "They were from other branches. Army. Marine Corp and Air Force. It was a bit strange on a noncom's naval uniform."

My eyes widened. "Did you tell Don?"

He lowered his face. "Not yet."

"I think you better!" Kathleen's face was stern as she walked over to the table and sat down a tray. "Pen's right. There is something really alarming about that guy."

I took a sip of coffee when the idea hit. "What are you guys doing for dinner tonight?"

Tom looked at Kathleen. "Begging," he said and we all laughed.

"Why not come for dinner?" I looked directly at Tom. "Get a front row seat. Don respects you and your opinion. Maybe you can encourage him to get that ass out of my house."

"That depends," Tom said smiling.

"On what?" I asked my voice too sharp for comfort.

"What are you having for dinner?"

Kathleen laughed. "He's an anatomical misfit. His brain and stomach is one organ."

I pushed my chair back from the table. "Then you'll come? Say six o'clock?"

"Sure," Kathleen answered. "But where are you going? You just got here."

I didn't let them see the panic I was feeling or let them know I needed to get back before Don discovered I was gone. "Food shopping," I said casually, "unless you'd consider eating ground Larry burgers."

Don snapped a glass of iced tea on the counter by the stove where I was cooking. "Why did you invite them to dinner without consulting with me?" His comment abruptly changed the atmosphere.

Continuing to cook, I stared at the stove while I spoke. "Why is it that when you invite guests, I'm just told about it? And if I invite someone, I have to ask you first?"

Don groaned. "I suggest you develop some protocol skills." His voice grew sharper with each word. "In a proper family, that is the way it is done." Grabbing the paper and his tea, he stomped down the hall to the bedroom and slammed the door.

I turned off the stove and followed. I stood in the doorway to the bedroom, my arms folded in contempt. "What is so bad about having your best friend for dinner?"

He crawled into the center of the made bed like a loggerhead turtle preparing to lay eggs, arranged the pillows to create a naptime nest and covered his face with his arm. "His wife," he said. "Kathleen challenged me several weeks ago about Larry and I don't like having to defend my decision."

He sat up, rolled the newspaper and flipped it off the bed. "Kathleen is a man hater. She spits insults faster than a mechanical pitcher in a batting cage. I don't like spending time with her. She's demented."

"And your house leech isn't?" I snarled. I walked to the end of the bed. "Kathleen is just a straight forward, no nonsense person who can't be charmed. If you give her a chance, you might discover that she is a nice, intelligent woman."

He propped his body up against the wall (we had never had a headboard), laced his hands behind his head and crossed his legs. "I don't want her here. And you are never to invite them again without my approval." His words were precise and chilly.

Anger displaced timidity. "This is my house, too. And I won't be treated like some child. I have as much right to invite people as you do. Tom is your friend; at least I thought he was your friend. I have had to tolerate Angelina's insults. You owe me."

He closed his eyes. "I make the rules around here. I pay the bills. This is the last time you invite anyone without my permission," he shouted.

I charged out of the bedroom and slammed the door.

It was after six o'clock. I quietly turned the handle of the bedroom door and pushed it open. The room was dark. Don was snoring. I walked over to the bed and gently shook him. "Don? Our guests are here."

He popped up in bed like a startled groundhog. "Why didn't you wake me sooner?"

"I tried. Several times. You didn't budge."

As Kathleen's laughter floated from the living room, Don scrambled out of bed, pulled on a pair of khaki slacks, grabbed a fresh shirt from the closet and headed across the hall to the bathroom.

"Your manners on loan, buddy?" Don's face tensed up, the lines in his forehead multiplied. He turned to face Kathleen who was standing in the hall and instantly forced civility. "You make it sound like napping is a felony," he said with a forced laugh.

I stood in the doorway, my heart pounding. "Domestic felony," said Kathleen. "Pen's been working her tail off trying to get dinner on the table."

I walked between them. "We're almost ready," I said smiling and walked down the hall to the kitchen.

"Cooking is her job, isn't it?" Don's voice filtered into the kitchen followed by the squeaking of the bathroom door.

Kathleen walked into the kitchen shaking her head in disgust.

"Just let it be," I whispered. "You don't have to live with him."

She stepped up next to me and whispered, "Neither do you."

Larry remained isolated in the playroom until I called him for dinner. He appeared in the dining room looking like he had walked to New York City and back. Unshaven, his clothes were wrinkled beyond the help of any iron. He sat down at the table and instantly introduced Tom and Kathleen to his reptilian manners before we even had napkins in our laps.

"Hey, pass them potatoes," he said, and without pausing added, "and I need one of you to write me up a resume."

Having successfully irritated Kathleen, Don's mood instantly improved. "I don't do clerical, Lar," he said laughing. "Better get the little writer in this house to help you."

The acid in my stomach was bubbling like some unattended stew on a burner as Tom turned his attention to Larry. "So what type of job are you looking for?"

"Something that pays well," Larry the idiot answered without looking up from his plate.

Kathleen choked on her water and Tom stifled what had to be an enormous laugh. "Do you have a degree?" he asked.

Larry nodded yes and continued to chew with his mouth open.

"What field?" Tom pushed on.

"Ah, '*cimmenatography*'," he replied, as a drop of mashed potatoes clung to his bottom lip.

I looked over at Don. His face was as flushed as a color of a flamingo. Apparently even he had never met anyone who held a degree in a field they couldn't pronounce.

Conversation was strained. In the middle of dinner, Larry tossed his napkin in his plate and pushed his chair back. "Got some TV I want to watch," he said. "I can't eat most of this stuff. I'm a vegetarian. I can't sit here looking at the poor dead cow on a platter anymore."

I glared at the children and they returned my stare. I knew my little talk with them had worked as they continued to eat. There was a collective sigh of relief when, forgetting his demand for a resume and his television commitment, Larry sprinted out the front door, jingling car keys in his hand.

Tom bellowed in laughter. "Different guy," he said, looking directly at Don. "Bit of a flake. He looked down at his plate. "I've never thought of prime rib in the primal form before, certainly while I was eating."

Don let his fork drop. "Come one. He's out of a job," he said defensively. "Anything wrong with the antique kindness of lending a helping hand?"

Tom sat back and patted his oversized belly. "As long as he doesn't steal the hand or kill the help, I suppose not."

Don polished off his wine in one gulp. "Come on, Tom. You think everyone's a criminal. The guy is harmless. Trust me."

The smile disappeared from Tom's face. "I wouldn't leave him alone with my family, Don."

Don laughed then stared at Kathleen. "Hell, I wouldn't leave him alone with your family either."

They ignited in laughter. Kathleen raised her water glass in a mock toast. "In Don we trust," she said.

Tom and Kathleen had been gone for over an hour and I had just finished cleaning up the kitchen. Don had not said one word since they left and my panic was building.

"We've got to talk," I told Don and closed the bedroom door.

"We have nothing to discuss," he said, with emphasis on the word *we*.

He was sitting up in bed reading. I walked over, sat on the edge of the bed and sighed. "Oh yes we do. I want that guy out of this house. Now!"

Don snapped his book in his lap and took a long drag on his cigarette. "That is not your decision to make. It is mine."

I clinched my teeth. "When was your lobotomy?"

He didn't respond at once, a fact I attributed to several glasses of wine. When he did speak, his delivery was slow, as if he was feeling his way through a dark tunnel. "Let's get something straight once and for all. I will not throw a friend out in the street. I make the decisions around here. I will handle it. Until then, you are to cooperate. Fully!"

The absence of hostility was surprising so I took advantage of it. "How comforting," I said and walked over to the closet to get my robe. "In light of your decision to let the guy stay here in the first place, I wouldn't brag if I were you."

He closed his book, put it on the night stand and turned out the light. "Just come to bed," he said. "And I don't want to hear another word about Larry Birkland."

I started out the door for the bathroom then stopped. "Why are you delaying the inevitable?"

He was snoring before I finished the question.

The next day, Don roared into the den with the mail. "There are three pages of calls to Utah, Arizona and California. Who do you think you are making calls like this?"

I was sitting at the desk as he shook the loose pages of the phone bill in front of me.

"I didn't make the calls," I said. I folded my arms in protest. "I don't know anyone in the west except for your mother!"

"Well, we have over two hundred dollars in charges."

I took the bill out of his hand. "Go show this to you chatty friend. And remember what the kids told us shortly after he got here."

"What?" He ran his fingers through his hair and swore.

Winning felt wonderful and I smiled. "They said 'Uncle' Larry knew Donny and Marie Osmond. If I recall, we both filed their comments under 'sure-he-does'."

Don scanned the bill again. Reaching over me, he grabbed the phone off the hook and dialed. "Mr. Donny Osmond?" he said. His face flushed red like someone was pinching his cheeks. "Oh, my apologies. I must have dialed the wrong number." He slammed the phone down. "That bastard!" he growled. "Where the hell is he?"

I shrugged my shoulders. "It wasn't my day to watch him. Could be in his room making dinner plans with Clint Eastwood or the President for all I know."

"Very funny," he snarled. I watched in silent amusement as he marched out of the den, and without knocking, opened the playroom door. I leaned back in my chair for a better look. Larry was lounging on an unmade bed, watching television. Don slammed the door behind him and I could hear him shouting but Larry's responses were too feeble to be audible. After a few minutes, Don left his room and came back into the den, the phone he had put in Larry's room dangling from the cord in his hand.

I leaned back in the desk chair. "Well? Did he write you a check?"

He wadded up the phone bill and threw it on the floor. "Hell, no. He says he never used the phone. Damn liar! Don tossed the phone on the couch and stormed up the stairs.

At noon the following Wednesday, Kathleen called and invited me to attend a restaurant grand opening in Worcester. It was difficult to hear her because the children were standing by me with an empty coffee can, crying. The three or four dollars they had made with their lemonade stand the day before was gone.

"Who's crying?" Kathleen asked

"The girls. Someone took the money they made selling lemonade yesterday."

"Leery Larry," she said without hesitation. "Did you tell Don?"

"Not yet. But I will." I paused then added, "The opening sounds great." I needed to get out of the house for a while.

"Aren't you eating?" Don asked as they sat down for dinner.

"Not here," I said, setting a basket of rolls on the table. "Kathleen invited me to Harris' restaurant opening."

Don stood up. "She called that little hole in the wall a restaurant?" He looked at me blankly. "Those people don't have the intelligence to ladle soup to the homeless."

I stood over Bridget and cut her meat. "We'll see," I said. "I think they'll surprise everybody."

He sat down and served his plate, hitting the ceramic surface hard with a wooden serving spoon. "A good mother stays with her family at night. She doesn't do running around town like some irresponsible gadfly."

"But you go out, Daddy," Stephie said.

"Eat your dinner," Don said gruffly. "And don't interfere in adult conversations."

Fear stiffened my neck as I walked to the front door. "Be good kids," I said, suddenly feeling awash in guilt. I didn't look at Stephie's pouty face when I added, "kids, mind your daddy." I closed the door gently behind me wishing I had never agreed to go.

It was past two in the morning when I slipped into bed. Don's head was buried under a pillow. Most of the covers were on his side of the bed but I didn't pull them away for fear of waking him. I lay on my back and was just beginning to fall asleep when he suddenly rolled over and clamped his arm across my chest. "Do you know what time it is, you slut?"

"Is it Howdy Doody time?" I said. Champagne permitted a free flow of words.

Crack! His hand stung my face. I hit him back and jumped out of bed. He grabbed my nightgown and spun me around. The force of the next slap to my shoulder knocked me off balance and I fell to the bed, screaming.

He slammed a pillow over my face. I tried to kick him. He lay on top of me. "What the hell were you doing out so late? Screwing around?"

I wrestled the pillow from my face. "You pig!" I yelled. "You stay out that late four nights a week. Are you screwing around?"

He hurled his fist into my shoulder. "I'm on business you worthless slut. Who do you think earned the money for you to waste tonight? It certainly wasn't you, Mrs. Hemingway!"

Suddenly there was a knock on the bedroom door. "Is everything okay?" Larry asked. "Penne, you need help?"

"Now look what you've done," Don whispered. He was still on top of me and beams of light from the streetlight illuminated his contorted face. "Sleeping with him too, are you?" He tightened his hand over my mouth and whispered a clenched teeth warning: "You ever tell him and you'll be sorry. Got that?"

Call the police. Yell to Larry. But I couldn't. Don would kill me before anyone had a chance to respond. Get a restraining order? Why? It was just some judicial makeshift shield. A piece of paper wouldn't protect me. Newspapers were full of the gruesome details of women who depended on that for their safety. The kids needed me. I wouldn't be any good to them dead. I rolled away from him and crawled under the covers. Minutes later he was crying, his face in my back.

"Pen," he whispered. "I don't know what came over me. I'm so sorry."

Sickened by everything, I vaulted from the bed into the bathroom, reaching the bowl just in time. When I staggered back to bed, Don got up, went to the bathroom and returned with a cold washcloth that he gently put over my eyes. "You never could hold booze," he said and snuggled down beside me. "My poor baby. You just need some sleep."

It took three days before I was confident to leave the house. Bruises were fading and I covered the ones on my face with makeup. Although it was summer, I pulled on a light cotton turtleneck to hide the bruises on my neck. It was far better for people to think I was cold blooded than to see the marks of a violent spouse.

I took the children to the grocery store and on the way home, stopped behind a car with a New Hampshire license plate. So affixed by the words at the base of the plate, I didn't see the light change. Horns honked me into accelerating. But the words still hung in my head like a banner: *Live Free or Die.*

I dropped the kids off at a friend's house to play and drove down to see Kathleen. Tom answered the door. "You look hot," he said. "Want some iced tea?"

Turtlenecks can make you sweat, I thought. "Where's Kathleen?" I said and took a seat in the kitchen.

"She took the kids to gymnastic practice." He put the glass of tea in front of me and sat down. "So how's it going with the pervert?"

I shook my head. "I need your help. Can you do a background check on Birkland?"

He pushed his chair back and stroked his beard. "I'm way ahead of you," he said. "Started just after your dinner and should have some information within the next few days." He was staring at my face so I lowered my head. "How'd you get those bruises?" he asked.

"Too much to drink and a stubborn door," I said.

"Really?" His voice rose on the last syllable.

The fact that he didn't believe me made me angry. "What would you rather hear, Tom? That Larry punched me?"

He was quiet for a moment. "I'd settle for the truth."

I stood to leave and my knees went weak. I bit my lip. "Call us if you get any feedback," I said and quickly let myself out.

Don arrived home early the next day and anxiously herded me into our bedroom. "Tom just called," he whispered. "You and the kids need to get out of the house for a while. We'll handle Larry when you are out of the danger zone."

His words made me laugh. "You mean the same danger zone you've kept me in for weeks? So what is he? An escaped convict?"

"I'll ignore that," he said, "and I don't have time to discuss the particulars. Pack some things for the kids and try to act normal around Birkland. Go see your parents for a few days."

"School starts in one week," I said. "I can't stay that long."

Larry stood lazily in the drive while I packed my car. "I insist you use mine," he said. "Your car isn't safe." He grabbed my hand and folded his fingers around his car keys. Drive safely. I wouldn't want anything else to happen to you." His emphasis was on the word *else*.

Don walked up behind Larry. I could tell by his expression he had overheard us. His brow rippled. "What's that supposed to mean, Birkland?"

Larry shrugged his shoulders. "I just want her to take my car. It's new and safer." Pointing to my car he added, "That car should be in a junk yard."

After several minutes of sparing, Don agreed and transferred the luggage to Larry's car.

"I'm going to Pennsylvania," I told Don as I started the car. "But not to my parents. I'll be at Patty's." The bruises were still on my face and I knew my twin would be easier to deal with. It had been a year since I'd seen her. As I backed the car down the drive, Don ran up to my window and motioned for me to put it down.

"You were right, Pen. He's weird. And I'm sorry I didn't listen to you in the first place." He handed me some money, then bent down and whispered: "You will come back, won't you? I'm sorry about the other night. I didn't mean to hurt you. You do know that, don't you?"

Without answering, I tugged at the turtleneck, turned up the air conditioning and found the power button for the window. It quickly rose between us.

And I was gone.

CHAPTER 11

September 1977
Lancaster, Pennsylvania

J sought refuge with my twin sister Patty who lived about six hours away from me and two hours away from our parents. It was the only place I could go at the moment without fear of oppression.

Patty and I had always been different, twins or not; like salt and pepper, affecting our worlds as differently as the condiments.

Like salt, Patty had moved through life sprinkling changes in planned obscurity, carefully blending in with her household until her changes were suddenly recognized. Too late to be challenged, she had carefully camouflaged parental wrath and appeared to be impervious to their domination. Or so I thought.

I, on the other hand, had blazed through life, peppering each change with attention-getting announcements. My bullhorn approach had caused many a confrontation with family, and without realizing it, I had created my own window for criticism.

Her brick, three bedroom home sat on the outskirts of an historical Pennsylvania town. White shutters graced the large front window which looked out to the street. Window boxes spilled over with lush red geraniums. Cottage curtains formed a billowy A in the window and framed the faces of my two adorable nieces as I rang the doorbell.

Patty opened the front door and smiled. Dressed in a stunning gingham dress, she looked like Good Housekeeping's queen of the perfect wife. Her hair was short, light brown and she wore small pearl earrings. We hugged and let the tears roll, the usual emotions given sisters who have not seen each other in so long.

While the girls raced to play with their cousins, we sat down in the cheery kitchen. Her pale face was sprinkled with darling freckles, something I never had. Then again, we had only shared a womb, not an egg. We were fraternal twins, two diverse souls who just happened to be born at the same time.

She stared at my face. "So tell me what is really going on," she said softly.

I explained the situation with Birkland.

"And Don?" she asked, staring at my face. "How are things between you two?"

"I think you can see," I said. "He's a difficult man to live with."

She was pensive a moment before speaking. "So Mom said." She stared down at the tablecloth. "I never told you this before, but Don has always scared me."

I tried to act nonchalant. "Oh? In what way?"

"Too flashy," she said softly. "I don't think he has ever approved of me."

She sounded like Mother. "What makes you say that?"

Patty was tense. Her eyes darted from pictures on the wall to the stove top as she tried to avoid my glare. "Remember the last time we were together? That barbecue we had here? And the tantrum my daughter threw?" She fidgeted with the corner of the tablecloth. "Don got pretty upset with her and acted like I wasn't even present. I have never forgotten his behavior that day, like he was some parent of the year and I was a complete failure."

I couldn't deny what she was saying. It was all true. But she was the first person who had rightfully put Don down that I hadn't become angry with. "I'm so sorry about that, Pat. He did act like a complete ass."

She stared at me with concern. "Did he bruise your face and your neck, considering you are wearing a turtleneck in August?"

I nodded yes but didn't want to pursue the discussion. "I don't want to talk about that, okay? And do me a favor. Don't say anything to Mom or Dad."

Patty was the most trustworthy person in the family, and, for that matter, the person I trusted more than anyone I knew. She put her hand on top of mine. "I promise, but you have to promise me something in return."

I looked at her and felt my face getting red. "What?"

She took a sip of her tea and looked at me with a pained expression. "Just promise me that if things get out of hand again, and you are in any kind of danger, you'll leave. I couldn't stand something happening to you. You could always come here. You know that. Deal?"

I leaned over and kissed her cheek. "Deal," I said softly. "Can you lend me a summer shirt? This turtleneck is going to give me heat stroke."

We had had less than two days to visit before Don called. He was nervous, agitated and I could hear him lighting one cigarette after another.

"Tom received a complete info package on Larry from the FBI. He was dishonorably discharged from the Navy two years ago. He spent six months in a military hospital for mental disorders. After his release, he went to Utah to stay with friends. These friends issued a warrant for his arrest. Apparently Larry stole many items from their home while they vacationed in Europe. He also purchased a new car and . . ."

"Don?" I yelled into the phone. "The Cougar I'm driving?" My heart was pounding so fast I stared at the floor expecting it to explode out of my chest and land on my feet. "Am I driving a stolen car?"

"Yes!" he said. "Purchased in his friend's name using stolen identity. And there's more. These people are missing a three hundred and fifty dollar dog!"

"A fugitive?" I shouted into the phone. "And you put all of us at risk because of that jerk?"

Don met my panic with calm instructions. "Listen to me. Leave Pennsylvania today and avoid being stopped by police for anything. Be brave. Everything will be okay."

I slammed down the phone and feverishly prattled through the events with Patty as I raced around her house gathering up our things.

For all the flap and commotion, Larry's exodus was uneventful. We traded cars when I returned, he packed what he could and promised to return for the boxes held captive in our garage. Tom had issued a Writ of Abandonment for the belongings and I pleaded with Don to open them. There was also a warrant for his arrest. He wouldn't get far.

"You can't do that," he warned. "Don't go near them until Tom says it's legal to do so."

I couldn't sleep knowing that somewhere in our garage might be the secret to Larry Birkland. Don was reading in the den when I got out of bed, made a pot of coffee and quietly walked down the stairs to the garage to play Nancy Drew.

I turned the handle of the door leading from the playroom to the garage, pulled the door open slowly and jumped. "What are YOU doing?" Don whispered. "You scared the hell out of me." He had pulled a chair from the den into the garage and was riffling through boxes strewn around the chair.

"You won't believe this stuff," he said. "The guy had everything from chandeliers to Cross pens."

"Cross country theft?" I said and joined him to comb through the remaining boxes searching for clues of Larry's past and perhaps uncover the present.

"Look at this," he said, holding up a handful of ties. "These are mine."

I rummaged through another box. "Well look here," I said. "Recognize these?"

He grabbed the candlesticks from my hand. "That damn thief! And he called himself my friend?"

I glared at him. "No comment."

He put the candlesticks on the garage floor and continued to dig. "Oh my God," he said, pulling a frame out of a box. He turned the frame around. It was a portrait of us with the children. But it had been defaced. Scrawled across the face of the picture in Larry's handwriting was the inscription: '*To Larry. We will always reserve a special place in our heart for the Godfather of our children. All our love, Doon, Peni Step and Briget*'

"Find any spelling bee awards?" I asked. "How sad. The guy was looking for love and approval and had to invent it when it couldn't be found."

How well I understood.

Two days before school started we held a yard sale hoping to collect enough to pay some of the phone bills. Larry's belongings—other people are belonging—sold quickly. Files found in one box, missing from Naval Headquarters in Washington D.C. were turned over to

Tom who gave them to the appropriate officials. Larry's medical records from Bethesda Naval Hospital offered the greatest insight into this guest. His history of mental illness, at least in those documents, began in 1967.

"I don't suppose you sold him disability insurance, did you?"

"Not funny," Don replied.

"Why did he come here?" I poured us both another cup of coffee and settled back on the den couch. "What was the lure?"

Don thought for a moment. "Guess he was running out of ties."

We laughed. "So now what happens to him?"

He put his arm around my shoulder. "I'm sorry what I put you through. He'll probably be picked up and taken back to Utah to face charges under that warrant."

"And the dog? Do we ship the slobbering beast back to the rightful owners?"

"No. I talked to the people in Utah. They thanked me for calling and told me to keep Bear with their blessing."

"Did their blessing include the pedigree papers?"

"I didn't ask, Pen."

Great, I thought. Technically we were still feeding a stolen animal.

CHAPTER 12

October 1977

$\mathcal{I}$t was almost five-thirty in the afternoon when Stephanie raced into the kitchen. I was on the phone with Don when she handed me a piece of paper she had found in our driveway. Scribbled in small letters were the name 'Abby' and a phone number. The handwriting was Don's.

"Can you do me a favor, honey?"

"Like what?" I snapped my anger building as I stared at the note.

"Pack me a bag. Put in the blue suit, white shirt, and tie. You know. The usual."

The usual what? "Where are you going?"

"Connecticut. The office is having problems. I've scheduled a meeting for seven tomorrow morning." His voice was anxious, his breathing heavy.

An hour later he dropped by to pick up his clothes. "Sorry about this," he said, grabbing his overnight bag. He pecked me on the cheek and patted my back. "Take good care of the kids."

"Are you giving me an option?" He didn't respond and the door slammed behind him.

"Abby," I said out loud as I cleaned up dinner dishes and dug my nails into the sponge. The name alone churned up negative feelings, fed by memories of a high school rival named Abby who made my life miserable. Prom Queen. Snowflake Queen. Homecoming Queen. We had been collectively nominated for each honor and she had won all. Beautiful, thin, rich and bright, she had flirtatiously solicited votes in her quest to capture all titles. Abby had stopped at nothing to win, including other girls boyfriends. Generalizing that anyone with the name Abby had to be a shallow creature capable of curling up in Satan's lap was childish, but I did it anyway. If I was going to baste myself in self-pity, at least it would be a spicy marinade.

I put the children to bed, went into my bedroom and shut the door. "Just do it," I told myself out loud. I fished in my jeans pocket for the slip of paper, lifted the receiver and dialed.

A shrill-voiced woman answered the phone. "Hello?"

"Is Don in?" I asked. It was one of my better voices.

"He just stepped out for cigarettes," she said nervously. "May I ask who is calling?"

Good, I thought. She was frightened. "His mother," I said.

"Oh wait," she said. "If you'll hang on just a moment I think I just heard him come in. . ."

I heard the all too familiar voice through the phone shouting, "I'm back," and hung up.

I slumped down on the bed, hurt and angry as usual. Why? Why did he treat me this way? What had I done, or, what did I do that made him want to stray like some alley cat?

Car lights flashed through the bedroom window. Someone was in our drive. I jumped off the bed, pulled the curtains back and saw Tom Hanson getting out of his car and felt a sense of relief. At least it wasn't Don. I walked to the front door worrying. Would the strange phone call I made to Abby make Don come home?

I tightened the belt of my robe and opened the door before Tom had a chance to ring the bell. "HI," I said. "What beckons you to my door at this hour?"

Tom stepped into the foyer. "Saw your light on. Thought you might have a spare cup of coffee."

I ran my fingers through my hair. "The coffee I have, but you may want to change your mind. Don's not home."

He lowered his eyes. "I know. I didn't come to see him."

He followed me up the stairs into the kitchen and took a seat at the table. I poured two cups of coffee, put a clean ashtray between us and sat down.

"Well?" I asked. "The expression on your face is so grim I'm almost afraid to ask what's wrong."

He pulled a cigarette from his shirt pocket. "You may think I'm out of line but I think there is something you need to know."

I closed my eyes briefly. When I opened them, Tom was staring at me. "Could that something be a woman named Abby?"

Tom's eyebrows arched in fuzzy white-haired A's. "You know?"

He cleared his throat. "Kathleen and I saw him, well, them, tonight at a restaurant. Don introduced her as a colleague. Kathleen was too furious to be consoling at the moment so I told her I would talk to you first."

I drew in a breath silently. "What's left to say, Tom? I feel humiliated, angry."

Tom looked unutterably sad. "Pen," he said, almost choking on my name. "There's a question I must ask you. Those bruises you had when Larry was here. Did Don do that?"

I pretended I hadn't heard him and fiddled with my wedding band.

"You just answered my questions," he said softly. "What triggered the violence?

"He always accuses me of soliciting the attention of other men, which I don't. He is just transferring his adulterous flings to me, probably to rid himself of guilt." I looked into his kind face, his tired, sad eyes. "I don't know if you'll understand this, Tom, and I hate myself for it. But I still love the man." My eyes watered but I pushed the tears away.

Tom patted my hand. "I'm your friend. I want to understand."

I got up and paced the kitchen floor. "A part of me wants to beat the hell out of him and then there's the other part." I sat down, leaned my elbows on the table and looked into his eyes. "I'm scared, Tom. I want to fight back. But I can't without risking further injury. And that makes me miserable."

"Can I ask a personal question?"

I laughed nervously. "Like you haven't for the past thirty minutes?"

He stretched his arms over his head. "How's your sex life?"

I suddenly saw him as an enemy. "What? You men. And I thought you were different!"

He held up his hands. "Whoa. Not so fast. Please don't misunderstand me. I'm just trying to help you, trying to find out why Don acts the way he does." He paused and took a sip of coffee. "I couldn't crave sex and be married to Kathleen at the same time," he snickered.

His admission made me uncomfortable but I needed his help. "Remember when Don and I went to San Francisco?" It was the greatest trip we ever had. The passion returned. The love was rekindled. It was storybook blissful."

His eyebrows arched. "And now?"

I sighed. "Back to sewer sex."

He laughed. "What the hell is that?"

"A waste," I said. "The boring norm."

He lit another cigarette. "Mind if I pry a bit?"

I looked over at the clock on the stove. It was after midnight and I was feeling anxious, fearful Don would return at any moment. "Sure," I said. "For whatever reason, I don't feel uncomfortable with you."

He smiled. "Thanks. Now what do you mean by 'boring norm'?

I sat back and gathered my thoughts. Should I tell him? I know he is trustworthy and wouldn't tell Don. Maybe he could help. "Well, a typical romp in the rack usually begins after he's been holed up in the bathroom which is his library as well."

Tom choked on his coffee. "Maybe all men are alike. If they can read."

I laughed. "At any rate, after reading what must be half of <u>War and Peace</u>, he walks out of the bathroom in a pair of old boxer shorts. Elastic threads spill from the worn waistband and crawls around his no-so-sucked-in tummy."

Tom roared and patted his ample stomach. "Sounds like we use the same tailor." His laughter was an intoxicating approval and encouraged me to continue.

"He keeps his socks on and they wallow around his ankles. He rarely bothers to brush his teeth before coming to bed."

Tom cocked his head. "So Romeo died, is that it?"

"Romeo?" I giggled. "Guess that persona was flushed with the rest of his crap."

Tom's laughter flooded the kitchen. "Go on."

"Well, Don flops on the bed, tosses his arm across my body and introduces his sexual desires with a term of impairment."

"Like?"

"Like, 'horny, babe'?"

"What do you do?"

"Respond," I sighed, "out of seasoned cowardice, I suppose and sense of duty. Three kisses later he asks, "Are you ready?" like we are starting some foot race."

"And?"

"I fake it. Better fake than sorry."

Tom strokes his beard. "Does Don sense it?"

"Nah. He just rolls over like a downed piece of timber and falls asleep." I paused and looked into his face. "I can't believe I just told you that. Are you writing a book or something?"

"No book, hon. I'm glad you feel comfortable enough to discuss it. I know you wouldn't talk to Kathleen like this. Right?"

"Right." Kathleen was too critical and wouldn't even allow the topic to be introduced. Sex was only for men in her opinion. Women were simply the recipients.

"Is Don affectionate?" he asked

"Not without an audience. I've tried to encourage him to kiss me tenderly or maybe even whisper those proverbial sweet things in my ear. But unless sweet nothings includes things like, 'Did you pick up my laundry,' the man is not educable.

Tom got up and poured himself some more coffee. I sat at the table and rested my head on my hands.

"Is he tender?" Tom asked.

"Tender?" I raised my head. "It might be the night or even the meat but rarely Don. Instructing him to be romantic would be like trying to teach German to a gerbil."

Tom propped his elbow on the table and leaned his face into his hands. "Have you tried talking about it?"

"A few times."

"And how did he react?"

"Angry. Hostile," I said.

"Not surprising," he said. "Don probably interprets it as a slap to his manhood. Did he ever threaten to leave you in search of a 'real woman'?"

I was startled. "How did you know that? Did Don tell you?"

"No. Certainly not. But you know I deal with macho men every day. That is textbook behavior." He paused then asked, "Has he ever become violent over these talks?"

I stared down at my hands. "A few times." I looked up and continued. "You know Tom, for a man whose charisma exceeded my wildest fantasies in the beginning, his sexuality has been replaced by such a self-serving lust, and it could just as easily be satisfied by a milking machine used on dairy cows. Or an Abby." Unwanted tears lined my lower lids. "There's no difference."

"What are you going to do?"

I stared at the table. "What can I do, Tom? Call her house again?"

His eyes widened. "Again? You mean you've talked to her?"

I got up from the table and retrieved the slip of paper from the bedroom. "Here," I said. "Stephie found this in the drive. He is at her house tonight."

"Suppose I talk to him, "Tom said.

The idea curled my insides. "No, don't." Panic showed in my voice. "You'll make things worse than they are. You know Tom, there is a part of me that wants to pack up and leave."

"So what's holding you back?"

It was exactly the question I had been asking myself for years. It had gnawed at me, beneath the surface, but I was always afraid of the answer. "I can't divorce him."

"Why?"

It was like working a crossword puzzle; the answers depended on so many others. Did Don want me? Did I need him for something more than a paycheck? And what did Don have, what did he offer that I couldn't get elsewhere or produce myself? "Fear," I answered. "And love. The combination."

"Are you afraid of raising the girls by yourself?" he asked.

I nodded, embarrassed to still be caught in that girlish web of wanting Don to change and wishing for that happily-ever-after ending in the story. "That's part of it," I said. "I just want him to love me as much as I love him."

Tom placed his hand over mine. "Did you know that during most of our conversation tonight you have been twisting your wedding band around your finger like it was a life preserver?"

A life preserver? I looked down at my hand. *Or was it a death wish?*

When Tom stood to leave, we both heard a car door slam and I panicked. "I hope that's not him," I whispered.

"I'll look," he said and walked into the living room. "Don't worry," he said. "It's just your neighbors across the street."

I took a deep breath. "Thanks," I said. "You better get out of here. Kathleen is going to accuse us of having an affair."

His eyes sparkled. "Not to worry," he laughed. "I'm fat, lazy and smoke too much. She knows no other woman would even split a sandwich with me. More important, she adores you."

I closed the door behind him, turned out the lights and wished I had someone like him to call my own. I shuffled down the hall to the bedroom knowing that would never happen if I continued to handle the problem by just wishing and not doing.

CHAPTER 13

January 1978

Sun streamed in through the icy windows as I tied the last cluster of balloons to the dining room chandelier. I took a step back to make certain the decorations were perfect and was pleased with the costly arrangement of Holly Hobby bobbles and bangles Bridget had begged for to celebrate her fifth birthday.

"Mommy?" Bridget's little voice echoed through the house. She walked in from nursery school and squealed. "I love it, I love it! Can I have my party now?"

She promptly took her seat at the head of the table, rested her cherubic face in her hands and stared at the presents. But it was only noon. She had rejected my idea of a party with her friends from school, opting only to have a family celebration.

"Daddy won't be home for a while," I said. "Why don't you have some lunch and go into your room and play? Maybe make room for all your new surprises!"

She continued her stubborn vigil at the table. I made her a peanut butter and jelly sandwich, a bowl of soup and put it down in front of her. She twisted her long pigtails around her fingers as she ate, never ceasing her focus on the stack of gifts. My analytical child stared at each package probably guessing at the contents. She was so quiet. Too serious for such a youngster.

By late afternoon the glow faded from her face. "Is Daddy working so hard he forgot about my birthday?" she asked. It was a sophisticated observation coming from a five-year-old.

"Of course not," I said and smiled, hoping I had told her the truth. She left the table briefly then returned to take up her vigil. By six o'clock she was asleep, her little head nested in folded arms on her plate.

"Do we have to wait for Dad?" Stephie whined. "I'm hungry."

I called Don's office. No answer. Frustrated, I called his secretary at home.

"He left a little after four," she said sweetly. "Is anything wrong?"

"No, Rachel. Thank you."

"Damn it's cold out there," Don said tossing his coat over a chair. He walked into the kitchen and his clothes smelled like they had been washed in gin and cigarette smoke.

"Where have you been?" I whispered angrily. "It's after eight."

"Working," he said. "Where else would I be?"

I ignored his attempt to make me feel stupid. "Have you forgotten what day this is?" I snapped.

He opened the refrigerator door and grabbed a beer. "No. But apparently you have. We were married in June."

I took his hand and pulled him into the dining room. Bridget was still asleep. "She waited all day for you," I whispered.

He cocked his head. "Well then, another few minutes won't hurt. I need to lay down. Give me thirty minutes."

I fed Stephie some garlic bread to keep her quiet and poured a glass of scotch for myself to keep me quiet as well. I took one gulp, my stomach turned and I poured the rest down the sink.

Bridget's head bobbed as she ate. I reached over and smoothed the loose strand of hair out of her face. "Honey? Do you want to blow out your candles now?"

Her eyes closed. "Stephie, would you please blow out the candles while I put Bridget to bed?"

Stephie got into bed without prompting. "Mom?" she said as I turned out her light. "I feel bad about Bridget's party, don't you?"

I covered her up and kissed her head. "Yes, sweetheart, I do, but these things happen. Bridget will be okay."

Minutes later I stormed downstairs to the den and closed the door. "Damn you," I yelled. Don was giving the television screen more attention than he afforded his daughter. "I don't give a damn what you do to me, but when it comes to the feelings of a little girl, I won't tolerate your self-centered crap!"

He responded with a silent look of disgust.

My anger overflowed. "I'll bet if it had been your girlfriend's birthday you would have been an hour early!"

He threw his pen across the room and jumped off the couch. I flinched and moved back toward the den door. "I don't have to listen to your dribbling crap," he yelled walking toward me. "Is your life so boring you have to invent soap opera diversions for excitement, at my expense? You stupid damn broad!"

I backed away from him. "Don't try and hide behind lies," I yelled. "If you don't want to be a father, just get out!"

He picked up his precious Cross pen off the carpet and charged past me. I stayed in the den and listened for the squeak of the garage door. I heard his car roar out of the driveway before I curled up on the couch and tried to sleep. I knew where he was going. And he wouldn't be back tonight.

At dusk the next evening heavy snow poured from the sky like fallout from some colossal pillow fight; a snow storm God kept a secret until the meteorologists signed off the air. I was standing in the front window of the living room when the front door suddenly blew open. Don walked in, removed his shoes and coat in the foyer and walked up the stairs into the kitchen. He was carrying a snow covered floral bouquet and a bag.

"Where's Bridget?" he asked.

I walked into the kitchen, kept my back toward him and shrugged my shoulders. The anger still shrouded my body and I couldn't be civil. "Probably in mourning," I said tersely.

He walked up behind me and dangled a teddy bear in my face. "Think she'll like it?"

I turned and faced him. "The bear?" I answered, "or you?" I heard Bridget's footsteps in the hall. "Find out for yourself."

Bridget took the teddy bear from him, offered a weak smile and weaker thanks then left the kitchen.

"Such appreciative kids you're raising," he snarled.

"What did you expect? A Father of the Year commendation?"

He walked over to the sink and placed the bouquet on the counter. "I'm really sorry," he said. His liquored breath made me nauseous. "But you need to understand that earning a living has to come before birthdays."

I left the flowers on the counter to die. He walked into the living room, built a fire in the fireplace then settled down in a chair with the newspaper. "We better make a run for the store," he shouted. "Looks like a nor'easter."

"Have fun," I said. I put detergent into the dishwasher and let the door snap knowing mishandling anything mechanical agitated him.

"Oh no," he said. "I just came in. It's your turn to brave the elements."

Close to exploding, I grabbed my coat out of the hall closet and exited through the garage. His car was parked at the top of the steep drive. Visibility was zero and snow lashed my face as I unlocked the door. City plows had already been by. Fresh snow had doubled the two foot base on the ground from the week before leaving a wall of white on either side of the drive. I started the car, backed it down the drive and deliberately plowed into the drifts. Feeling smug, I climbed the drive, plowed through the front walk up to the front door and yelled for Don.

"You did what?" he shouted.

"The car skidded into a drift. You can blame Mother Nature."

I could hear him rummaging around in the hall closet. He walked in an irritated gait down the walk, opened the garage door, retrieved a shovel and stomped down the drive. "You stupid, dumb, broad," he shouted as he walked.

Suddenly he slipped. His right leg buckled and his body gave way as he fell to the ground. I stood at the top of the drive and watched.

"God damn son of a bitch," he yelled. His profanity echoed off the snow drifts as he struggled to get up. He limped to the car and began digging around the tires. When the car was freed, he hobbled back up the drive and opened the playroom door. I followed and watched as he had trouble removing his boots. He rolled up his pant leg, grimacing. I looked down. His leg had begun to swell. Sweat dripped from his brow.

"I'm calling an ambulance," I said.

"Forget it." He struggled to remove the other boot and pushed me away when I tried to help. Dumping his coat, gloves and hat on the floor, he limped up the stairs groaning.

Once in our bedroom, he fell down on the bed. Guilt had me fluttering around him like some misguided moth. I arranged pillows on the bed so he could elevate his leg and moved the good TV (on a rolling stand) into the bedroom.

It was just before dawn when he awakened me. "Oh, God," he moaned.

"What's wrong?" I asked and turned on the light. His face was contorted in pain. The covers were tossed back and his injured leg lay exposed, swollen to a point where the skin would have screamed if it could. "That's it," I said and reached for the phone. "I'm calling an ambulance."

"It's not that bad," he moaned.

"Save the macho for another time," I said and dialed 911. I stared at him while I waited for someone to pick up on the other end of the line. I had never seen Don in a helpless mode before and actually dependent on me. "They're on their way," I said hanging up the phone.

I changed into street clothes and tried to make him comfortable while we waited. Thirty minutes later a station wagon with a mobile flashing light clipped to the roof backed up in the drive, the tire chains grinding through the snow and ice. I opened the front door and found two men standing there who looked more like deer hunters than an emergency crew. Dressed in wool hats, storm coats and mittens, the two old men had seen more winters than I had lived.

"Are you paramedics?" I asked.

"Kind of," said one. "We're covering for them. Lots of accidents tonight. We take the easy stuff."

I let them in. "Follow me. He's upstairs in the bedroom."

"No I'm not," yelled Don. His voice was coming from the den.

Heckle and Jeckle of the emergency world took turns examining his leg. "Yup," said the older of the two. "It's broke for sure. Trouble is we don't have any splinting equipment. The wagon, she jest has a gurney."

As he spoke, Heckle gazed around the den. "Can we use some of that kindling', lady?"

"Sure," I said.

"Got some old belts?"

I raced upstairs and pulled a handful of belts from Don's closet and returned quickly. When his leg had been secured in the makeshift splint, the men pulled the gurney into the den and despite Don's protests, made him lie down.

"Pen?" Don tugged at my sleeve and motioned for me to come closer. "I'm scared," he whispered. "I've never been in a hospital before, as a patient." His hands trembled. He rolled his eyes in torment as the men pulled the gurney out the door. "I'll get Tom to stay with the kids," I told him, "and I'll be there."

I watched from inside as they struggled to lift him into their wagon as the snow and wind whipped at their faces with a debilitating force.

I arrived at the hospital as the doctor was walking into Don's curtained cubicle.

"Well, well," he said, adjusting his glasses. He was a slight man, frail in body with thinning brown hair. His eyes were close together, his face gaunt. "So who brought you in here?" he grinned. "Daniel Boone?"

It was past six in the morning by the time we got home. X-rays showed a bad break in the left calf. He would be in a non-walking cast for six weeks. Tom greeted us at the door and helped Don up the stairs and to the bedroom. The girls were still asleep.

He was obviously in pain. "Did they give you pain medication?" Tom asked.

"Yes," Don moaned. "But I don't want to take it."

Tom laughed. "Don't be stupid. Take the pills. At least you will get some sleep."
I walked into the bedroom with a glass of water and two pills. "Tom's right. Don't suffer." Actually, I needed him to be drugged which equated to peace very four hours.

"Thanks for all of this, Penelope," he snorted, trying to get comfortable. "You'll have to take me to work for six weeks thanks to your stupidity."

Tom spoke for me. "Come on good buddy, don't blame your wife. She wasn't responsible for the snow storm. And I can drive you to the office when you're up to it."

Don fell asleep quickly and Tom left. I walked back to the kitchen wondering if Tom would drive him to Abby's as well.

CHAPTER 14

May 1978

*D*on walked across the new carpet beaming. "Like it?" he asked

"It's beautiful," I said smiling. The installers had just left. Soft beige carpeting rolled across the floor like a windswept desert. "But it won't look great for long."

He turned and faced me. "What do you mean? A lot you know about flooring. This is the best quality on the market."

I sighed. "Bear," I said, "as if you didn't know." New carpet was a perfect reason to sell the dog who insisted on defecating in the house each time he heard a car start and he wasn't invited to go along for the ride. The habit had become unsanitary. Enjoying the mercenary prestige of owning the rare breed, Don was against it. I walked into the kitchen. "Have it your way," I said. "Three thousand dollars of financed carpet is an expensive bathroom."

Don sat at the kitchen table and turned to look at his pet. "So keep my boy in the kitchen," he said.

I gazed at the dog. Fluffy white fur covered his eyes and that large pink tongue dangled out of his mouth like bleached liver.

"Just look at him, Pen. Isn't he the most magnificent animal? If he could talk, my boy would be the ultimate pet." Snapping his fingers, Don summoned the furry behemoth to his side. "Be careful of that lady, boy." He patted his fur. "She has it in for you."

I stared at the over fluffed beast. His eyeless face reflected no shame. He looked stupid, as if given the ability to speak, all we would say was, *ah dah.* "His poop isn't so magnificent," I said and continued to peel potatoes.

"Like I said, Pen, just keep him in the kitchen. Follow the training suggestions in the book I bought you."

Without wiping the water from my hands, I opened a junk drawer and pulled out a badly chewed paperback. "Here you go." I tossed the book on the table. "Bear read it first."

He laughed but I kept my back to him. "Confining a hundred-and-fifty pound dog in the kitchen would be like trying to confine you," I said. "It won't work."

"Very funny," Don replied. "Just block the openings with table boards."

One afternoon, Don came home while I was picking the girls up at school. We walked in the door and found him standing in the kitchen, gagging, holding my new spatula in his hand. "Where have you been?" he said angrily, waving the spatula in the air.

"A quick trip to Thailand and then to school to pick up the girls," I said. I pointed to the spatula. "What are you doing with that thing?"

He gagged. "Scraping up Bear's poop." He threw the utensil into the sink. "Don't worry. You can still use it. Just disinfect it in the dishwasher." He dumped yards of paper toweling into a trash bag and began to tie the top.

"Wait," I said. I grabbed the fecal instrument out of the sink. "Throw this out. I won't ever use it again."

"Easy to say when you don't make the money to pay for it," he snapped.

"Fine, Don. Would you like me to use the turkey baster to douche with and save you money as well?"

He ignored the analogy. "You need to watch Bear more closely."

"I won't have the time. I took a part time job."

He frowned. "Doing what? And who is going to care for the children?"

"A part-time secretary for a local church. My hours are commensurate with school hours. I will pick them up on my way home from work. It's a perfect arrangement."

On Saturday, Bear ripped apart the garbage while I was at the store. Don ordered the girls to clean it up and was swearing at them when I returned.

Tonight Bear's garbage diet created a never ending bout of diarrhea in the dog. Don and the girls gagged as they cleaned up one mess after another and Bear was exiled to the back yard where he was fastened by a large rope. Dissatisfied with the new accommodations, Bear barked continuously.

A week later Don found a home for his pet. And I heard through the company grapevine that Angelina Arigone was not too thrilled about a large dog and I doubted it had anything to do with the color of his fur

Just the name Abby Denton made me choke. As Don walked through the kitchen on his way to the garage, I picked up the checks and fanned them like a poker deck. "You sure have written a number of checks to a person you said was my soap opera diversion." I waved them in the air. "Who is she anyway and what are these checks for?"

"And good morning to you too," he said crisply. "Quit creating problems, Pen. She is just a friend who works in the same building I do. When I can't get to the bank, Abby cashes checks for me. Anything wrong with that?"

"Strange," I mumbled.

"What's strange?" He stood over me, his hands firmly planted on the table.

I took a deep breath. "How difficult is it to run to the bank when your office is in the same building? And just out of curiosity, what does the "B" stand for in her name. Babe?"

"Birkland," he blurted out in frustration. Suddenly, his face drained of color as he walked briskly toward the door, looking at anything but my face. I pretended not to care but watched his eyes fill with horror and felt a surge of accomplishment muddied with anger and hurt.

"Any relation to your feckless friend?"

"Come on," he said, with a contrived breeziness. "It's not an uncommon name. Are we going to play your mind games again?" Shaking his head, he walked outside to mow the grass.

October 1978

The dress on a mannequin in the store window so I stopped and stared. It was black, the same color as my disposition, had long sleeves with a straight skirt. I guessed the fabric to be wool. It was perfect, I concluded, but only if Don died in the fall or winter. I walked into the store and bought it.

I was home before he was and as I hung the dress in my closet the guilt was staggering. I didn't remove the tags as if this was only a temporary purchase to remind me that his death could be an escape route out of the marital tunnel. As the sole beneficiary of his life insurance policy, I could keep the house, educate the children and wouldn't have to struggle on limited earnings. I could do as I please and not have anyone questioning me. More important, I wouldn't have to agonize about the other women any more or placate him in the name of peace.

Hollow sounds haunted my head; the conversations he and this Abby person must have had. Did they giggle together like we once did? Did he brush his teeth for her at night? Did he take off his socks before going to bed? Had he ever HURT HER? I wished the intestinal fortitude that had eluded me all my life would suddenly surface and I could hurl the hurt at deserving persons. I wouldn't stop with Don. Abby would be history and if I could find her, so would Diane. Depression was spreading deeper day by day. It was a mental cancer which was beginning to erode everything around me.

At ten-thirty on Tuesday morning the phone rang. I was still in bed. The children had been treated to a day off from school due to their mother's complete lack of responsibility.

"Mom?" Stephie yelled from the kitchen. "It's Mrs. Hanson."

I picked up the phone. "What's wrong?" she asked. "The kids said you were sick."

"Nothing," I told her, too intimidated by this strong willed woman I called my friend. By elementary precepts, we were friends. We share secrets and jokes about that rotting institution of marriage but she took it a step further. In her world all suffering was caused by men. Kathleen had little sympathy for spineless wimps who tolerated male dominance. Like my neighbor, Patricia. Like me. But then she had a loving, respectful husband.

"You sound depressed," she insisted.

I feigned nonchalance and yawned. "It's nothing. Just general laziness." We exchanged a few banal comments and hung up.

I sat up in bed and stared out the window at the bleak gray sky and the almost leafless trees and found that same bleakness was fogging the bedroom. Dust coated the top of Don's dresser and mine. Too many ties hung from his valet; folded laundry from last week sat piled on an old chair, hiding rips and tears. The bedroom walls were papered in a poverty print; faded blue and white stripes looked like they belonged in some Civil War museum. Of the two white lamps in the room, one was cracked at the base and sat on my dresser. His lamp, the once white shade now yellowed from nicotine, was crack free. The furniture seemed symbolic of our marriage, heavily marred with splintered legs. It was mine before we married and we had antiqued the early attic collection and turned the gray French provincial pieces to an olive green the first month we were married. I had wanted new but it wasn't affordable.

Now the furniture didn't need any help to look old. Scratches, dents and missing drawer handles said it all. I slithered under the cover and was just falling asleep when the doorbell rang.

"Hi Mrs. Hanson," I heard the children say. "Mom is in her bedroom".

Kathleen knocked lightly on my door and entered before I invited her in. "Start talking," she said and closed the door. She removed her coat and sat at the end of the bed, her eyes piercingly focused on me.

Something made me ignore a self-prescribed vow of silence. Wallowing in a trance like state, I closed my eyes at times, rambled on, and told her what I knew about Abby. But I didn't say anything about physical abuse.

"You can't go on like this, Pen," she said straightening her shoulders. "And you're a fool if you do. You don't have to put up with adultery or abuse of any kind." Her eyes were fixed on me in a trance-like state and she knew more than she was telling. "Tom and I will help you get on your feet. You have to divorce him."

"Please don't tell me what to do," I said. *Why had I confided in her?* Tom was so much easier. Of course he wouldn't have said anything different but I didn't want to hear the truth. Not from Kathleen, the woman who had it all. Sure, in theory, divorcing him would be simple. In practice, it seemed completely beyond my grasp. "Do me a favor, Kathleen, and don't use the word adultery. He had affairs. Simple, flighty, affairs."

She sighed deeply. "You're in denial, Pen. The term is adultery. A knife by another name still cuts. Don has betrayed your trust, your vows. You're just using the word 'affair' to your advantage—because it sounds less serious. Answer me one thing. Why can't you divorce him?"

She sounded like my mother. But I kept reminding myself she was my friend. "I can't support my children, this house, on a meager little income. And what you and Tom don't seem to understand is that, crazy or not, I still love the man. He can be a good person and I think in time he'll come around. I can't give up." I folded my arms stiffly in front of me. "Not yet, at least."

"You're as much of an idealist as Tom," she said. "But you're not making any sense. I think you may be confusing love with dependency."

Dependency. How would she know? "Kathleen, with all due respect, please do not tell me how I feel. You can't begin to understand. You are married to a kind, gentle man who adores you and you also earn more money than he does. In fact, you are completely self-reliant. "My vocal chords suddenly sounded rust coated.

She smiled. "My situation is completely different, Pen."

I leaned my head back against the wall. "You're telling me?"

She stood up and placed her hands firmly on her hips. "We'll all help you. The courts will make certain you and the girls are given ample financial support. And you are underestimating your own abilities. You can find a good job. You're bright and well educated. You've written some amazing letters to the editor of the paper. You're talented. But you need to begin now. Today. No one can help you if you are unwilling to help yourself. And to do that, I think you need to begin by being honest with yourself as to what is happening and why."

Honest? I thought silently. Okay. I am married to a man with a vile temper that also has good sides. I have weathered his cruelty hoping I could cure him with love, fidelity and acceptance. No, I haven't weathered it. I've tolerated it in the name of staying together. I would never admit that to Kathleen. And I had caused some of the problems. To avoid her stare, I pulled the covers up around my chin. "You can't solve my problems, just as I can't solve yours."

She frowned. "For a smart woman, you certainly are acting stupid."

I popped up in bed. "And for a good friend, you certainly are being insensitive."

"Insensitive?" Her mouth dropped. "Am I insensitive because I want the best friend I have ever had to live?" She paused and closed her eyes briefly before continuing. "You are just frightened." She jangled her car keys. "Toss him out. Because if you don't, the alternatives could be deadly."

"Daddy! Daddy!" the girl's squeals floated up from the den.

My pulse rate quickened. As I threw the covers back, I could feel Kathleen's stare. "See?" she said. "You're afraid of your own husband. Is that any way to live?"

I jumped out of bed, pulled off my nightgown, grabbed a pair of jeans and pulled on a sweatshirt. I walked past her, opened the door and froze.

"Hi," Kathleen said coldly. "I was just going. I'll see myself out."

He waited for her to leave before speaking. "What's going on here?" His voice was accusatory like we had been planning to eliminate the male race.

"Nothing." I shrugged my shoulders and walked down the hall to the kitchen. "What's going on with you? Why are you home so early?" I had no idea if he had heard anything Kathleen had said and tensely pretended everything was fine.

He followed me into the kitchen. "Just stopped by to get some papers I left on the desk. Are you sick?"

"Just a bug. Kathleen stopped in to see if she could do anything. Good neighbor policy."

He eyed me with disbelief. "And the kids? Why did they stay home from school?"

I slumped down in a kitchen chair. "Because I felt too sick to get them ready. You have a problem with that?"

He took a seat across from me. "I have a problem with everything I'm seeing. You don't look sick and something was really bothering Kathleen. What were you talking about in the bedroom with the door shut?"

I got up from the table. "Just leave me alone, Don. I don't feel like answering questions. "I walked back to the bedroom, crawled under the covers and feigned sleep. I heard his footsteps in the hall. He walked into the bedroom and slammed the door.

"Wake up," he said much too loudly.

I didn't move.

He jiggled my shoulder with his hand. "Did you hear me? I know you're not sleeping."

The sight of tears rolling down my face softened his demeanor. "What's wrong, Pen? Why are you crying? Was another article rejected? Did you get your period?"

Such convenient answers for him, guilt free and an adequate shovel for covering up the truth. I sat up and wiped my face with the back of my hand. "I can't talk about it."

He clicked his tongue like some missionary. "Since when do we have secrets from one another?"

Since the day we were married. I changed the subject. "Will you be home tonight?"

He stood up and tugged the cuff of his shirt even with the sleeve of his suit coat. "Of course. Why wouldn't I be?"

It was eerie the way he seemed to blot out the truth. Couldn't he sense what it was doing to me? Or did he really believe I was that naive? Abby must be busy tonight, I thought and waited until I heard his car start before I rolled over and tried to sleep. My body was tired but my mind was too active to cooperate. I could hear the television blaring downstairs. The girls were fighting but I couldn't move. *What are you going to do?* I asked myself.

Everyone seemed to have a recipe for my happiness but me. I couldn't make Kathleen understand. If I left, I would forfeit all the good I had struggled to achieve. I'd always given up anything that was difficult. To give up on this relationship was like throwing out tarnished silver without any attempt to uncover the original luster. Don had an original luster buried somewhere. Why couldn't the tarnish be removed?

There were too many questions for which there were no answers. How could I resurrect that person deep inside me who would not be so accepting of the premise of being a lowly wife? Could I continue to relinquish my character and dreams? Or would I spend the rest of my life being dominated to a point of voiding my soul? Why did I exist as an observer to the human race instead of being a participant?

Flip, flop, flip, flop. Hate him. Love him. Leave him. Stay. The kaleidoscope of emotion engulfed me. I pulled the pillows over my head. I didn't have the strength to do anything about this today.

And tomorrow? It could be a better day if I made it one.

CHAPTER 15

March 1979

*T*here was a chill under the ash-colored sky which had nothing to do with the weather. Don's mother had arrived for what has become her annual visit. But as I settled her into the bedroom, I was overcome by a feeling of awkwardness in the presence of this stranger who called herself Mom. She had lost almost thirty pounds. Her face was gaunt and her eyes had a flat glint to them. "Are you feeling okay?" I asked as I helped her unpack.

It took effort for her to smile as if someone had overdrawn her happiness account. "Just a long trip. A big change from sunny California. Proves I'm getting old."

No it doesn't, I thought and closed her door. It proved something was wrong.

"Would you mind if I took Donnie out to lunch alone today?" she asked the next morning. "I don't want you to think I don't enjoy your company."

I was fixing a late breakfast for us. The girls had left for school and Don for work before she ever got up. "I think that's a great idea," I answered. "You two need to spend some time together. It's been awhile."

I sat down at the table and she put her hand on mine. "You look a bit tired yourself," she said.

"You know how it is," I said, rubbing my cheeks and hands. "A job, children, a house and a husband.

Sometimes it can be overwhelming and tends to wear me out."

She smiled. "So how is your job? Donnie said you were working as a secretary for a small church."

I took a sip of coffee. "I like it. The pay won't take care of the mortgage but it's a job. Actually, I earned so little I cash the checks instead of depositing them to avoid sarcastic comments from Don. Money, after all, is his only barometer of value or success."

"You're a gem," she said. "Few people would be as flexible as you've always been. And kind. I hope Don appreciates his jewel of a wife."

So do I, I thought.

It was almost dinnertime and my heart began to pound in my chest like there was some small being in there trying to get out. When Don and his mother returned from lunch, their eyes were red from crying. Their cumulative appearance suggested the air was contaminated. Collectively, they were a portrait in misery.

"Would you mind if I skip dinner?" she asked.

"No," I said. "Of course not. Can I get you anything?"

She patted my shoulder. "I just need to rest." She shuffled down the hall to her room and closed the door softly.

I raised my eyebrows at Don in a questioning grimace but he was too saturated in grief to respond. "I'll be downstairs," he mumbled and left the room. I fed the children in a fog of worry and whisked them into bed.

Don was sitting in the den, his head in his hands. Respecting his solitude, I sat on the arm of the chair and stroked his head in silence. There was so much I wanted to know but couldn't violate his choice to be mute. Something was seriously wrong and I felt a deep sorrow for this man and for the events in his life over which he had had little control.

He didn't speak until we went to bed. "Oh God," he sobbed. "She's going to die, Pen. My mom's going die."

I held him, felt his shudders against my body and cried with him. He suddenly sat up. The glare from the street lights highlighted his face. He rubbed his eyes fiercely with the heels of his hands then laid his head on my shoulder. "It's cancer. Diagnosed four months ago. It has metastasized into her lungs and spine."

He was gulping for air as I stroked his back and felt the potency of his fear and grief in my hands. "Can't they operate?" I whispered.

He nodded no.

"Does Veronica know?"

"Only that Mom is sick. She doesn't know the prognosis."

It was a rainy Saturday as Mom prepared to leave on the six-thirty a.m. flight out of Logan airport in Boston. Mom and I stood in the foyer as Don loaded her luggage into the car. Tears flooded our cheeks. She reached up and touched my lips. "Please keep loving each other," she said. We hugged and I walked her down to the car. There was an unbearable finality in that walk. I stood at the top of the drive and waved until they were out of sight then walked back into the house and sobbed uncontrollably.

One month after her departure. Don said he would be home for dinner but staggered in the door at midnight. I had worried and fretted to the point of exhaustion wondering where he was and almost asleep when he roared into the bedroom. Drunk.

Suddenly the lights went on. "Where the hell's my dinner?" he shouted. "Did it ever enter your feeble mind that I've worked all day and might be hungry?"

I had to be kind. "Honey, please calm down," I said, and threw back the covers. "I'll fix you something."

But I couldn't move fast enough. He thundered out to the kitchen, opened the refrigerator door and threw the contents everywhere. Bottles took flight and crashed to the floor. Fruit squashed under his feet as he hurled bowls of leftovers into the sink.

"Don," I screamed. "Stop!" I physically tried to restrain him by grabbing his arms. "I know you're angry. Upset. But this won't solve anything."

He pushed me away with his forearm and then lunged toward me. I raced outside, onto the deck then into the backyard. He chased me, grabbed my waist, picked me up and screamed, "Why should you live and her die?" He tossed me to the ground with such force my head hit a rock. I heard his footsteps back up on the deck before I passed out. Hours later I came to, crawled through the yard and made it up to the deck. The left side of my head was bleeding; the blood obliterating my vision. Pain shot through my left temple. I stumbled into the house, crawled to the couch and laid down.

I had been the scapegoat, beaten because the woman who had placed him on an unchallenged throne was slipping away and there was nothing he could do to save her.

The children awakened me the next morning. The wife of one of Don's salesmen was standing over me. "Pen," she said. "The kids told me you fell in the backyard when I called this morning. I rushed over to see if I could help. And you do need help. I'll clean you up and then I'm taking you to the emergency room."

She paused. "Do you want me to call Don?" I shook my head no and she reluctantly obliged my request.

Beth Collier was a kind, young woman who waited with the children while I was X-rayed. They found a small fracture in the left mastoid of the skull. And although the doctor wanted to admit me, I told him I had to go home, that there was no one to care for my children. My head was bandaged and he reluctantly released me under the condition I would stay in bed and handed me a prescription for pain killers. "I want to see you tomorrow. If you are still the same, I will have to admit you. Understood?"

Beth stayed with me until Don returned from work. When he walked into the bedroom, he panicked. "What happened to you?"

"She fell outside last night and hit her head on a rock," Beth said.

"Why didn't someone call me?" he asked.

"She didn't want me to," Beth said sheepishly. "Believe me, I tried."

His hands were trembling and he was anxious for her to leave. "Thank you for everything, Beth. I can take over from here." He quickly walked her down to the car, returned and sat on the side of the bed, patted my hand, and cried. "I did this to you, didn't I? Pen, please forgive me. I'm so sorry. Just try and rest. I'll get anything you need. You didn't deserve this at all."

He held his head in his hands. "I'm losing my mind."

June 1979

"Pen?" Don yelled from the den. "Pick up the extension. Veronica's on the phone."

"Hi Pen," she said, her voice sounding surprisingly perky.

"Hey Vic. How are you?"

"Great, now that Mom's feeling better." Her voice was animated. "She's getting stronger!"

"How?" Don asked. "New doctors?"

"She went to Mexico," Victoria said. "Saw some specialist. I don't really know what he did or what she is taking but I do know she is so much better. She's even talking about trying to get her job back at the bank."

I hung up to allow brother and sister a private chat and silently thanked God.

Transfused with new hope, he rallied. Clinging to family with a duct-tape allegiance, his original charm emerged. And with his action came a treasured peace.

Don struggled through the kitchen door one afternoon carrying a large box wrapped in a memorial-sized ribbon. He called the children into the kitchen and asked me to open it. He was animated, chuckling and fuller of life than I had seen him in a long time.

"A new typewriter!" I shouted. "What's the occasion?"

He pointed to a piece of paper rolled into the carriage. *To the writer we know you can be. We're all behind you. Love, Don, Stephie and Bridget*

Tears. Why did I always cry? "I don't know what to say." I hugged each one of them. "But I'll begin with thank you."

"Why are you crying?" He stared at my face. "I thought you would be happy?"

"Oh Dad," Stephie said. "Those are her happy tears. Sad ones roll lots faster."

We laughed. "I'm way beyond happy. I'm overwhelmed by all your support."

He put his arm around my shoulder. "You've deserved this for a very long time. And you have always backed me. Now it's my turn. Don't give up." He pulled me closer and whispered, "and I'm sorry for everything. I love you."

I had mentally returned to that day frequently, like it was an elaborate ceremony for the presentation of a lifetime achievement award. The memory had no rival.

November 1979

The house hummed with contentment as the girls and I worked side by side in the kitchen creating Don's birthday dinner. It was almost five-thirty. "Let's get his present wrapped," I told the girls as I pulled Bridget's finger out of the bowl of icing. "But wash your hands first."

I retrieved the gifts from hiding places, grabbed the wrapping paper and put it on the table. Stephie reached over and picked up a box marked 'Canon.'

"Is this a camera?" she asked

"Neat, isn't it?

Stephie frowned. "But he already has one. Why didn't we get him something different?"

I smiled. "Because that old camera he has doesn't work right and he won't use it."

Actually I had read the report from his doctor's office on the results of his physical the month before. The doctor had suggested Don take up a hobby to vent his frustrations and lower his blood pressure.

"Can this be just from me?" Stephie asked.

"It is from all of us, okay?"

"Does he know how to work it?" Bridget asked

"Of course, honey. Let's hurry. He'll be home soon."

"Fantastic!" Don said as tore the paper off his gift. "I've always wanted one of these. But everybody has to help me learn how to use it. Okay?"

Stephie frowned. "Mom told us you already knew how, Daddy."

"Oh, pumpkin, I do. But there are many fancy things on this and I will have to practice. I can take lots of pictures of you guys, okay?"

Excited with his new toy, the amateur photographer soon wore us out as he moved from subject to subject with a literal translation of still life: still first, life later. Lurking everywhere that night was a comical 35 mm Frankenstein mumbling about aperture settings, ASA's and commands to freeze which made me question whether his hobby was photography or cryogenics.

"Sit with your back to the camera," he told Bridget one night.

"Okay," she said and plopped down on a small stool. Don moved about five feet from her back and crouched like a war correspondent for UPI.

"Okay, baby girl. Now turn your head slowly over your shoulder, look at Daddy and smile."

She turned as directed and with the expertise of Raggedy Ann, fell toward the camera in a blob."

"Bridget?" he said, rushing to pick her up. "You okay, honey?"

Holding back tears, she hugged him. "Did you take my picture?"

"Not yet, honey. Want to try again?"

"Nope," she said backing away. "Your camera hurt me."

"Why don't you just take natural pictures of the children at play?" I suggested after they were in bed.

"Can't," he said, fiddling with dials on the camera.

"Why not?"

"I'll blur the picture. Until I get the hang of it, everyone will have to be completely still."

I thought for a moment. "How about mannequins?"

He laughed. "Try patience, hon. I'll get it right eventually."

A week later some excellent shots of Massachusetts winter scenery finally made him focus on Mother Nature. She didn't seem to mind, as the mountains and forests stayed in place with only an occasional wind to remind him of her flexibility. "These are great," I told him. "Stick to wildlife, okay?" I wanted to add *not the female variety* but had the common sense to keep my mouth shut.

December 1979

My mind was tumbling in a drum of success. I was a published author. FINALLY. Not on any grand scale, maybe a step above bubble gum wrappers, but it was a beginning. My parody of the poem *"Twas the Night Before Christmas"* was titled *"Twas the Bike Before Christmas"*. I had sold my first piece to a New England newspaper. The earnings wouldn't cover the mortgage but dollars were immaterial.

To honor the milestone, I served a for-company-only-dinner, waiting until dessert to display the published poem. "I want to show you all something," I said and unrolled the paper to the full page spread they had given the poem. "I did it!"

Don smiled and applauded. "Well, well," he said. "Congratulations! So how much did you get, Mrs. Hemingway?"

Why did he always equate success to dollars? I thought silently. "Well," I stammered,

"They paid me twenty-five dollars. But the money is not important here. I have a chance now. I have been validated and am on to new beginnings."

He nodded his head as if bowing to royalty. "And a good one," he smiled. He then turned to the children and added, "you guys better wait to pick out your new cars."

"Oh no," I said. "Pick them out. But you'll have to wait a few years to buy, okay?"

Don cleaned up the kitchen and built a fire in the den fireplace while I put the kids to bed. We cuddled on the couch like teenagers. Then silently, he reached down beside the couch and pulled up two champagne glasses and a bottle of pricey champagne.

"So who told you?" I said.

"No one." "He raised his glass in a toast and clinked his against my rim. "Here's to a Pulitzer Prize for you someday and the trip of a lifetime for us."

I took a sip with registering what he had just said. "Wait a second. Trip? What trip?"

He rested his head against the back of the couch. "Let's see," he mused. "Where have we always wanted to go?"

"Hawaii." I paused for a moment before it hit me. "Don? Did your region qualify for the big one?"

He fumbled in his shirt pocket and pulled out a piece of paper. "It's official. Read it."

"We are going!" I beamed. "I'm so proud of you! When?"

"March."

I sat my glass down and threw my arms around his neck. "I can't wait to tell the kids. Hawaii!"

He snuggled his face into my shoulder. "Hon, I'm afraid they can't go this time. We'll have to leave them with your parents. That's why I waited until they were asleep to tell you. They won't understand."

I felt bad but tried to push the thoughts out of my head. He had earned the right; we've earned the right. Tonight was a time to celebrate. "I understand," I said softly and cuddled next to him. But the guilt had already taken root as usual.

CHAPTER 16

February 1980

*L*egal reminders Don had of his mother's life lay inside the rich leather briefcase he carried off the plane. I watched as he walked down the jet way in a slow, droopy gait. His face was sunken, he had lost ten pounds. He hadn't shaved for several days and as he came closer I could see his once crystal blue eyes were now streaked with red, like some careless teacher had marked changes on the originals.

"How are you?" I asked, not knowing what else to say.

We hugged. "Orphaned," he whispered.

The word was so dramatic but unbearable, even at his age. There wouldn't be any more phone calls on his birthday or cards at Christmas from his mother. He wouldn't have a parent to share his joys of the next promotion, a raise or a new home. Worse, Victoria was still in college, a baby who had lost both parents before she herself had reached adulthood. "I've been the stabilizer for my brothers and sisters," he said as we watched the baggage carousel revolve. "Especially Victoria. Mom's death has worn me out more than anything else in my life."

I was uneasy, afraid to say anything that might further trigger his fragile emotions. "Will she move back here with us?"

"Can't," he said. "She has to finish school. But I'm the executor of Mom's will."

His voice had an all-consuming sadness. "So I'll have to go back to California several times until her assets have been distributed." He paused, grabbed two suitcases from the carousel and struggled to lift them. "It's so awkward trying to carry out her wishes."

We walked to the parking garage in silence. "I wish I could have been there for you," I said as I helped lift his bags into the trunk.

"Just be here for me now." He patted my shoulder. "I hope you understand why I couldn't fly you out. Besides the expense, it was best that I be there alone."

"I'll always stand by you, Don." I kissed his check. "You want to drive?"

"Not really. Do you mind?"

I slid behind the wheel. He turned his head toward the passenger window. I could tell he wanted to cry but knew he wouldn't, his tears imprisoned more by anger than a macho aversion of displaying emotions.

"I'll never forget this month," he said as we pulled onto the highway. "Can you believe it, Pen? The only person who always believed in me is gone." He closed his eyes and in minutes was asleep. *I believe in you,* I thought. But it wouldn't do any good to mention that.

I stopped to pick up the girls at Kathleen's on the way home. Both she and Tom walked out to the car. Don got out, hugged each one and bravely acknowledged their condolences.

"Daddy," yelled Stephie. "You're back." She raced toward him. He wiped his tears, gathered her up in his arms and hugged her with a gentle passion.

"Miss me?" he asked

"Of course," she said.

Bridget was right behind her. "My turn?" she said, holding up her arms.

Don swept her off her feet. "Your turn, baby girl." He kissed her forehead. "Sure missed you, Pumpkin."

Bridget bent her head back and stared at him. "Did you miss Mommy too?"

Don smiled. "You bet. Now let's go home."

I made Don a stiff drink and took it down to the den where he sat working at his desk.   He mumbled a thank you, raised the glass to his lips, downed the contents in several gulps and handed me the empty glass. "Get me another?"

Although it was not the time for me to be an AA advocate, I poured less alcohol into his glass and was back quickly. This time he nursed the drink.

"What are all those papers?" I asked

He leaned back in his chair. "Victoria's college stuff. She has a partial scholarship and her grades are exceptional. Success is more than a goal for her; it's a burning passion that must become mine as well. Where scholarships fall short, I'll have to find some way to fill in."

It was too soon to ask about his mother's will. So I carefully broached the topic of the Hawaiian trip. I stood behind him and rubbed his neck as I spoke. "You know, honey, I'll certainly understand if you want to postpone your trip. You need time to come to terms with things."

"No," he said without looking up. "I don't think you understand what I need at the moment. Then again, how could you?" He didn't actually say, *hey, you still have parents* but the words hung in the air as if he had. Defensively silent, I continued to rub his neck.

He opened his briefcase which was full of legal documents and sympathy cards. "I hate these stupid things," he said. "So many people wrote, 'It was God's will'. What kind of a God would let my mother suffer in such intense pain, die at any early age and leave a daughter behind who hadn't even begun her adult life?"

He dropped the cards in a pile on his desk and put his head in his hands. "The only way I can push some of this in the dark for now is to be busy. Activities. People."

"You're sure?"

"I'm sure." He took my hand and pressed it to his cheek. "Don't worry. I'll be fine." He reached over and turned off his desk lamp. "Let's get some sleep. We've a lot to do before we leave."

March 1980

Snow swirled through the sky like flakes of dandruff and the temperature hovered at twelve degrees as we boarded the flight for Hawaii. We had dashed around for days to get ready. My parents had agreed to care for the children so I collected their school work and drove them to Pennsylvania—round trip in one day which meant twelve hours of driving-- while he handled the sundry but necessary chores.

We sat next to each other as mute partners, our hands entwined. We were both guarded, unable to speak for fear we would cry.

Traveling with three couples from Massachusetts, Don ordered enough drinks in flight to own stock in Seagram's. Wary of vomiting in his lap, I stuck to Coke.

Always the showman, Don stretched across the aisle to get the attention of Ted Samson, his top salesman, who was dressed in a traditional Hawaiian shirt and sporting his normal arrogance.

"Hope you packed some warm clothes, Samson," Don chided. "The company changed our destination at the last minute."

Ted laughed. "Maybe someone should have told the pilot."

"He knows," Don said. "He's just covering it up."

Samson stroked his mustache. "A lying aviator. Some job description."

"Good background," Don teased.

Samson playfully raised his eyebrows. "As what?"

Don smirked. "Nixon's personal pilot." They both erupted in laughter, joined by many passengers who had heard the exchange.

Maui was Chamber of Commerce perfect and the warm tropical breezes were a welcome respite. Scheduled as a three day hiatus prior to the beginning of the conference in Honolulu, Maui was supposed to provide some relaxation in the sun and surf without the strains of a corporate performance the conference would command.

It was after dark when we reached the hotel. The grounds were well lighted. The green grass and lush beds of flowers mirrored the dreams I had had of the tropical utopia.

But our room was a disappointment. It was much smaller than expected with twin beds. Don didn't seem to notice so I didn't voice any complaint. "Hurry up and get unpacked," he said and emptied his suitcases in a whirlwind, carelessly tossing underwear, socks and toiletries into a top drawer of the large dresser. "The guys are waiting for us at the bar."

After twelve hours of traveling, my feet were swollen, my head pounding. Unlike Don, I didn't have the buzz of alcohol to keep me going. "Would you mind if I went to bed?"

He dropped his brush on top of the dresser. "We finally made it to paradise and you want to sleep? Fine," he said without disappointment. "I'm going anyway. And don't forget. We have to be up by 4:00 a.m. to get to the Haleakala crater."

I had overheard other couples discussing this on the plane. Don was the only one who wanted to go. "Four?" I said. "Can't we reschedule?

His anger permeated the room. "I didn't come to Hawaii to sleep. But if that's what you want to do, I can't stop you." He sighed in disgust and left the room, slamming the door behind him.

I awakened the next morning and he was gone. I showered, dressed and went to find the others. Only one man had met the demand of a four o'clock wake up call. The rest of the people, who had made inebriated promises to go, failed to show.

We had a leisurely breakfast and I answered their questions about Don's mom.

When Don returned, the atmosphere became more oppressive than a child's wake. "So how was it?" I asked with an artificial gaiety.

"Buy postcards," he snapped. Hastily changing his clothes, he left the room.

At dinner he resumed his part as a typical, loving spouse in front of his colleagues but privately we moved around each other in an uneasy silence as bottled up feelings spread like an emotional bacteria in our minds.

On Friday we left Maui for Honolulu and after checking into the Sheraton on Waikiki, he readied himself to leave the room. "I'm going to meet some guys from other regions. Get our stuff organized. We have a busy schedule the rest of the week. I'll be back in a bit to get ready for the dinner tonight."

I took my time getting ready and sat waiting in the room for almost an hour. Suddenly there was a key in the lock. "Get my clothes ready," he shouted as he rushed to take a shower. Twenty minutes later we were out the door.

In the elevator he took my hand. "Do you know where this event is being held?" I asked.

"No," he said smiling. He pulled me close. "But we'll find it." He kissed my nose. "Have I told you how gorgeous you look tonight?"

Pumped up for the social affairs I loved so much, I opened my eyes to the beauty which surrounded us as we strolled through the majestic lobby with marble floors and glorious potted fan palms.

We moved arm-in-arm through the maze before we found the ballroom, his sense of direction impaired by a few martinis. His eyes widened as we entered the lavish ballroom for the traditional beginning of any Leadership Conference: a cocktail party and dinner.

Women dressed in summer dresses and men in light colored shirts and jackets strolled about laughing and chatting above the music of a live orchestra. Familiar faces bobbed among many unfamiliar ones. Couples we had met in San Francisco noticed us before we saw them. The warmth and genuine tenderness radiating through the room of winners was an energy which was almost mystical.

Don and I circulated then stopped to talk to friends we had met in San Francisco. Marge Kingston, wife of the regional Vice President, warmly welcomed us. "Well, did you bring the kids? she asked. "I'd love them to meet ours. The last time we spoke, I think our children were about the same age."

"Yes, I remember. But we couldn't bring them this time," I said.

"Are they spending time with their grandparents?" her husband asked.

"Yes," I answered, not wanting to continue any grandparent conversation. They bantered for a bit about their children then continued to merge into the crowd. As they disappeared, Don suddenly excused himself. "See you in a bit, Pen" he said, and abruptly left me alone. Conversations swirled around me like I was a statue in a park. Feeling awkward, I watched as he was quickly surrounded by an entire civilization of insurance executives, and their wives. An obvious favorite, his peers greeted him with an exuberance akin to welcoming a dignitary.

I roamed around the ballroom feeling awkward, looking for familiar faces. After an hour of idle conversations with a variety of people I hardly knew, I went searching for Don. Unable to find him, I went through the buffet line. Juggling a plate of food and glass of water, I roamed amid tables until I heard his unmistakable laugh. He was seated with members of our region and almost finished with his meal.

The table was full. I walked up behind him. "Hon? Can I squeeze in here?"

The conversation stopped as he looked back at me. His smile had vanished as he leaned back in his chair and said much too loudly, "Go find your own goddamned table."

His bark hit me with the force of an electric shock. Tears jammed my eyes like floor waters against a dam. His peers lowered their heads in collective embarrassment while Don sat fixed, continuing to entertain the now disinterested masses, too drunk to know what he was doing.

My body quivered as I walked away to find a table in the immediate vicinity. Three couples I had never met sat at an almost empty table talking as I approached. Strangers. My appetite faded. I put my plate down on a serving tray at the far end of the room and disappeared into the lobby.

Minutes later I heard someone call my name. "Penne?"

I turned and saw Angelina Arigone, her lips outlined in such bright red lipstick she looked like an ad for ketchup. "Get back in there," she demanded, pointing to the door, "and tell that miserable son of a bitch to go to hell!"

"Forget it," I said and continued to walk ahead of her.

She pulled me back by my arm. "You're crazy," she said. "I wouldn't let him get away with that garbage for one minute. You don't deserve it!"

Yes, I thought, and I don't deserve to have you screeching at me like some strangled pig. "You're forgetting, Angelina. Don just lost his mother. I have to be patient. Fair."

"Fair?" She tossed her head back and laughed much too loud then snapped her head forward. Her long black hair swirled around her face like a whip. People walking past us stared as Angelina continued her loud diatribe. "Something tells me that ass can't even spell the word fair!"

I was mute. Never in our marriage had Don behaved so disastrously in public. There was no need to go back. He had done it one time and would certainly do it again. "Stay out of this Angelina. I'll handle him." My knees wobbled and I was getting very light headed. Two drinks were beyond my limit, especially without food.

"You're really stupid," she said and stomped her way back to the ballroom.

I fumbled for the room key in my purse and walked the great lobby, blindly checking elevators, looking for something remotely familiar.

Finally I took the next available elevator relieved to find it was the right one. I leaned against the gold bar surrounding the interior until the elevator stopped on our floor.

I checked the key to confirm our room number and followed the arrows down the hall to the door. As I struggled to put the key in the lock, the door suddenly opened. Don stood there glaring, his face snarled. He reached out, grabbed my arm and flipped me into the room.

"You stupid bitch," he growled.

I pulled away. "Stop it! Let me go!"

He charged toward me, grabbed me by the back of my head and covered my mouth and nose with his hand.

I kicked. Squirmed. I wrestled to get free but was no match for his strength. He threw me against the glass doors leading to the balcony and I screamed. "Let go of me!"

Grabbing the front of my dress he hauled me to my feet and pounded his fist into the right side of my face and then the left. Blood spurted from my mouth. I tore away, only to be trapped again. He pulled at the pearls around my neck, and, with a fierce tug, snapped the strand. Pearls flew like spitballs around the room.

A full fist hit my stomach. I doubled over as he snarled, "I'm gonna kill you, bitch!" Clutching me around the throat with his left arm, he opened the sliding door and started to push me outside. I grabbed the drape. With a karate chop, he slammed my hand against the glass.

His hands tightened around my neck and he shoved me to the floor. Part of my body was on the balcony, the other was pressed against the inside carpet. The metal tracks of the sliding door ground into the back of my neck.

He was shouting. I couldn't understand him. He released his grip and with a clenched fist, pounded my face, my arms, my legs and I passed out.

Night was swallowed by morning the next time I tried to open my eyes. A wet, cold cloth had been tented across my face. My head pounded without pause. Pain surged from my nose through my face into my ears.

Memory; how I wanted my memory to die. I pulled the rag off my face and struggled to sit up. Everything hurt. My body felt crushed. Naked from the waist up, I focused on my arms. They were bruised. Cut.

Tears. My eyes burned as if they were coated in acid and the vision in my right eye faded rapidly. I inched my body out of bed and tried to walk, listing like a storm wrecked ship. I dropped to my knees, crawled over to the dresser and pulled myself up to the mirror. The image made me scream.

My eyes were filled with blood. My nose had swollen into my checks like a misplaced mound of flesh. Shades of purple, black and blue were everywhere on my body like a wall desecrated by graffiti.

The bathroom door opened and Don stepped out, his face red, his eyes swollen. He walked up behind me and I flinched. "It's okay, honey," he said softly.

Putting his arms around me, he lifted me to my feet and guided me back to bed. Standing over me he began sobbing. "Oh, God, Pen. I don't know what happened."

He slumped down on the bed, laid his head on my chest and continued to cry. "I don't even remember doing such awful things to you."

A knock at the door made us both jump. Don bit his lip. I slithered down under the sheets and covered my face with a pillow while he answered it.

"Good morning." The male voice was unmistakable. It was Gene Arigone. "Got worried when you didn't answer your phone," he said.

"The phone never rang," Don said, his voice cracking.

Despite Don's attempt to block his path, Gene walked into the room. "Is Penne okay?" I could tell by the way Gene's voice rose on the word 'okay' that he knew I was not.

"We've had a bit of a mishap," Don stammered. "I was racing to get into the shower and didn't know Pen was behind the door. I shoved the door open and she went flying."

Gene walked over to the bed and lifted the pillow. "Judas Priest. You need a doctor!"

He walked over to the night stand, picked up the phone then slammed it down. "You're right. It's dead." Gene walked back to me and gently patted my shoulder. "I'll go to the lobby and find you a doctor," he said and walked out of the room.

Don sat down on the bed and wrapped his arms around me. He was shaking badly. "We'll get you some help, hon. Just hang on."

In under an hour, Gene was back. "There's a doctor at the Royal Hawaiian," he told Don. "He can see Pen now." Gene's voice was tense, frightening. And I know he knew exactly what happened.

I was lying on the bed dressed as best as Don could dress me. Gene walked over and handed me a pair of sunglasses. "They're men's glasses, but light will hurt your eyes without them."

No, I thought, that's not why he bought them. He wanted to cover my eyes from the glare of inquisitive strangers, or worse, people we knew.

With Don on one side of me and Gene on the other, we walked through the lobby and outside to a waiting cab.

"Call me when you get back, Don," he said and closed the cab door.

As soon as we arrived the nurse took me into an examining room and allowed me to lie down on the table. She was a master of diplomacy, never staring, just smiling. On the verge of vomiting, the horizontal position quelled the nausea. I swallowed hard as the door opened. A rotund man with a sunburned complexion walked in. "I'm Dr. Hardy," he said. He examined my entire body before speaking. "You want to talk about this?" he said. His voice was soft and surprisingly not accusatory. But I couldn't look at him.

"Not much to say," I stammered. I used the bathroom scenario as explanation and strengthened my credibility by stating I had had too much to drink and was more accident prone as a result. My voice trembled and I could tell he didn't believe me. But I was terrified of what the doctor could do to Don if I had been honest.

I was six thousand miles away from my children with no money or credit cards of my own and the only person I could depend on was my attacker.

The diagnosis was as expected. Broken nose, eyes had hemorrhaged, contusions, cuts and a possible concussion. "I'm sending you over to the hospital for X-rays," he said. "When are you scheduled to go home?"

"End of the week," I said.

He turned his chair around. "You cannot fly until the hemorrhaging in your eyes has stopped. I'm going to give you a prescription to reduce the bleeding, antibiotics for possible infection and some pain medication. Allergic to anything?"

Just my husband, I thought, but nodded my head no.

X-rays took the balance of the day and Don treated me like an infant, taking great care to keep me as comfortable as possible. He had been asked the cause of the injuries by the admitting clerk at the hospital. "She fell into a tub," he said. I couldn't see the clerk's face but heard her feeble mumble of "oh really," with a verbal question mark.

Dr. Hardy suggested I spend a few days in the hospital for observation but I declined. The fear, pain and mental confusion were so overwhelming I couldn't tolerate the thought of being hidden away in the nosey sterility of an institution. As an attendant wheeled me into X-Ray, I felt like I had been cast in some grade Z movie and no one had bothered to yell 'cut'.

Back in my room at the hotel, I slept for days. The nose and neck were painful but medication helped the pain, swelling and discoloration. And every four hours a pain pill temporarily dulled the horror. All I could think about when I was awake was how I could disappear out of my own life.

Don never left the room. Resigned to servitude, he tended to my every need and cried. Too much. Surrounded by bouquets of flowers he and others had sent, I imagined viewing my own funeral and wondered why there wasn't one of those yellow crime scene tapes around the room. Around him.

When I awakened one afternoon, I watched from the bed as Don stood at the window of our room, looking out at the ocean as the late afternoon sun cast a flicker of light on Diamondhead. When he turned I could see tears rolling down his face. He walked over and sat on the edge of the bed. "This was supposed to be a trip of a lifetime," he said, "a benchmark of success. And I destroyed it."

I had nothing to say and feigned sleep.

"You awake?" he whispered.

"Kind of," I mumbled.

He put his head in his hands. "I'm so humiliated, Pen. Look what I've done to you and yet you helped me save face. Do you think people are suspicious?"

"Yes," I said bluntly. "Wouldn't you be?"

He got up, walked over to the desk and slumped down in a chair. He looked lifeless, as if part of him wanted to die to avoid the turbulence he now faced. The most difficult part was his inability to remember how he did this awful thing or what I had done to encourage it. "I hate myself," he cried. "And my memory was erased by booze." He put his head back and sobbed.

The emotions barely thawed my icy feelings. "We'll have to work to dismiss what people could be thinking," I said, knowing the foundation of that statement had nothing to do with him. I was more afraid of being embarrassed than he was.

"Can we do it?" he asked. "Can you?"

"Do what?" I asked.

"Face everyone?"

I raised my head off the pillow. "We have to. Our presence will help convince everyone of the accidental origin of the injuries. But continued absence will feed the mouths of the gossips." I rolled over and cried. How could I go on defending him?

Don was quickly at my side. "Why are you crying? Do you need more pain stuff?"

"No," I said. "I just can't stand the thought of people thinking of me as a fool to stay married to you. We both need professional help, Don."

He patted my shoulder. "You're not the fool, Pen. I am. And yes, we do need help."

By Friday Don was pacing the floor. "You look much better," he said as he stood behind me in the mirror. "Think you feel up to going to the formal dinner tomorrow night?"

My throat tightened. "All I have is a strapless gown, Don." I looked down at all the bruises on my arms, chest, face and neck. "I can't go looking like this."

"I know, sweetheart." I watched him in the mirror as he scanned my reflection. "Tell you what. I'll go shopping and find you an evening jacket that will cover everything. How does that sound?"

"Frightening. Unless you can find one with a hood and a mask." I got back in bed. "Wake me when you come back," I told him and fell asleep. It was the only escape I had.

The room was dark when he returned. He sat on the bed and ran his hand gently over my forehead. "Hon?" he whispered. "I found it."

He reached over me, turned on the light and pulled a long, gold satin jacket from the box. Standing up, he put it around him. "See?" he said. "It will cover everything you want to hide. I also bought some expensive makeup for you."

Without a reply, I rolled over and went back to sleep.

I stood in the mirror for hours the next night staring at my face. Makeup hid quite a bit of the damage but I would have to wear sunglasses. At night. In a ballroom. No makeup would hide eyes still tinged with blood and surrounded by bruises.

I was envious when Don walked out of the bathroom in his tux. "You look beautiful," he said to me, but the mirror did not reflect his artificial sincerity.

Tell him, I thought. *Tell him now.* "Don, before we leave I have something to say."

"Sure sweetheart," he said, scooping up change off the dresser.

I kneaded my arm with my hand. "I'm willing to participate in this thing tonight, but not for you. I'm doing this for myself."

He squirmed, pulled a cigarette from his pocket and lit it. I turned my back to him and continued to talk. "I will never, ever tolerate your abuse again." I turned around and faced him. "I can't even promise you I'll stay your wife. I haven't decided yet. What I can tell you is that as much as I have loved you, as much as I have cared, I would rather be dead than go through anything like this again."

Don walked over to me. Tears collected in his lower lids. "I can't tell you why I did this or how. What I can tell you is that I will spend the rest of my life making it up to you." He paused and asked, "So will you come with me tonight? I'm too scared to go alone."

My stomach constricted as we stopped in the lounge before going into the ballroom and watched Don ingest three drinks in less than twenty minutes. With his discomfort modified by liquor, we joined the others.

Ted Samson was standing at the door and his stare made my heart beat much too fast. While Don left to get a drink, Ted and I struggled with unwanted conversation. He was my least favorite person in the company, brash and arrogant, but Don was still his boss. His sun tanned face looked healthy under the lights and the dark, rich man's tux he was wearing fit his body like each seam had been sewn on him. He wasn't handsome and his dazzling white—yet bonded—teeth did little to improve the long, hooked nose which begged for remodeling.

"I can't believe all this damage was the result of a fall in the bath tub," he said taking a deep breath.

I swallowed hard. "Hard for me too. It ruined our trip. But you know the old cliché. Truth is stronger than fiction."

Ted cleared his throat. "Except in this case," he said abruptly. "So how long are you going to lie for him?"

My throat was parched. The emotional turmoil sent my head spinning. I looked pass Ted and saw Don walking toward us. "You're wrong and out of line, Ted," I said in hushed tones.

"Really?" Ted said. "My wife divorced me because I was a mad man. It takes one to know one. Don needs help and so do you." Catching a glimpse of Don, Ted patted my cheek and disappeared into the crowd.

"Take me back to the room," I told Don. "Now!"

He scowled. "What's wrong? You look beautiful?"

"My insides are showing," I said and walked out the door. He followed then scooted around in front of me to block my path. "We're both fools," I said tersely. "That's what's wrong."

CHAPTER 17

March 1980
Los Angeles, CA

*T*he plane rolled slowly up to the gate at Los Angeles International Airport and stopped. I didn't want to stay here but Don and I agreed in Hawaii that the layover was unavoidable. The bruises and marks on my face needed to disappear before I saw my parents. The children. They weren't stupid. They would never allow me to go back to Massachusetts with Don.

We had spent the entire flight hammering out a logical story to explain my appearance to Victoria; planning intensely as if we were putting together an ad campaign for Lizzy Borden. Fine tuning details, we concluded the best cover would be to say I'd been hit in the face with a ball, broke my nose and fell to the concrete court on impact. For my parents, we decided to stick to that story with a different venue. The ball game would have taken place in LA, not Hawaii. Long sleeves and a turtle neck would cover other marks. Nothing, however, could camouflage my depression.

California held no joy, no excitement as it had in the past. His mother's house was cold, wallpapered in death. And despite Victoria's façade of cheeriness, the loss was there. Boxes of unwanted memorabilia were stacked in the hallway leading from the living room to the bedrooms. Beds were not made; bathrooms reminded me of a gas station facility. The kitchen sink was piled with dirty dishes, remnants of food left on plates all over the house. The dining room table supported yards of newspapers and textbooks. And every picture of any family member had been removed as if all had died with his Mom.

"I want out of here as soon as possible," I whispered to Don. "And when Victoria graduates, we should consider having her move back east." I looked around at the debris and neglect. "This is too much for a young girl to cope with."

"So how was your trip" Victoria seemed genuinely interested.

While Don and Vic chatted, I snuck down the hall to the bedroom to call my mother who answered on the first ring. "Hi." I said, adding as much perk to my voice as I could muster. "How are the girls?"

"Fine," she said, "but missing you. Where are you? When are you coming back?"

My hands were trembling. "We're in LA with Victoria, Mom. But we've been delayed."

My voice faltered. "I got hit in the face with a ball. Broke my nose. The doctor doesn't want me to fly for a few days." *It's just a white lie*, I told myself.

Mom's voice changed abruptly. "Since when do you play ball?"

I laughed. "Victoria's friends needed one more player. How could I say no?"

There was a momentary silence on the other end. "You're sure it was a ball and not a fist?" Mothers' words were sharp, penetrating.

I cleared my throat. "That wasn't necessary, Mom."

Her voice was grave. "Give me your flight number and the date."

I gave her the information and asked to speak to the girls.

"They're not here. Your Dad took them on a nature walk."

"How nice," I said. "Thanks for taking such good care of them."

"Just take care of yourself, Penne. We can handle the children just fine."

I hung up feeling guilty. I was a liar.

The California sun was behaving like a travel brochure the next morning, beginning its golden ascent over the mountains. I was sitting in the kitchen of his mother's house, drinking coffee, when Victoria walked in, her tall willowy frame moving as gracefully as a Swiss watch. Her long, white blond hair shimmered down her back, coming to rest on the lace trim of her nightgown at the middle of her back. As tired as she looked, her face still held incredible beauty. Sea blue eyes like Don's, a long sculptured nose and flawless tanned skin gave Victoria the look of that perfect sun n' surf girl.

"Coffee, sweetheart?" I asked.

She nodded and looked around the room. "Wow. This place looks great. Thanks for cleaning up. I just haven't cared much lately."

I poured her a cup of coffee and put in on the table. "I don't blame you," I said. "Would you let me help with the rest? I'd feel much better if you didn't have to live in so much clutter."

Her eyes brightened. "You wouldn't mind, I mean, with your problems?" She shook her head and stared at my face. "I never knew volleyball could pack such a wallop."

I touched the bandage on my nose. "Almost healed," I said. "But I need something to keep my mind off my stupidity."

She put her hand on top of mine. "We don't really know each other well, but I'm really glad you're here."

We talked briefly of the past and then quickly turned the conversation toward the future. "Vic? Would you consider moving east when you finish school? You could live with us, or your brother Gavin or get a place of your own. With a degree in marketing, especially one from USC, New York may be just the place you want to be!"

She nodded. "I don't know, Pen." Her voice was very soft, borne out in a long trembling breath. "Everything I've ever known is here. I don't know if I could stand the winters, the people or the loss of all the friends I have here."

"Just think about it, okay? Now, why don't I get started straightening up around here? Can I sort through the boxes in the hall?"

She stood and stretched. "Sure. Be my guest." A smile returned to her face. "Most of that stuff is old school papers of mine. Mom saved everything I did." She paused and chuckled. "You know; the early years stuff with the 'you-are-wonderful stickers on them'."

Don was still sleeping as I carried out several cartons from the hall to the back porch. Victoria was right. In the first carton, large enough to house a small television, I combed through stars and bunnies and smiley-faced papers for an hour yet didn't have the heart to toss any of them.

The second carton was more of the same. I reached in and pulled out a huge stack. Victoria's years in school had been carefully preserved by her mother. As I neared the bottom of the box, I found a small notebook, its once blue face covered in ribbons of teenage doodling; *I love Bobby/ I hate Bobby/ Jennifer loves Bobby/ I hate Jennifer.* Eighth or ninth grade, I decided as I opened the cover and flipped through the dated pages; month and day only. No year.

I opened the tab labeled *ENGLISH* with the word *YUK* after it and found a folded sheet of paper. I opened it and a shiver ran through me. It was a letter written to her father, bearing a full date, written six month after his death. One sentence caught my eye: 'I know what you did to Mom.'

Suddenly I heard a noise in the kitchen behind me. Stuffing the letter in my robe pocket, I quickly tossed the notebook back in the box.

"Find anything interesting?" Don asked.

"Just the papers of a young scholar," I said.

April 1980

One week later we returned to the east coast to pick up the children. My face looked much better although some slight bruising still remained which I had covered with thick makeup. A turtleneck and long pants covered everything else.

"Tell us what happened," Dad said as he and Mom walked with me through the airport. His face was a portrait in anger. Mom's face remained emotionless.

I focused ahead on Don and the children who were holding hands and skipping about thirty feet in front of us on their way to the baggage carousel. "I already told Mom," I answered. "A ball in the face. Nothing exciting. I am obviously not meant to play sports." I giggled as if the laughter would give me added credibility. "But you guys already know that from my P.E. grades in college."

Dad remained grim. "Or you weren't meant to be married to that man," he said. Again I focused ahead refusing to look directly at my father. "Everything is fine," I said. "We had a great trip and we're thankful you two could care for the children."

Although they had been polite to Don when we deplaned, I knew how nervous he was, and saw the relief on his face when the children created the perfect diversion as they raced to greet him.

The trip back to Massachusetts was delightful. Elated we were home but a bit moody at the thought of returning to school, the kids willingly unpacked then left with Don to pick up the animals. I made a quick run to the store and picked up our mail, happy to discover I had sold another article. But the success melted in the fumes of an unforgotten Hawaiian Armageddon.

Eager to stay busy, I planned an elaborate evening for Stephanie's tenth birthday at her favorite restaurant. Dressed in a bright yellow dress, her blond hair flowed in waves to her shoulders. Her face beamed when her lobster was served. She seemed so worldly as she cracked the claws with precision then diligently poked each piece of shell in search of another delectable shred of meat.

The restaurant environment always brought out the best in Don. As waiters stood by, Don began his gift presentation. He pulled a new watch out of his pocket and a card with fifty dollars enclosed and presented them to Stephie as if she was royalty.

"Wow!" she squealed as the waiters applauded. "Thanks, Daddy."

Don endeared himself to her this blissful evening. Anxious to become part of an adult world, Stephie basked in his treatment of her as a young lady. Raising his glass in a toast, Don said: "To my big girl. May you always be as beautiful as you are tonight."

Stephie's faced glowed as he leaned over and kissed her gently on the cheek. "I love you, Dad," she said.

He beckoned the waiters who arrived at the table with a small cake. Ten candles flickered on top while an entourage of waiters sang Happy Birthday in perfect harmony.

I sat back watching my daughter, as smiles danced off her little lips. Don's attentiveness had made her birthday more special than anything else she had experienced with him and I was thankful that the shadow which engulfed he and I was not visible to our children.

On the way home, Don suddenly stopped at a Toys 'R' Us. Acting mysterious, he left the car running. "Be right back," he said and disappeared into the store.

"Maybe he's getting you a Walkman, Steph," said a cheerful Bridget who had the unique maturity at age seven to be sincerely happy for others.

Don returned quickly, got in the car, turned his head around to the back seat and handed Bridget a bag. "I messed up your birthday a few years back," he said. "Hope this will make up for it."

I watched Stephie's face in the rear view mirror. It was not that she couldn't be happy for Bridget, but, it was her birthday.

Bridget pulled a Raggedy Ann out of the bag.

"You like it, Pumpkin? Don asked.

Bridget didn't answer him. She turned to her sister and said, "Here Stephie. It's your birthday. This should be yours."

Two weeks later, I struggled to open the door of the house balancing two bags of groceries when suddenly the door popped open. Stephie and Bridget were smiling, tingling with excitement as only little children could do. "Boy do we have a surprise for you!" Stephie shouted.

I handed her one bag and followed her up the stairs to the kitchen. "What kind of a surprise?"

"You'll see," Bridget giggled. "Now put the bags down." She cupped her hands around her mouth like an empire. "You ready, Daddy?" she called down the hall.

"Ready," he yelled from our bedroom.

"Now close your eyes," Stephie said. "We'll hold your hands and guide you. Okay?"

The girls pulled me down the hall and took pigeon steps to avoid bumping into walls. "You're at your bedroom door," Bridget announced. "On the count of three, you can open your eyes."

"One-two-three" they counted in unison with Don. "Okay, Mom," they yelled. "Open your eyes NOW!"

My stomach flipped. Don stood by our bed. Waving his arm in an introductory manner, he pointed to the wall above our bed. Spanning the width of our king bed were three large framed pictures of Hawaii.

"You're kidding," I whispered and glared at Don.

"Didn't Daddy do a great job taking pictures?" Bridget asked.

"Yes, honey. He's great with a camera." *He's great with his fists too. Do you have pictures of that?* I thought silently.

With the excitement over, the girls raced out of the room to play and I was left standing in front of a Kodak nightmare. "How could you do something like this?" I stammered. "Of all the pictures, of all the places, why that?" I was too angry to cry. "Is this what you meant when you told me you would spend the rest of your life making up for Hawaii? You insensitive bastard!"

Don stood there, his hurt feelings quickly drowned by anger. "Talk about insensitive?" he said. "I paid a lot of money to have these blown up and framed. And for your information, I took them in Maui, before our problem."

I grabbed the pictures off the wall, slammed them on the bed and left. For the next week, I slept in the den while the angry silence grew like a tsunami between us.

My intolerance for being in the same house with Don grew daily and was especially debilitating on weekends. So I started taking the children on day trips on Saturday's and Sunday's, never inviting him to go. Surprisingly, he never quizzed me nor asked where we spent our days.

It was a perfect Spring Sunday for a picnic at the beach. At eight a.m. the temperature had uncharacteristically stayed in the seventies. The ocean was too cold to swim in but the beach offered a variety of diversions. A gentle breeze ruffled through the kitchen window as I finished putting our lunch together. Don was sitting at the kitchen table drinking a clear liquid out of a coffee cup so I kept my back to him as much as possible.

We were walking out the door when he came to life and called the girls back into the kitchen. He remained seated and put an arm around each of his daughters. "Be good to your mom," he said in a slurred, pathetic whine. "She'll always be good to you."

He walked us down to the car and handed me a piece of paper. "Victoria's new phone number," he said. "Thought you might need it."

Need it? I thought. *What for?"*

I backed the car down the drive knowing he was going to try something stupid and was sickeningly happy. For days he had been showing an uncharacteristic contentment, as if he had had a disposition transfusion. He offered little or no opinion on anything or anyone and had ceased raising his voice.

He was home by six-thirty every night and in bed by ten. But he never seemed well rested.

The children and I stayed at the beach until the sun set. They were getting cold and hungry but I ignored their pleas to leave until I felt it would be safe to return. I wanted everything to be over, the easy way, so we could begin again. Just the three of us.

It was dark when I pulled into the driveway. Don's car was gone. A chill skipped down my arms as I turned off the ignition and opened the driver's door. There was a car engine running.

"Run and get ready for bed," I told the girls. "I'll be in shortly."

When they were out of view, I grabbed a rag from my trunk, opened the playroom door and walked over to the door to the garage. Before I turned the handle, I wrapped the rag around my nose and mouth and tied it behind my head. *If you were smart, I thought, you would just call the police.*

The driver's door was open. Don was slumped over the wheel. I walked around the front of the car, slipped between the open car door and garage wall, reached in and turned off the ignition. I pushed Don back from the wheel. His face was colorless. The smell of liquor was heavy as I grabbed for his wrist to see if he still had a pulse. He did.

I dragged him out of the car and he started to rally. With his arm slung over my shoulder, he took baby steps as I half dragged him into the playroom and laid him on the floor. Leaving him there, I hit the garage door opener to air out the garage. His skin color slowly turned pink and I knew he was more drunk than asphyxiated. I covered him with a blanket and went upstairs.

The next morning, he was gone. I called his office and he answered on the first ring.

"Are you all right?" I asked.

"Why shouldn't I be?" The softness in his voice scared me more than anger would have and his voice trailed off as if he was trying to avoid being overheard.

"Just checking," I said and hung up. My head was spinning from the domestic vertigo. I went back to bed and cried, trying not to question whether my tears were because he was still alive or because I was.

CHAPTER 18

June 1980

It was the last day of school as I dragged myself out of bed and headed to the kitchen. Don had made coffee before he left so I poured myself a cup then awakened the girls with a cheery, "Hey it's the last day of school. And the best one. You'll just play and have fun today."

They sprang out of bed with energy akin to Christmas morning. They ate and dressed quickly. "See you at noon," I yelled as I dropped them off and drove home.

It was just before eleven and I was cleaning up the kitchen when Don roared through the front door waving a checkbook in the air. "Who the hell told you to transfer money into this account?"

It took me a minute before I remembered transferring some funds from our savings to checking. Not that I had purchased jewels or clothing. American Express had been calling. Over fifteen hundred dollars had been charged in Hawaii. And the payment was overdue.

He stood in the middle of the kitchen, his face red, and his eyes radiating with his *I hate you* look. "That was my mother's money," he screamed. "You spent my dead mother's money!"

"No, Don, I paid the American Express bill you ran up in Hawaii, you know, the card you depend on?"

His screams were so shrill I became a reincarnation of Lot's wife as he raced around the kitchen lobbing dishes at the cabinets. Plants were airborne. Books flew off the coffee table in the living room. I cautiously moved toward him and tried to grab his arm but he shoved me out of the way with a force that said he was unstoppable.

He dashed into the kitchen, grabbed a book of matches and returned to the living room. He lit match after match and flung them on the new carpet. In his rage he did not see that his flailing arms made each match burn out before it hit the floor.

I slowly backed out of the living room into the kitchen like I was inching my way from a coiled rattlesnake. When I felt the kitchen counter in the small of my back, I blindly fumbled for my car keys. My hand landed on the metal ring. As I picked them up he was suddenly in front of me, his eyes glaring, his jaw set in a menacing snarl. He jerked the keys out of my hand and I saw a face so riddled in anger it did not look like Don at all. This was not a drunken rage.

Don was sober.

I barreled out the back door, ran through all the neighbor's back yards to Kathleen's and pounded on her door like some crazed hippie.

She quickly tried to calm me down. "Deep breaths," was her mantra. "Let's go and get the girls from school," she said calmly. "We'll bring them back here. We can't take a chance that they could walk home."

I pulled myself together on the short drive to school and superficially joined in the gaiety of my children on the summer reprieve. Back at Kathleen's, her daughter took the children downstairs to the den juggling a plate of cookies. Kathleen listened in silence as I outlined the morning tirade, telling her everything I had concealed from the past. When I finished, I sat back in the chair and was surprised by the fear I saw in her face.

Without prelude, she reached for the phone, called Tom and briefly told him the events. "He'll be right home," she said, then added he told me not to let you go home."

I sat at the table in a stupor, treading the fine line between sanity and hysteria. "I need to get some clothes for the kids," I mumbled.

Kathleen glanced at her watch. "It's almost three o'clock. You need to wait for Tom and make sure Don has left the house before either one of you go up there."

She joined me in trembling and I reached over and put my hand on hers. "I'm sorry to cause you such pain."

Kathleen's eyes brimmed with tears. "I probably never told you this before but you are a very special person and one I count on as my best friend as well. I don't want to lose you to the same marital disease my other friend succumbed to." She wiped her nose and put her head in her hands. "It seems everyone who has lived in the damn house has met with the same domestic atrocities."

"Don't blame the house, Kathleen. I brought these problems in from out of state.

"Tom was home by five. He walked into the kitchen, kissed Kathleen's forehead and gave my shoulder a squeeze. "Don's car was gone when I passed the house," he said. "Think he went back to the office?"

I shrugged my shoulders. "Perhaps. But I need to get into the house before he comes back."

Tom stretched his arms over his head, his belly girth momentarily shrinking in size. He sat down at the table. Stroking his beard he said, "Pen, only if I go with you." He patted the revolver he wore in a holster under his arm and I remembered the story he had told us about being attacked by an escaped prisoner whom he had put behind bars years before; an attack which enforced his need to be armed. "Let me call Don's office before we go," he said and picked up the phone. "I want to make sure he's there. You and Kathleen can listen in on the extension."

He waited until Kathleen and I were in their bedroom by the phone before dialing. "Pick up, he said quickly. It's ringing."

"Well Thomas," Don said cheerily. "You are still alive. What's new in the cloak and dagger world?"

Tom laughed. "More cloaks and an abundance of daggers. Just thought I'd check in. I haven't talked to you since you came back from paradise. How's the world treating you?"

There was silence at the other end. "Not exactly like royalty," he said, "but the day isn't over yet."

"And Pen? The kids? They okay?" Tom quizzed in a nonchalant tone.

Don laughed. "About as close to the perfect family as one could have."

Tom let him ramble for a moment before he hung up. He was leaning against the wall when Kathleen and I walked into the kitchen. "Don's a sick man," he said, shaking his head wearily. "You and the kids need to get out of here before you're all killed. So let's go get your things but we'll have to hurry."

I hadn't quivered that much since Hawaii. Tom walked beside me to his car, steadying my arm with his hand. "Why don't we just walk?" I suggested.

"Not a good idea," he said, opening the car door. "If Don does come home, I want him to see my car in the drive. It will be a deterrent. He won't want to come in if I'm there."

The dog was barking when we reached the back door of the house. Don had locked Gnook, our new golden retriever, inside. Tom wrapped the handle of his gun in a handkerchief and smashed the pane of glass closest to the handle, reached inside and opened the door. I felt like I had been miscast in someone else's dream. There was a haze around me which prevented clear thinking. Or thinking at all.

We stepped into the kitchen and a jolt of apprehension sprinted down my spine. The house looked like a hurricane-ravaged beach. The refrigerator door was ajar, the contents littered the floor. Magazines were shredded all over the living room rug; shade less lamps lay smashed in the foyer. Candles on the mantle had been snapped in half and the handle of a kitchen knife peered out of the arm of the couch.

"Oh my God," Tom said anxiously as he followed me back to the bedrooms. "The man has snapped. Are you sure he wasn't drinking?"

"Positive," I said and reached for the handle of our bedroom door. I pushed it open and screamed. Many of my clothes had been cut, ripped, shredded and eerily draped on lamp tops, the dresser and the closet door. He had carried my typewriter up from the den. It laid in pieces on the floor.

Standing by Don's dresser, Tom gripped my shoulder. Typewriter keys had been lined up in a message: *You are Dead.* "Let's hurry and get out of here," he said.

"I need my purse," I said as I frantically clawed through the ruins.

"You don't have time," he said sternly. "Forget it."

"Car keys, Tom. My wallet."

We combed through the debris in each room without success. "Get a suitcase. Grab some clothes for the kids. I'll keep looking for your other things."

Suddenly we heard a car door slam. Tom raced to the window and turned around, relieved. "Just your neighbor," he said breathing hard. He wiped his brow with his hand. "Have everything you need?"

I nodded, followed him through the kitchen, stopped to give Gnook water and food and then pulled the door shut behind me. By the time we got to Tom's car, I was so overcome with nausea I vomited in the brambly bushes by the drive.

"Can I use your phone?" I asked Kathleen as we walked through the door.

"Yes, of course. Use the one in our bedroom so you'll have some privacy."

It was time. I needed to call home. I couldn't stay in Massachusetts.

"Mom?" I broke down when I heard her voice.

"Penne?" Mom's voice was etched in alarm. "What's wrong?"

I offered a few rambling details ending with, "Tom thinks Don is having a nervous breakdown. We have to get out of here."

"Your brother is just finishing a job on Cape Cod. He is scheduled to leave tomorrow morning for home. Give me Kathleen's number and let me try and reach him. You can drive down together."

"What would I do without you?" I said.

She sighed with discomfort. "I shudder to think. Love to the children."

I walked back to the kitchen. Tom stood and spread his arms. "I think you need a hug," he said. There was such comfort being in his ample arms. With his left hand on my shoulder, we walked into the living room and sat down on the couch. Kathleen followed and sat down in an arm chair across from the couch.

"Pen," Tom said, "You know I deal with violent people every day. And one thing I've learned is that despite today's episode, you have to recognize the situation for what it is before you can begin to come to terms with your life." He paused and then said, "So, say it."

My mouth became a twisted line. "Say what?"

"Acknowledge the fact that you are a battered, abused wife."

It was not something I wanted to verbalize. Think about. Battered wife? Of course I was but I had always aligned such words with people living in impoverished surroundings, unemployed and hungry. Me? "Maybe in the past," I told Tom. "But this is different. Don's sick."

Tom shook his head in disapproval. "You need to be honest with yourself and discard the guilt, the shame. This situation isn't much different than others you have described today. You tried to make this work and you have not done anything wrong."

His voice deepened on the words: *Have not done anything wrong.* "With one exception. You have continued to stay with him. Only when you finally acknowledge the truth of the situation will you be able to begin the road to recovery as well."

I made no effort to camouflage my anxiety. Classified under nervous breakdown, Don's behavior today seemed less humiliating than in the past, perhaps because it was more socially acceptable. I didn't feel like a battered wife that day. I felt like the wife of a man who had lost his mind and was plying myself with those thoughts when the phone rang.

Tom quickly grabbed it. "It's your brother, Pen."

Art was difficult to talk to. He was not a conversationalist and had an economy with words that precluded me from knowing exactly what he thought. "I'll be there at five a.m. or so tomorrow. Just stay where you are."

"Thanks," I said.

"And Pen?"

"Yes?"

"Be honest with the kids. They probably know more than they are acknowledging."

I hung up slowly. "I need to talk to the girls," I told Kathleen. "Alone."

Minutes later I was settled on the living room couch. "Uncle Art is picking us up in the morning," I told the children. "Daddy is sick and needs help." I hugged them and made that maternal cure-all promise that everything would be okay.

Suddenly Stephie pulled away. Her cheeks flushed. "Why did you lie to us?" she snapped. "You weren't hit by a ball on your trip, were you? It was Dad, wasn't it?" She jumped off the couch and ran downstairs to the playroom.

I groped for words. Looking at their faces, I knew I had never kept them from harm and pain as I had intended.

I had only delayed it.

CHAPTER 19

June 1980
Easton, Pennsylvania

a much too fragrant lilac bath oil glistened pink in the morning light. I laid back in the pungent, foamy bath, watching birds fly in and out of the Pennsylvania pines and tried to relax.

The trip from Massachusetts in Art's Volkswagen was anything but comfortable. The children were tired and whiney and I couldn't seem to discard the feeling that I had abandoned Don when he needed me the most but steeled myself against the rising tide of sympathy.

After fifteen minutes in the tub, I got out, dressed quickly and walked downstairs to the front porch. I heard the children squeal as they played hide and seek with Uncle Art while butterflies fluttered in and out of Mom's flowerbeds. The valley was luxuriant and green and a stream bubbled down the far side of the property coming to rest in the pond. I watched unnoticed as Art, a self-proclaimed but well educated naturalist in his late twenties, busied himself as the children's guide, filling their hungry young minds with new discoveries. It was a rare treat for Stephie and Bridget to have such honest attention from a man and as I stood on the porch I wondered if they ever thought the same.

Tall and lean, Art's face was shadowed by a well groomed beard. He had become their heartbeat, their reason to jump out of bed that morning, a walking *Field and Stream*. I could hear bits and pieces of information float through the air as they walked.

Without telling them a mama raccoon had given birth to several babies the night before, Art tapped their curiosity. "Come here," he said, beckoning each with his index finger. "I have a surprise for you." Following like dwarfs, he took them up a path into the woods. To get a better view, I left the front porch, walked through the house to the side porch and stood at the edge as they rounded the corner. "Be real quiet," Art said.

They tip toed up the path and approached a tree; the children's version of tip-toe much too exaggerated for any quiet approach. "What's up?" Stephie asked. "Something die?"

Art laughed softly. "No. Something was born last night while you slept. New babies. "They were about four feet away from the tree when Art pointed to a small cage, the door open.

"Look in there and tell me what you see," he directed in hushed tones.

From my vantage point, I watched their faces as they spotted the baby raccoons and reveled in their excitement.

Lunch was served on the picnic table just under a large willow tree. "You have a neat world out there, Uncle Art," Stephie said.

Art laughed. "It's not just mine. It's yours too."

"And mine?" Bridget asked as the jelly from her sandwich oozed down her chin.

"Of course," he said and gently wiped her chin.

A great world, I thought, popping the last bit of sandwich into my mouth. But where we came from, the world was not so great at all. I stared at my brother thankful he had finished his stint with the Coast Guard and was home for now. His gentleness was a gift. His love was unconditional. He was a peacemaker of infinite abilities.

I spent the first two weeks trying to unwind. One night after the children were in bed, I sat out on the screened porch. Crickets, lightening bugs and a host of unknown critters provided an underlying symphony for the process of healing.

"Pen?" Art whispered through the screen. "I have a surprise for you!"

"What kind of a surprise?"

He laughed. "Turn around. You have a visitor."

My sister Bug (nicknamed in childhood) stepped out onto the porch. I hadn't seen her in so long. She was five years younger than my twin and I, in great shape and had earned her master's degree in nursing.

"Bug!" I hollered. Jumping up from the chair we hugged each other like we had never hugged before.

"Wow, Pen," she said. "Mom just filled me in. You have got to get rid of that bastard."

"I'm trying to work this out, Sis."

She sat down and stared at me. As blunt as Dad, she was never one to keep any opinion to herself, but her intentions were good. "Work it out in court," she snapped. "You've tried. He's a monster. I've always detested that bastard. It's time to go after him, kick him out of your life before he kills you."

"You're right, Bug. Just give me time."

"Look, I can't stay, but I had to see you and let you know I'll always stand behind you."

"Can't you spend the night?" I asked.

She stood up. "No, have to be at work early in the morning. But I didn't want to miss seeing you. She laughed. "You know I wouldn't miss an opportunity to throw in my two cents."

Art, she and I joined in a circular hug. "Take care of you," she said and left as quickly as she had entered.

When she was gone, Art pulled up a lounge chair so we were facing each other.

"So which way is your mind tumbling?" he said.

I shrugged my shoulders. "In a vacuum of indecision. I'm getting older by the minute."

He laughed. "You're not old. Troubled minds just make us feel older." There was a momentary silence. "So what will you do?"

"I don't know yet. I can't decide if Don and I are conjoined by habit or love at this point. There's a tragic gap between the good man with admirable intentions and the man who is so possessed by anger he doesn't know what to do with it."

Art folded his hands like a choir boy. "He needs help. That's obvious."

"Yes, he does. I think if his mental health could be restored we might have a shot at normalcy. But. . ."

I hushed when Mother walked out and pulled up a chair. "Are you still thinking like Cinderella?" she asked. "Haven't you had enough?"

The crickets grew louder. "Forgiveness, Mom. Didn't you raise us all to forgive?"

Her eyes focused above my head. "Yes, but there are limits."

I sighed. "Not in the bible there aren't."

She shrugged her shoulders. The wrinkles in her forehead squeezed together like creased paper. "For me, there are. And there should be for you. All your father and I want to see is for you and the children to live peacefully, without fear." She stood and stretched. "We want that for ourselves as well." She hung her head and walked away. "Don't stay up too late," she said before closing the door.

"Poor Mom," Art said. "She worries about all of us. But you are on the top of her list for now. You really need to think this thing through, Pen. Not only can you not continue to live like this, you can't expect Mom, Dad or the children to exist like this either."

"I know. But this time is different. This was not like the abuse in the past. Don is sick."

Art removed his glasses and pinched his nose in thought. "Don has always been sick." He put his glasses back on and stood. "Get some rest. You won't solve anything without sleep."

July 1980

"Penne?" Mom called from the kitchen. "Kathleen is on the phone." I sprinted to the kitchen.

"How are you holding up?" Kathleen asked.

"Fine. I just want to solve this thing and go on. How are Tom and the kids?"

"Tom's fine," Tom said picking up the extension. "I just stopped by to see Don."

"Oh?" A pinch of jealousy flicked in my head. "I haven't heard from him. What is he doing?"

"Well, the house is cleaned up and he's going to work. He doesn't bring up the fact that you are gone. Let's face it. He's basically a nice man who is screwed up." Tom cleared his throat. "Hope you don't think I'm cavorting with the enemy, Pen. But everyone needs support and love if they are going to survive."

"Then I'm thankful you are around."

"I'm thankful he is too," Kathleen quipped. "If it was up to me, I'd never look at Don again." She paused then added, "And Pen? This may or may not be the time to tell you but Patricia Bernard is in the hospital."

An image of my bird-like neighbor flashed in my mind. "Oh? Is it serious?" Patricia had always been so frail.

There was silence on the other end of the line. "Yes," Kathleen said. "She slit her wrists."

A shiver took off through my body like a fast acting poison. "What? I don't understand. She never appeared to be the self-destructive type. She adores her children. How could she do that?"

Kathleen didn't try to hide her contempt. "I've known her for many years, Pen. She always kept her bad feelings about that arrogant bastard of a husband locked up in her head until she was on over load. She's made excuses for him since they were married. Her father treated her the same way. Her bruises weren't visible but they were there. A mental hemorrhage."

"No wonder she rarely invited me to her house," I said.

"Did you ever invite her to yours?" she asked.

"Yes, but she always had something else to do."

Could I have helped her? I wondered. And I realized, no. No, I couldn't have helped her when I was denying the same thing was happening to me.

Several days after that conversation, I was sitting in my parent's living room when the phone rang. Everyone else was asleep so I snapped the receiver off the hook before it could ring again.

"Hi," Don said. "Since when do you answer their phone?"

His voice startled me. It was the first time I had talked to him since we left. "When they're asleep." My head began to pound. "How are you?"

"It's hot down here," he said, his voice wooden. "Even Gnook can't stand it. I try and get home early every day to make sure he has water."

"That's good." I didn't recognize this person. Why talk about a dog when our lives were in chaos?

"So when can I expect you to come back?" He was so unemotional it was as if he was updating a page in his Day-Timer.

My timidity momentarily disappeared, replaced by conviction. "That, Don, is up to you. You need help. We won't come back, can't come back, until you are under the care of a doctor and only if you want us to be a violence-free family."

"You're such a drama queen," he said. There was a rustle of papers at the other end and then a click.

August 1980

A summer thunderstorm hit the valley Thursday afternoon. It was as if God had saved rain from all over the world to be dumped in one day on Pennsylvania.

Art stomped his feet on the front porch and I raced to open the door. He was clutching the mail under his slicker. He removed his rain gear and we walked into the kitchen. "Here's something for you," he said, and thrust an envelope into my hand.

There was no return address but the handwriting was Don's. I ripped it open and my driver's license fell to the floor. There was no note, just copies of some bills. "Oh my God," I said.

"What's wrong?" asked Art.

I smiled. "Maybe something is right for a change," I said handing him the billings. "It appears that Don is seeing a doctor."

As we scanned the papers, Mom walked into the kitchen. "What are you reading?"

Art handed her the paperwork. "Don sent these to Pen. Apparently he's seeing a doctor."

I stared at her face as she scrutinized each line. "Hope it's true," she said with little change of heart. "You need to verify this before taking it to heart. Don is devious and clever when it suits his purpose."

It was the first time she had ever complimented him in any fashion. *Clever*, I thought. At least she gave him that much. "I'll check it out," I said and vanished to what had become my thinking porch to watch the rain and think.

Art was quick to follow. He moved a chair away from the screened side of the porch and popped it in front of me like he was about to fit me for shoes. "Well?" he said.

"Well what?"

"Do you believe him?"

I closed my eyes. "I want to, but I know Mom doesn't. I knew it would be difficult for her to ever accept the fact that he was sick as opposed to evil or that she would believe anything but her own opinions."

"Dad will be back from his trip tomorrow. Why not discuss it with him?"

I shoved the papers away in my jeans pocket. "Art, he and I have butted heads so many times over Don. He has never approved of any of my ways of handling it. And, he knew I was lying about Hawaii. He has reason not to trust me. And I have reason not to like him, father or no father. He is self-aggrandizing. Always has to be right, even when he isn't." *Should I confess that I am also afraid of my own father?* I thought.

Art stood up and patted my shoulder. "I think you should begin to depend on yourself, sis."

An hour later I was on the phone with Kathleen and Tom.

"I've never heard of that doctor before," she said. "But I'll do some checking. Could you spell the doctor's name and give me the address?"

"You don't believe this, do you? " I asked.

Kathleen sighed into the phone. "I want to believe, for both your sakes." She sounded almost apologetic. "But I don't want you to base your future on Xeroxed promises. Okay?"

"You're right. By the way, how is Patricia?"

"Recovering. Slowly. She made her husband her life. And he ruled her for years. The pressure whittled her down to nothing, to a shell that was afraid of everything around her. Especially herself. It will take time." She paused then added, "She also asked about you."

I was surprised. "And what did you tell her?"

She cleared her throat. "That you were recovering slowly as well."

Several days passed before I heard from her. But it was good news. Tom confirmed Don was seeing a psychologist. But I already knew he was. Our phone conversations the past few days had become warm and animated. He talked to the girls every other day and without them knowing, I listened in on their conversations and was amazed at Don's sudden ability to listen to what his children had to say.

After dinner the night my father returned, Art made good a promise to take the kids on a nature walk.

"Watch them closely," Mom said. "And don't be gone long."

Dad, Mom and I remained at the table and I suddenly realized this time had been orchestrated.

"Okay," my father began. "I understand Don is getting help, which is good, and I think it's time for you two to meet face to face." He looked over at Mom who was frowning.

He leaned back in his chair. "Now although your mother may not agree, I think you and Don should meet on neutral ground. It is not a good idea to return home just yet but I do think there is plenty to be gained by talking in person."

"You're right," Mom interrupted. "I don't agree. Seeing each other is not going to resolve the past or improve the future. Don still refuses to admit he has done anything wrong and without remorse, there can be no honest reconciliation. We've been through this before."

Dad listened patiently and waited until she finished speaking. "There is more to my suggestion than I have shared with you Mildred."

He turned to me and put his hand over mine. "Little daughter? What do you think is the main thing Don wanted in you as a wife?"

It was not a question that allowed any spontaneity in answer so I remained silent for a few minutes. "The usual, I suppose." I shrugged my shoulders. "Love, companionship, family."

Dad sat back and digested my words. "Do you think Don would have married you if you were not such a pretty woman?"

Mom folded her arms stiffly in front of her. "It's a little late for that."

"It's never too late for honesty," Dad responded.

It wasn't so much the question that made me quake, but the answer. "You know, Dad, I hate to admit it, but no, I don't think Don would have given me two seconds. He flirts a lot at social functions, but only with pretty women."

Dad cleared his throat. "With that said, I want you to try something." He pushed his chair back from the table and paced while he spoke. "I want you to arrange to meet Don in the next week or so in some public place, somewhere close to this house. When that is arranged. . ."he paused, walked over, placed his hands on the table and leaned toward me. "I want you to meet him as you look right now."

Embarrassed, I ran my fingers through my uncombed hair. It had been weeks since I introduced even a curl to my limp strands which fell around my face in an unkempt defiance. I hadn't bothered to open my makeup case and my pale skin looked chalky. Black circles lay under my eyes like I was some football player all charcoaled up for a game. "But I look awful," I said. "You can't expect me to go out in public looking like this."

He sat down. "It's time for you to focus on who you are, and what you are beneath the washable veneer of paint. If you only see what is in the mirror, or put more emphasis on what is on the outside than what is in your soul, your heart, I do not believe you have a chance to reconcile. You have used your looks as if you created the image, when in fact; your beauty was a gift from God. This is why your mother and I always objected to the beauty pageants in high school and college. You took credit for something you did not create. It is time to redirect your thinking. Looks will not cement any marriage."

It was time to just say what was on my mind. "Dad, I sit here looking at you with your perfectly groomed beard, tended to by a Swedish barber, the blessing of perfect white teeth, your tall, firm body dressed in a Brooks Brothers suit, and quite frankly, am a bit confused. Your good looks and superior mind have served you well in your career. And yes, you do occasionally try to appear humble in bib jeans and a flannel shirt, but you are, and have always been, totally cognizant of your appearance as well."

He stared at me, patted my head and left the table.

I walked down the stairs on Saturday morning dressed as Dad suggested. My face was scrubbed and

plain. I wore jeans and a clean blouse but no jewelry—
including my wedding band. I felt awkward, timid, as if
I was walking out into the world naked. But I had lived
my life relying on beauty of face and of the rewards it
brought—Miss Marine Corps in college—Miss this and
Miss that, when in fact, it was now unimportant to be
Miss anything except misunderstood.

"Here" Dad said, handing me some money. "Tuck
this in your sock, just in case." He hugged me tightly.
"Drive safely and show Don consideration without
compromising your own feelings. And know that God
is with you."

I reached the Holiday Inn in record time and found
Don sitting slouched on a bar stool, smoking in a
suitably grim cocktail lounge, dressed in jeans and a
Polo shirt. I walked up to behind him and took a seat on
the next stool. We didn't hug nor touch.

He looked at me and scowled. "What the hell
happened to you, Pen? You sick or something?"

I feigned confusion. "Sick? What makes you think
I'm sick?"

Don turned his back to me for a moment, picked up
his beer glass and drained the contents. Then he slowly
turned on the stool and faced me. "You don't look like
my wife." He raised his hand slightly and motioned to
the bartender. "The same," he said. "You want
something, Pen?"

"A Coke will do just fine. Thanks."

Don raised his eyebrows. "A Coke and no makeup?
You become ordained?"

I looked down at myself for a moment then met his
stare. "I'm just in a plain brown wrapper mood." My
stomach made an audible growl and I used the sound to
change the subject. "You hungry?" I asked him.

He looked at his watch as if I was keeping him from
some appointment. "Sure. I have time for a bite." He

looked beyond me to the back of the room. "But let's go and sit over in a booth. I'll order sandwiches here. Hamburger okay with you?"

"Fine," I said.

He picked up our drinks and I followed him, more embarrassed than he was, looking the way I did. He wasted no time once we were seated.

"You said you wanted to talk," he said. He lit a cigarette and offered me one but I declined. "OH brother," he said, and shook his head disparagingly. "Do you have a bad case of bible-perfect or what?"

I leaned across the table. "Can we really talk now?"

He laughed. "Has the last thirty minutes been on tape?"

I sat back in my seat, silently reminding myself not to be defeated by his bull moose attitude. "I only want to know one thing. Do you want us to make it as a couple? A family?"

He ran his finger around the top of this glass. "Stupid question, Pen." He stared at my face with an uncompromising gaze. "You really don't look good at all. Did mommy and daddy confiscate your makeup or is that look one of choice?"

I took a deep breath. "No. I just wanted you to see the real me. As for my question, it is not stupid and I expect an answer."

He looked down at the table. "You know the answer. Of course I want us to make it. Do you think I would have wasted several hours driving down here if I didn't?" His guileless face registered every emotion aroused by the awkward reunion. "Because I love you and my children and I don't want to live without you."

We lingered over each bite of food as if once it was consumed; we would have no reason to continue talking. But we had only scratched the surface. He didn't apologize but promised new beginnings. Somehow, I wanted to believe him.

"Are you staying here tonight?" I asked when he walked me to the car.

"Can't," he answered. "I don't want to be alone."

"Won't you be alone at home?"

His eyes watered and he walked to his car without answering.

Art had accepted a job in Alaska but waited until two days before leaving to tell me. At the airport, I wrapped my arms around him not wanting to let go of this sensitive brother who had guided me so nonjudgmentally during the past weeks.

"Thanks for everything," I said as tears trickled down my cheeks. "We're sure going to miss you. Especially the kids. You've helped them through a very difficult time."

He awkwardly returned the hug. "You're going back to him, aren't you?"

I pulled back from him and nodded. "Yes, but this time I'm going to have it my way."

He tossed his backpack on the baggage scale. Then as we walked through the gate, he stopped me. "Pen, you remind me of a salmon. You are constantly fighting to swim upstream." He paused, adjusted his pack then added, "I don't want to discourage you from making things work but I don't want you to end up like the salmon either."

"How so?"

He lowered his head. "After fighting their way upstream, they finally reach their destination, only to die."

I fought back tears. "I'll be careful, Art. I promise."

We sat in the waiting area and he pulled an envelope out of his pocket. "Here," he said. "Take care of yourself and the girls. And don't ever give up on your dreams. You write well but you must write often. You'll hit it someday. I have faith in you."

"And I in you," I said, knowing how well he paints and how many he had sold. He would be a successful artist in time. "Are you still going to stay with Luke?"

Luke was our youngest brother with a spirit of adventure who was in school in Sitka.

Art laughed. "Yes, and looking forward to it. Haven't seen him in a long time."

"And I haven't seen him since he pointed that rifle at Don!"

"Glad Dad stopped him," Art laughed. "Or I'd have to visit him in jail." We were still laughing when he stood up. "Time to go," he said. We hugged and I watched him walk out to the tarmac up the ramp to the plane. He stopped at the top, turned, waved and blew a kiss. I clutched the envelope in my hand and waited until I got to the airport parking lot before opening it.

Dearest Pen: I want you to follow your heart and do what only you think is best. You have a lot going for you raising two little girls. But I trust you won't continue to jeopardize your freedom for anyone. Here are the keys and title—signed off-- to my Volkswagen. It's no prize, but it's yours. The engine is new and it has four new tires. No one knows I named her, but I call her the 'Eagle' because she is free and clear. That's what I wish for you. All my love, Art.

CHAPTER 20

September 1980
Auburn, Massachusetts

*D*on turned off the television, pulled me toward him and kissed my head with the grace of an Elizabethan Knight. "God I missed you," he whispered. "Life without you wasn't any life at all."

I snuggled closer and stroked his hand. It felt limp, cold. But it was, like all of him now, a pliable being. "Let's really make this work," I said.

"It's me who has to try," he said, "not you. I know how lucky I am to have you all back."

That you are, I thought, *that you are.* He had erased the past few months with only one reference. "We know what happened," he had said this morning. "But I don't ever want to talk about it again."

The comment left me feeling vacuous but curled up in his arms, I was not willing to risk what we were becoming for what we had had.

December 1980

I don't really know why but I have always felt awkward when someone gives me a gift. I suppose I was afraid I would not display the reaction the giver expected, or, worse, my true feelings would betray me.

So when Don pulled out a small box one night, I just sat there, not really knowing what to do.

"It doesn't bite, Pen," he said. "And you don't have to feed it." The little boy twinkle had returned to his eyes and his mouth curved in nervous expectation.

I removed the paper and pulled out a silver heart. Holding it up, I let it dangle from the ornament hook. "This is beautiful. When we pack up the Christmas decorations, this will have to go in a box marked 'Gold, Frankincense, Myrrh and Us."

He turned the heart around to the inscription. *To The Christmas in my life. I love you, Don.* "I knew you'd cry," he said, dabbing my tears.

"And if I hadn't?"

"I would have taken it back and bought the lump of coal," he laughed. "It was half-price."

February 1981

The ever present edge of cautiousness hovered between us as we pushed forward in the New Year with a unified effort to continue in peace. The children felt the contagion of security and had begun to relax in the positive environment. I had been offered a part time job as an editor for a small ecumenical paper and threw myself into the responsibilities with wild abandon, comforted by the absence of guilt.

"I tried calling you all afternoon," Don quizzed at dinner. "Where were you?"

"Working," I answered.

He looked up and smiled. "It's becoming a bit more than part time, isn't it?"

"Sure. Why? Does that bother you?"

"Of course not," he smiled.

Work had become a joy, but not just because of the editorship. A new minister had been appointed as my boss. A bachelor, Dr. David Kingsley was rumored to be the best catch in New England. And it was no wonder. Brilliant, witty and well educated, David's personality was unique and yielded the fruit of a learned man. Educated at Harvard, he was a man who had lived through so many of the difficulties he spoke about each Sunday. He never pretended to be that extraordinary giant of piety which seemed to trap most members of the clergy and was so good looking, most of us on the newspapers staff found it a bit difficult to concentrate on editing when he was present.

David was extremely supportive of my family responsibilities. My self-esteem was on the rise and for the first time in many years, I was closer to finding the peace and contentment I had craved for so long.

July 1981

Early one morning, I received a call from the editor of the town paper. "Really enjoyed your material in the Gazette," he said. "And I'd like to see more of your work. I need a columnist and if your prose is as creative as your poetry, maybe we can work something out.

"What?" I said, sounding like some star struck kid. "Are you serious?"

He laughed. "How about this. When time permits, write two light-hearted sample columns about anything that is Art Buckwalish. Stay away from anything sensitive like the Pope or the Kennedy's. Interested?"

I could hardly speak. "Sure. I'll have them for you in about two days if that's okay."

We agreed on a delivery date and time. I hung up happier than I had ever been in my life. In twenty-four hours I quietly produced three columns based on regional and national events. They were sarcastic, cynical and I was ready for my Monday meeting.

Seated in a dingy little office located near an out-of-business fruit stand, I stared at the editor, Adam Strong, who was a squirrelly little man with the personality of baking soda. I sat across from him as he slouched at his desk and watched his eyebrows move up and down like a puppet. "We'll run the first one this week," he said. "I had a strong hunch you could do this. You have a lilting way with words."

On Thursday afternoon the paper was jammed in mailboxes. And by evening the phone started to ring; not a volume AT&T would consider profitable but sufficient to infuse my ego. "Great stuff," Rachel, Don's secretary said. "I didn't know you could write. And write so well!"

By the time I got off the phone, the doorbell rang and my head felt like a large balloon over a used car dealership.

Kathleen was at the door. Laughing, she held the paper up in a cheer. "Bravo! This is ingenious," she said. 'Someday My Prince Will Come. . .' Great title! Why didn't you tell me you were going to do this?"

"And risk exposing failure if I didn't make it?"

She was reading aloud in the foyer when Don pulled up the drive. I heard my words. I had compared my wedding to Lady Di's. . .and thought about what Kathleen had said, *Write like you talk.* I had done just that, ending the piece by saying the only chance I would ever have to sing 'Someday my prince will come,' would be standing in front of a Fotomat chanting, 'Someday my prints will come. . .'

"I can't wait to see Don's face when he reads this!" she said. Suddenly my stomach contracted into a knot. The words sounded so funny when I wrote it. Read aloud, they now sounded vindictive. No, Don wouldn't like this. He wouldn't like it at all.

"Another time, Kathleen, okay?"

She stared at me. "You don't think he'll get angry over this, do you?"

"I'll let you know."

She patted my arm. "No matter what he says, this is great. Okay?" I watched her walk down the front walk and was relieved she only waved to Don.

November 1981

Early Christmas shopping at a department store in downtown Boston was not something I wanted to do but Don had insisted. After waiting almost twenty minutes in line, a cashier rang up our purchases while Don practiced his *I'm-an-important-businessman-who-is-tired-of-waiting-inline-sighs* behind me. I handed her a check. And waited. And waited. She was taking an inordinately long time scanning the information.

Don poked his finger into my back, his signal for me to do something about the cashier.

"Is there a problem?" I asked.

She looked away from her register. "On, no not at all," she said smiling. "It's just that your name looks familiar. Aren't you that new newspaper columnist?"

From housewife to columnist was difficult for me to assimilate. It did not matter that my thimble of fame only appeared in a few local papers, or that most subscribers used the pages to wrap their garbage. "Yes," I said. "I am."

I looked up at Don expecting to see a proud smile on his face. There was nothing. Not even a smirk. We walked to the car in silence, an uncomfortable hush with no basis. Why wasn't he excited? Why wasn't he proud? Was he still angry about my first column?

He unlocked the passenger door. "Sure your head will fit in the car?" he snapped.

I turned and faced him. "And just what is that supposed to mean?"

"Simple. Your ego is light years ahead of your talent. Just because some minimum wage clerk treats you like you were Erma Bombeck doesn't call for that tidal wave of pride I just saw sweep over you. Five or ten bucks a column isn't exactly income. It's more like lunch money."

I stared out the window on the drive home so he couldn't see my anger, tears, and watched the miles of familiar landmark flit by, thinking only of the distance which continued to separate us and suddenly feared the distance yet to come.

December 1981

"Isn't this place beautiful in the winter?" I said as we drove over the bridge into Cambridge.

"Not as beautiful as you are," he said. "And I like the new hairdo. Just like Victoria's."

I patted my hair and smiled. "I sure miss that kid. Has she ever said anything more about moving back east?"

"No, but keep that thought," he said and pulled the car into the restaurant parking lot. He handed the valet the keys then walked around to help me out of the car.

"By the way," he whispered. "Where did the silver fox coat come from? Has your column been syndicated?"

"No, but my friendship with Kathleen's sister has. The coat is hers."

Another corporate dinner, I thought, but in truth I did love most of them. This one was promotional, according to Don, a bit of a midweek pep rally for management. "Are you sure my hair looks okay?" I said as we walked in.

He stopped and smiled. "Are you kidding? It may be short, but just keep it blond and I'll always love it, no matter how short, no matter how long." He pulled me to his side. "No one could ask for a better looking wife."

I envisioned Dad's no-makeup experiment then let it go. We walked with measured steps toward the maître d'. "Good evening sir," he said.

"The Arigone party," Don replied.

We followed him to the table where about twelve people from his office sat drinking cocktails and laughing. After Don and I had been served our drinks, Gene Arigone stood up and proposed the first toast.

"I've asked you all to dinner tonight so you can share in Don's latest success."

I looked at Don. He caught my stare and winked. *Gene made such an impressive Vice President,* I thought as he raised his glass.

"Please join me," Gene said, his rich baritone voice floated down the table. "A toast to the new Regional Sales Manager of Los Angeles. Don could you stand?"

As Don got to his feet, glasses were raised in a spontaneous toast. Then thunderous applause. I fought to keep the corners of my mouth from trembling as I struggled to hide my shock. Throughout dinner I managed to engage in casual conversation, thankful only for the fact that I was seated furthest away from Angelina. But my composure crumbled on the drive home.

"I take it those aren't tears of joy," Don said as he turned onto the expressway.

"Here I am. Your Drag Queen again. Why didn't you tell me? I'm happy for your success, but everything we've ever wanted is here. We have friends, family.

Why move now? I've worked so hard to achieve the harmony we have." Then I thought, *and I've finally made a name for myself.*

"Drag Queen?" he laughed. "As usual, Penelope, you don't understand slang phrases. I'm sorry this upset you," he said with a touch of bitterness in his voice. "I thought you'd be jumping up and down for a chance to move to the Golden State and be near Victoria." He paused then added, "Women. I'll never understand you."

"To begin with, I used the term 'Drag Queen' because you feel you can just drag me anywhere as long as I look like a queen. And I abhor the fact that you never even have any consideration for me. Husbands and wives are supposed to discuss life changes first. But not you. You just make the decisions and I hear about it from strangers. It isn't just your life involved here. It's four lives."

He let out a long, deep sigh. "I know you hate change Pen, but we can give our kids a lot more in California. Living in different places will help them grow up well rounded." He glanced at me before continuing. "Look at what happened to you. You moved two times in all the years you were growing up and it has made you afraid of change. You can't see the opportunity because you are blinded by fear."

"I'm not blinded by fear, Don. I crave stability. Promotion or no promotion, it was not right to keep such a big thing from me."

He reached over and patted my leg. "Because I knew how you'd react. But this is a chance of a lifetime, to live well, be free of snow and ice and have a home with a pool. Doesn't any of that appeal to you at all?"

Mile after mile and I couldn't begin to feel any happiness for his success because it required me to give up everything I had struggled to achieve. But there was something much more important to address. "I won't move any place else with you until you promise me there will be no more abuse. I refuse to drag the same problems three thousand miles away. Only if you agree to that will I even consider moving."

He was speechless and slammed the accelerator to the floor.

December 1981

"You should see my view," Don purred into the phone. "All of Los Angeles. The City of Angels."

"And you should see mine," I said. "Snow covered hills, green pine trees and a roaring fire in the fireplace."

He ignored my narrative. "Only one thing is missing here. I'm staring at a large oak credenza, and more specifically, at my family, sitting in a frame instead of here. I don't have you to come to at night or the sounds of the children."

"They are both coughing," I told him. "So much for sounds. Besides, this won't last forever. At least you have a roof over your head that isn't costing anything."

"I'm living in my dead mother's house." His voice was cold. "And it cost me plenty."

I stood my ground. "You have Victoria, Don."

He groaned. "Yes and she's almost twenty years younger than I am. I have to put up with loud music at crazy hours, her countless friends who parade through this house—all of which are members of some born again church group which you know I can't handle."

"She worships you, Don. That should spark your ego."

He grumbled and cleared his throat. "Worships me? She called me a chauvinist the other night because I asked her to clean up the kitchen."

"If it was your mess, she was probably right." We hung up without goodbyes.

The day before Don's plane touched down in Boston, the girls and I scurried about creating Christmas. I had decided not to depend on him this year to pick out the tree, or be the annual Saint Know It All of tree trimming.

This year the children and I had done it all, from chopping down the tree in a snowstorm to lugging it home. Of course it fell off the roof of the car twice on the way home but no one complained, we had the freedom to laugh, retied the tree then rolled down the car windows so we could each hold onto a branch while the snow blew through the windows and left us all looking like weakened versions of Frosty the Snowman.

We'd spent the last few hours trying to get it to look straight when it had grown for years in a defiant bow we never noticed until it was inside. "What would Dad do?" I asked the girls as I stepped back from the tree.

"Swear," Bridget said. "A lot. But wait 'til he sees this. "Won't he be proud of us Mom?"

Stephie placed her hands on her hips like she was suddenly an adult and cocked her head like the decorator of the National Christmas Tree. "Boy we're good, huh Mom? And to think we did it all by ourselves!"

My face was glowing. We had accomplished what Don had always done and with better results. And the best part? I had paid for all of it with money I earned writing and editing. The self-satisfaction lubricated my parched self-esteem. I sat back on the couch and mentally hummed along with the stereo. . 'Let there be peace on earth and let it begin with me. . .'

"Wait outside, Daddy," Bridget told Don after picking him up at the airport. He stood on the sidewalk leading to our front door rubbing his hands together.

"Hurry up, pumpkin, make it fast. It's cold out here."

The girls scampered inside to turn on Christmas lights and music.

"Hope this doesn't take long," Don yelled from outside. "It's three days before Christmas. We don't have any time to waste." I glanced out the front window and watched him as he irritably tapped his foot on the walk. My insides tingled as I thought, We have plenty of time. This year, the season has been cheerfully provided by your family.

"We're ready," they yelled in unison from the front door. 'I'm Dreaming of a White Christmas' filled the air, well, it was so loud it filled the neighborhood as Don walked into the house, climbed the stairs to the living room and stopped on the landing.

"Surprise!" the girls yelled in unison. They spread their arms as if they were presenting the next act at a circus. The tree stood floor to ceiling—over six feet—and the glitter of little white lights danced off the branches. Petite red velvet bows were tied on many of the branches. All ornaments we had used in the past were carefully placed. Fresh pine garland curled endlessly around the banister. Thick folds of garland hung in scallops from the mantel. Red tapered candles stood in waxed symmetry amid the greens. Inside the arched doorway leading from the living room into the kitchen, another rope of pine garland carefully followed the arch. Small white lights were woven throughout the lights and seemed to twinkle in time to the music.

"Well Dad?" Stephie coaxed. "You like it?"

"It's just magnificent, pumpkin. But what happened to the colored lights Daddy always used?"

"Outside," Bridget answered. "We put them around all the bushes. It looks like Disneyland at night. You'll see when it gets dark."

He gathered his children in his arms. "Great job," he said. "And just think, you will get to live near Disneyland in just a little while!" He picked up his suitcase and a shopping bag from Saks and walked down the hall. "Daddy's going to take a short nap, okay?"

Stephie and Bridget stood silent; their lips collectively curled in disappointment but said nothing.

After a pleasant, friendly dinner, we all sat on the couch to stare at the tree.

"Its beautiful guys," Don said. "The tree is full and straight. Did you do it by yourselves?"

Stephie laughed. "We sure did. Lots of work we saved you, right Daddy?"

"Sure did, sweetheart," he said and hugged them both. "It's time for you guys to go to bed. I'll come and tuck you in when you're ready, okay?"

After the children were in bed, he walked over to the tree and pulled out the Saks bag and handed it to me. "Go ahead, hon. Open it."

"But what about our rule of no Christmas presents before Christmas?"

"You guys made changes to our ritual. Can't I?"

"Of course," I said. I opened the bag and pulled out an expensive black bikini. "Wow! And where am I supposed to wear this little thing?"

"In our pool," he said.

"Our pool? Did you buy a house without me?"

"No, of course not. I'm just holding it until you see it."

I checked the label of the suit. "This might be a tad too small for me, hon. It's a three. I've never been that small before."

"Oh, sorry. I thought the salesgirl had checked it. I'll exchange it. Size six, right?"

I nodded and wondered where he ever got the idea I was so small.

"I've decided you and kids will move to California in January," he said, as he set the turkey platter from Christmas dinner on the counter. "And I won't take no for an answer."

I stood at the sink and continued to rinse dishes. "Sorry," I said. We had an agreement. Not until school is out. And not until you promise me that there will never be any abuse."

He stood next to me and pushed his body gently against mine. "Come on, Pen. We can't continue this way. I do promise never to abuse you again. I've said it before. Just believe me. Now, that said, the week after New Year's, would you please come to California to look at the house?"

I dried my hands and faced him. "Sure. Love to. But we're not moving until May."

"Are you forgetting who the bread winner in this family is?"

"No, of course not." I smiled. "You and I both are."

"You promised me you would move," he said angrily. "You need to keep your word as well."

"I am. Moving in May as I agreed. Quit trying to make this more difficult than it already is."

He returned to California before New Year's leaving us to greet the New Year in peace. I was relieved that his company would only pay for him to come home once a month and thrilled at the prospect that he probably wouldn't even do that.

April 1982

It was my last Sunday in church and I sat in the choir loft as usual, contributing an extra body only. My vocal abilities probably left people wondering if there was a key of 'Z'. So I simply moved my mouth without sound.

David Kingsley sauntered up to the pulpit, his snow white teeth shimmering like small ceramic tiles beneath his mustached rainbow of a smile. "When a minister leaves a church," he began, "usually that person gets to preach a farewell sermon, offering up whatever reminiscence, words of wisdom, cautions or other tidbits he or she feels may fit.

"Penne is leaving Massachusetts. This is her last Sunday and although she has been a minister to all of us in every sense of the word, she's not preaching a departing sermon so I'll do it instead. It will be good for me anyway because in my heart I have not really accepted the fact that she is going. I'm stuck at the psychological level authorities in the field call denial."

As he ended, tears washed my face of all makeup and filled every tissue choir members could find. Most people shook David's hand as they left. I hugged him so tightly I embarrassed myself. "Don's a lucky man," he said. "You have strength and courage you haven't even used yet. I know how you feel about moving, about him, but God will guide you."

He started to walk away, and then stepped back. "I was hoping I would meet Don this morning."

I didn't tell him Don left right after Christmas or that I hadn't seen him for two months. I walked down the front steps of the church and stopped.

For the first time in our lives, I realized I didn't need Don to be happy.

CHAPTER 21

May 1982

"*You* can't take it." Don's voice was calm. "It's too expensive to ship and too far to drive." He sounded like he was next door but I was glad he was back in Los Angeles.

I sighed. "But the Eagle isn't just any old car."

"The what?" He was irritated.

"Never mind. When do the movers come?"

"Friday morning. Early. I'll be back Thursday night."

"Whatever," I said.

"Pen, you put attachments on the wrong things."

You're telling me, I thought. *Like my attachment to you.*

"It's just a car," he said blandly. "Not a family heirloom. Maybe Tom and Kathleen's son could use it. What did you call the car?"

"A car."

He sighed. "Just focus on how much you liked the new house when you toured it. The pool. The yard. Thirty-six hundred square feet of living space. Your own office. Who could ask for more?"

I could, I thought. "I'll see you in a few days."

WELCOME TO CALIFORNIA. NOW GO HOME. It was my favorite bumper sticker. But, cynicism aside, California did offer promise. We had paid way below the asking price for the house as someone had been murdered in the back yard. I knew that shallow part of me had a deeper root than I thought as the crime didn't concern me.

The new house had majesty to it, from the double oak front doors to the massive living room with a Palo Verde stone fireplace which dominated one wall. Each room was designed to service the owner. An eight foot wide foyer was enhanced by newly laid Saltillo tile. The dining room had a built in oak china cabinet and large floor to ceiling windows. There was the convenience of a serving bar which separated the newly tiled kitchen from the dining room. Architecturally, the design made the bar very handy yet obliterated the view of messy meal preparation from the dining room. A gleaming copper rack held shiny pots. Of course I scrubbed them. A maid was not part of the purchase price.

With the exception of the foyer, kitchen and baths, beige carpeting offered a padded path from room to room.

We had friendly neighbors on either side; retired but kind, and, of course, no children for the kids to play with.

"You sound miserable," Kathleen said on the phone one night.

"I am." Depression had again engulfed me and I couldn't seem to shake it.

"Why? Don back to old habits and new girl friends?"

No, I think. "Actually he's being wonderful. I'm just wallowing in my usual, pathetic wish-we-hadn't-moved phase."

"Then why did you?" Her voice was abrupt.

"Kathleen, I've asked myself that question daily."

"And how did you answer yourself?"

"The answers are all the same. Even though my marriage has negative components. . ."

"You can say that again," she interrupted.

"It has an advantage over the unknown, which was going it alone."

"Why would that be so bad, Pen?"

"Oh, you know my resistance to change. The status quo of staying married is more predictable than the unknown I would have faced had I stayed in Massachusetts and divorced him. Status quo means a modicum of security and, in the long range. . ."

"And in the long range," she finished, "status quo means a minimum of risk. Translation: You are afraid to be on your own because you just don't believe in yourself."

"You're right. But let's change the subject. Is the Eagle running okay?"

Kathleen laughed. "Sure, she works fine. I drive it quite a bit so I renamed it."

"Huh? What do you call her?"

"Penne."

I laughed. "Before you hang up, how is Patricia?"

"Doing better. She took the kids and moved in with her mother. She's in the process of filing for divorce. Jealous?"

I thought for a moment. "Yes, but good for her."

The backyard had become my daily haunt with the children. A tropical ambience with lush lawns, swaying palms and luxuriant foliage surrounded a large, free form in ground pool with a caterpillar curved slide and diving board. Gas tiki torches and a warming pit made us feel like we were on vacation. When we tired of the water, the monotony of television had to handle the balance of entertainment. There were no kids in the neighborhood and the girls would probably be stuck being each other's friend until school began. With no column to write, no job and no car, I struggled to hide my boredom.

Weekends were a different scenario. Don wasted no time inviting corporate people over for elaborate pool parties. The extraordinarily friendly people made me feel like I had been part of the group from inception.

Don was standing by the pool surrounded by his peers one time when Bridget walked up to him. Looking down at her little head, he wrapped his arms around her and patted her back.

"Daddy?" she asked.

"Yes, pumpkin?"

Bridget leaned back and looked up into his face. "How come you only hug Stephie and me when we have company?"

I watched Don force a laugh. "Because that's the only time you two behave," he joked.

Bridget walked away glumly.

June, 1982

By twelve noon I had to turn on the central air even though I worried about the cost. I was lamenting the fact that my life was void of excitement or friendships as I adjusted the sprinkler heads in the front yard. Suddenly Gnook, our golden retriever, bolted out the front gate and made a dash for the neighbor's yard in pursuit of their dog, which could be heard in our yard but not seen because of the block wall which surrounded the back yard.

I threw down the hose and went chasing after him as he bounded over snarls of thick ivy in the neighbor's yard. I was a few feet away from collaring him when he let out a yelp and fell to the ground.

His cry beckoned the neighbor who ran out of his house as I bent down over my dog. There was blood everywhere and the dog just laid there, his eyes closed.

"My God," said John. "Look!"

I followed the old man's finger and my eyes came to rest on what looked like a piece of flesh a few feet from Gnook. "What is that?" I gasped.

Stooping down, John's face flushed as he pushed the white hair out of his eyes which flopped in his face like an aging mop. "I think it's your dog's penis, Penne," he said without shame. "He must have gotten it caught on a sprinkler head."

He helped me wrap Gnook in a towel and ran into his house to get a plastic bag full of ice for his dismembered part. Panting, he ran back outside. "Saw this on TV," he said. "Should keep it alive." His wife, Ethel, followed close behind. She was a sweet looking lady with a southern drawl that reminded me of my mother. "I've seen your cute little girls," she said. "Can I watch them for you while John takes you to the vet?"

"Thanks so much for your help. I'll run and get them. Just don't tell them what has happened to their dog, okay?"

The kids were thrilled to go someplace different. Ethel took each by the hand and started chatting with them as they walked back into her house.

John laid Gnook on my lap in the cab of his truck and we raced to the local vet. The attendants quickly put the dog on some form of a stretcher while I walked behind him carrying his missing part like I was bearing a gift to the pagan god of reproduction.

I filled out the necessary forms while he was in surgery and named Don as the registered owner but skipped over his work number. I needed to tell him first. The vet's office would keep him for several days to make sure the attachment worked.

"How the hell could you let this happen?" Don ranted when he got home.

Here we go again, I thought bitterly. *Always my fault.* "The gate kept snapping shut. But Gnook persisted. He read the gate operation manual and finally learned how to make it through."

Don was sitting in the den half watching television. "Stop being a smart ass. It's not like you have a million things to handle. I hope you won't be as careless with the kids."

I stood in the doorway between the kitchen and den and put my hands on my hips. "Gnook was easier to train," I said as snotty as possible and let out a theatrical sigh. "Every time I let the kids out of the gate, they just keep coming back!"

September 1982

Endless summer days finally bled into the beginning of the school year and the shallow root friendships they made the first week of school helped ease the girls into a carefree lifestyle as they mixed and mingled well with a variety of other kids. Introduced to the ins and outs of the California girl, they denounced New England as backward by the second week of school and begged to have pool/slumber parties. Having suffered for so many months with no friends, I couldn't say no and allowed them each to invite five.

It was seven o'clock Friday night and music blared from the stereo in the den. Twelve little girls looked like a human train as they pranced through the kitchen, their hands around the waist of the girl in front of them and chugged through the house to the beat.

"Make them turn that down," Don bellowed from our bedroom.

I walked down the hall and pushed the door open. He was sitting in the middle of the bed, like some guru, trying to read.

"They are just having fun," I said. "It's the first time they have had anyone their age around since we moved here. So lighten up, big daddy."

"Too much noise," he said. "It's time for them to go to sleep."

"At ten o'clock? No, too early. Just like you once said when you insisted we move out here, there is a lot for them to do. Now, they're doing it. Aren't you glad we moved?"

He looked up from what he was reading. "Check with me the next time you want to do this," he said. "I'll make sure I'm away."

"Okay. And you check with me with next time you want to go away." I walked out, slammed the door and gave the children free reign on when they wanted to go to bed.

Lights were finally out at one thirty in the morning.

December 1982

The holiday season snuck in through the smog and lack of cool weather and the constant blight of afternoon sunlight dampened my Yuletide spirit. We had been in California for eight months and I had yet to see a drop of rain. Meteorologists seemed to be as useless in Southern California as snowshoes. What education did it require to say "the sun is out" everyday?

The first corporate Christmas party approached too quickly. I was trying on the red slinky dress I had purchased when the phone rang.

"I missed my flight so I won't be back from Phoenix in time," Don said. "So Marty and Brian will pick you up."

Brian was the Director of Personnel. He and his wife had gone way beyond the expected to make me feel welcome. Marty was very much like me but I rarely got to see her. "I don't want to impose on them, and, more important, it is my first function in this region. I'll just skip the party."

Don was impatient. "No you won't. You are my wife and we need to attend as the team that we are. I will be there. I just can't get there in time for the beginning."

"Fine," I said. "I just feel awkward walking in there without you."

Marty and Brian escorted me to the corporate table and made the introductions to the few I had not met.

"Where is Don?" one of the managers asked.

"Missed his plane out of Phoenix," I said. "He should be arriving shortly."

"That's strange," said his office manager, Anne Hampton. "Kathy's here. I guess they didn't get the same flight."

"Kathy?" I asked Marty. "Who is Kathy?"

"His new assistant," Brian answered. "She basically handles everything for him; keeps him on track."

Dinner was almost over in the lavish ballroom of a Los Angeles hotel when Don finally arrived. Marty was sitting next to me at the corporate table and tapped my shoulder. "He's here," she said.

I turned around and watched Don walk through the large double doors. I started to push my chair back from the table and readied myself to greet him when a dark haired girl beat me to his side. I flipped my head around and stared at Marty. "Who's that?" I whispered.

She turned her head for a quick look then promptly snapped it back. "Kathy, Don's assistant," she said loudly. "Kathy the Pit Bull."

Don spent a few minutes with her before joining us. Walking up behind me, he planted an obligatory kiss on my cheek, greeted the others at the table and took his seat beside me.

"So how's Phoenix?" asked one of his managers

"Full of snow birds and heat strokes," Don laughed. He took a bite of prime rib and grimaced. "God, this is awful."

I tried to act nonchalant, lit a cigarette and turned my head toward him. "It was excellent when it was hot," I whispered.

He waived over a passing waiter. "Could you get me a gin and tonic good buddy?" he said and pressed a folded bill in his hand. In record time, the waiter returned and Don gulped down his drink while the rest of us ate the dessert he had not touched.

As lights twinkled in the glittery ceiling of the ballroom and the band began to play, Don abruptly excused himself with a brisk, "have to fulfill a promise to my assistant" and headed for the dance floor.

"That bastard," Marty said, blowing a stream of smoke out of her mouth like the north wind. "Who the hell does he think he is?"

"It is okay honey," her husband said, patting her hand. "He's the one looking foolish. Not Pen."

"I'm with your wife, Brian," I said and rested my elbows on the table. "Why the hell am I sitting here alone?" I glanced over at the dance floor. Don and Kathy were moving in perfect time to the music, both laughing.

"Good question," Marty said. "Just remember the old phrase—'A woman needs a man like a fish needs a bicycle.'"

Wonderful, I thought, California's version of Gloria Steinem. Except in my world, fish seemed to be riding ten speeds. I still needed his paycheck and stared at Kathy while they danced and ordered another drink to blur the view. Kathy was petite, just barely five feet tall. Short, black hair fluffed around her childish face and she smiled continuously at Don; a smile that said she knew him beyond the office. She was what a charitable person might call cute in her snug little non-virgin white velvet dress. But I felt no sense of charity. Don seemed to be delighted holding her in his arms, impressing his peers with his Arthur Murray skills on a girl closer in age to his daughter than him.

"Where did she come from?" I asked Marty. "Camp Snoopy?"

Marty laughed out loud. "Before you start imagining things that aren't there, Don spent most evenings with us before you moved out here. Brian said he's training her to become his right arm."

I stabbed my cigarette out in the ashtray between us. "Looks like she's become more than his right arm right now," I said. Liquor acted as the conduit, feeding thoughts onto the tongues of others who probably would have kept silent.

Muriel Gibbons, Brian's secretary, was the first to pass a slurred speech judgment. "It's no wonder they threw her lily white ass out of home office, always worming her way in around men of 'thority'." She turned to her husband, a balding little man of few words. "I better never catch you doin' somethin' that stupid," she scolded. He gave her a practiced nod, tipped his glass up and downed his drink in one gulp.

I tossed my napkin on the table, walked out to the dance floor and tapped Kathy on the shoulder. "My turn, young lady. I don't believe we've met." I extended my hand. "I'm Penne, Don's wife. Been married to this old man for a lifetime." I laughed just to increase his anxiety.

She slinked away without shaking my hand. Don grabbed me around the waist. "What are you doing?" he snarled into my ear.

"Claiming what's mine," I whispered. "For a man who begged and pleaded to have his family in California, for us to behave as the ultimately happy couple, you certainly aren't behaving like any Czar of domestic bliss."

His hand dug into my back as he tried to move his anger to music. "Quit being a bitch" he said. "You're acting like some jealous school girl."

I pushed away from him. "I'm not acting LIKE some jealous school girl," I hissed. I am REACTING to YOUR school girl. And you, Mr. Regional big shot, are behaving like some old man who just raided a day care center for a date."

Don smiled, not at me, but for the benefit of his peers he knew were watching.

"Just stop," he said and flashed a phony smile. "You are making a fool out of both of us."

When the music stopped, I tossed my head back and laughed. "And you're not?" I walked back to the table, my head held high, and grabbed my purse. "Nice to have met you all," I smiled. "Happy Holidays. I look forward to seeing you again." Behind my mask of a smiling face was total contempt.

As I left the table, Marty scurried after me. "Way to go," she said. "But now that you've made your grand exit, how to you expect to get home?"

I reached into my purse, pulled out a set of keys and dangled them in front of her. "He drove that old car he bought for me to the airport," I said. "And he drove it here. He could have a problem getting home, at least to our house."

Marty hugged me. "I knew I liked you," she whispered.

The sounds of the organ filled the old cathedral. Candle flames danced throughout the sanctuary and dozens of brilliant poinsettias marched up the sides of the historic altar. Heads turned reverently as the priest in his flowing white robe walked down the center aisle led by rosy cheeked altar boys.

Stephie was leaning on one side of me, Bridget on the other, too sleepy to appreciate the majesty of a Christmas Eve mass. Marty, Brian, their two sons and Don filled the balance of the pew. Every so often Marty looked over at us and smiled; a smile that said *I'm so glad you're here.* There was no look I could offer, no signal I could use to convey my surprise that we were actually there. Don had willingly accepted their invitation as if church had been an integral part of his Christmas tradition.

"A blessed Christmas to you all." The priest's voice wafted through the microphone, his voice as celestial as one might imagine God's to be. He raised his arms skyward and the sleeves of his robe gracefully billowed from his outstretched arms. "Please join the choir in singing our final carol."

As we rose to our feet, Don thumbed through the hymnal, located the page and handed me the book. "You can use it," he smiled boastfully. "I know the words to this one."

As his rich voice filled the air, I could only stare at him with pure loathing. "Oh Come All Ye **Faithful**. . ."

CHAPTER 22

March 1983

"*L*et's see," Don said and reached into his suit coat on the back of his chair. We had just finished dinner and he was suddenly all smiles as he produced several envelopes. "Here's one for Bridget, one for Stephanie and one for Mommy."

Stephie ripped her envelope open the fastest. "Plane tickets," she shouted. "To Pennsylvania in July." She grabbed Bridget's arm. "We're going to see Grandma and Grandpa!"

A scowl formed on Bridget's face. "To stay? I don't want to go back there to live."

"You ninny," Stephie said. "We're not moving. We're just going to visit our old friends and our grandparents. A fun time Bridget! For two whole weeks!"

I looked at Don. "What's this all about?"

"Keeping a promise," he said, cocking his eyebrow. "Or don't you remember?" His voice was more accommodating than sincere.

"Refresh my memory." I had no idea what he was talking about or where he was getting the money to pay such airfares.

"Hon, I promised you before we left Boston I would make sure you could visit."

Am I experiencing senile dementia in my thirties? I thought. "I don't remember that. At any rate, aren't you going too?"

"Can't," he said. He stood and carried his plate out to the kitchen. "July is a busy time for me. Business before pleasure."

Business is pleasure was more like it. "But you have three months before the trip. Won't that be enough time? Even the president of General Motors takes a vacation."

He stood behind my chair and gently put his hands on my shoulders. "When I'm the President, sweetheart, I will too." He kissed my cheek and disappeared down the hall.

April 1983

Stephanie hit her thirteenth birthday and had blossomed into a beautiful girl; her long blond hair and pixie features had made her the envy of many of her friends. But she had also reached that age when her entire lexicon was reduced to the B word----BOYS.

"Mom," she wailed. "Tell Dad to stop."

I walked into the front hall. There was a young boy I didn't recognize at the door and Don was talking to him. "Well little fellow," he said, which was embarrassing because the young man was as tall as Don. "I'm afraid Stephanie's a bit too young to entertain boys. Perhaps you can come back in a year or so."

Stephie pulled me back into the kitchen. "He's making a fool out of me," she cried. "The kids are talking at school. He always humiliates me in front of them."

The front door closed and Don roared into the kitchen. "Go to your room, young lady or you won't date until you're twenty-one! I won't have your little boyfriends popping up at this house at all hours or tying up the phone. You're too damn young for this!"

Stephanie raced down the hall to her room and slammed the door.

"Knock it off, Don," I scolded. "This is a difficult time in any young girls' life. If we don't handle this carefully, we'll have more trouble than we ever dreamed about."

Don put his hands on his hips and scowled. "Considering the way you turned out, you had better leave Stephanie's guidance up to me."

I laughed. "Oh? Does being a habitual womanizer certify you as the better parent?"

"You're so damn stupid," he said. "And your daughters will probably be just the same."

Stephie imprisoned herself in her room any time Don was home and her continual sulking around him pushed his anger button to high. At ten, Bridget sat on the sidelines knowing enough to watch in silence.

"Stephanie?" he yelled. "Get out here and clean up the kitchen!"

He was being grossly unfair. He had made the mess. But it didn't stop at that. He accused her of taking his precious Cross pen and later found it in his car. There was no apology.

When he answered the phone and it was one of her friends, he demanded that she tell any boys to stop calling. But Kathy the Pit Bull called continually. According to Don, it was always business related which was difficult to believe. He always took her calls in our bedroom with the door shut.

I was torn between proper parenting and defending Stephie just to air my pent up grievances against him. It was so confusing I had to force myself to think ahead---

think of our trip back east—to maintain my sanity and I secretly encouraged the girls to do the same.

July 1983
Easton, Pennsylvania

Pennsylvania was wonderful this time. To be there on vacation instead of an escape to safety was refreshing. We were relaxed, my parents were relaxed and the visit was a memory in the making.

The second week on the east coast, I rented a car and drove to Massachusetts. Without Don around to dampen her spirits, Stephanie glowed in the admiration of old friends who were stunned by her transformation from the little girl in braces to a beautiful young lady. Bridget, once a shy, almost reclusive child, had become a mystical, adorable young lady, unusually introspective, sensitive, with a dry sense of humor. It's so exhilarating to see you!" Tom said. "You all look great. California must hold the secret to lasting beauty."

Their children raced up the stairs. "Stephie, Bridget!" They all hugged and dashed downstairs to the "fun place" as the kids often referred to it.

I rolled my eyes at Kathleen. "It holds secrets but not to lasting beauty, just lasting cutie.

"Another girlfriend?" she asked with disgust.

"Pretty sure. I'll know more when I get back. But I don't care anymore.

"And has the abuse stopped?"

I chose my words carefully. "Physical, yes. But I still suspect another woman although he makes me think I am inventing the relationship."

"And?"

"And, I probably won't last much longer. I'm not sure what I'm going to do or just how I'm going to do it. All I know is that the children and I deserve a better life."

I left their home feeling comforted and knew I had the support of two people who didn't consider me mentally disabled. There was a glorious peace between Stephie, Bridget and I which I could only explain with one thought: *Don was not around.*

For two weeks we traveled and laughed without a cross word and the calm was so treasured.

But it didn't last long. "Do we have to go back to California?" Stephie cried at the airport. "I like being with nice people."

I squeezed my eyes shut for a moment to gather strength. "I thought you liked it, honey. It's your home now."

"Mom?" Bridget asked as we boarded the plane.

"Yes honey?"

"Didn't you feel more love back here?"

The truth of her question burned in my throat and the girls reclusive dispositions remained throughout the flight. I wanted to cater to them but knew better. I put my head back and closed my eyes. But there was no escape from the truth. I had made the wrong decision. We never should have moved to California.

Home was not where anyone's heart was, including Don's. We came home to a dirty house, bills piled on the dining room table like a mail out campaign, and our expensive bedspread had been thrown away. "What happened, Don?" I asked

"Animals," he grumbled. "I was late for work one morning and locked the dog and cat in the bedroom. It was such a mess I threw it out."

I sat down on the bed and rubbed my chin. "Interesting," I said calmly.

Don turned from his dresser. "What's interesting?"

I stood up, walked toward the bedroom door then stopped. "We don't have a cat."

Don's face drained of color. He grabbed his briefcase. "Oh, Pen, you know what I mean. Dogs, cats. They are all the same."

December 1983

I shoved Kathy's invitation to her Christmas cocktail party under the newspapers in the den while Don watched with disgust. "You can toss this out with the trash. I'm not going."

Don slammed his hand down on the newspapers. "What's with you? You used to love parties. You'll make us both look foolish if you don't go."

"You do that very well by yourself, Don. And for the record, I'm not attending the company dinner either. Not after last year."

"All right," he said. "Let's compromise. We'll skip the cocktail party if you'll go to the dinner. They are both on the same night. We have to attend one, for God's sake. I'm the Regional V.P. How would it look if I'm not there, or worse, there alone?"

I had yards of answers backed up on my tongue but swallowed all. "Fine. I'll attend the dinner. But only the dinner. Have I made myself clear?"

He shook his head. "What's gotten into you? You haven't been the same since your trip. Did Mommy and Daddy anoint your spirit in Christian dogma?"

"No. We had a great time. Coming home anointed me. With total contempt."

On the night of the party I was doing my usual thing of daydreaming while Don drove, not paying attention to anything. When Don parked the car in a residential area, I suddenly woke up. He got out of the car but I sat there frozen. He walked around to my door and opened it. "This will only take a minute, Pen. I have to make an appearance for the sake of the company."

"Then make your appearance. I'll wait in the car."

He grabbed my arm, pulled me out of the car and pushed me up the walk to a condo and pressed the doorbell. And surprise, Kathy answered with a cheery, "Merry Christmas."

I couldn't respond much less smile as Don nudged me in the door. "Shape up," he whispered in my ear.

"You first," I shot back.

Marty joined me in a corner and we watched as Don, ever so acquainted with the whereabouts of everything in the kitchen, played host by Kathy's side for the hour we were there.

At the company dinner, Marty dragged me off to the ladies room. "You can't just sit back," she said. "You need to do something."

"I'm not even close to sitting back. I have to make certain of what is happening and get everything in order before I make my move."

"Like what?"

"Money, a job, a place to live. You know minor details."

"Oh," she said before we left the restroom. "I should warn you about something. I overheard Don offer your home for his new salesman's wedding reception in May. Just thought you might want to know."

"Wedding reception?" I laughed out loud. "At our house? That would be like having a barbecue at a crematorium!"

We walked back to the dinner laughing.

"Dress up tonight," Don said on the phone. "I have a surprise for you."

I was in the mood for a lynching, not some celebration. "What's the occasion?"

"You're kidding," he said and sounded genuinely hurt. "I can't believe you didn't remember our anniversary. Seventeen years, Pen, seventeen years. Doesn't that mean anything to you?"

A marital parole for my good behavior I thought. "For the record, our anniversary isn't until Sunday."

"I know that. Are you forgetting how you celebrated it on our first anniversary?" He laughed out loud. "I had to show you the inscription in your wedding band to prove you had the wrong date!" He laughed again. "Just be ready at seven thirty, okay?"

Don had reserved a table at an elegant restaurant in downtown LA and oozed affection as he sat down across from me. Tender words gushed in a torrent equal to his consumption of wine as I just sat there and stared at him.

And then dessert. A miniature wedding cake was brought to the table. And hidden on the cake tray was a box. Don flipped the top open. Nested in the white shiny folds was a beautiful ring. One medium diamond peaked above a row of smaller ones which marched around the band. He removed the ring and held it up to the candle. "There are seventeen diamonds," he said proudly. "One for each year."

Only the waiter standing by responded. "It's beautiful, sir," he said.

"Give me your left hand, Pen," Don said with enough tenderness to melt cold wax.

I pushed my chair back and grabbed my purse. "Give it to Kathy," I said and left the table.

Don raced after me, pulling me back by my arm. "What are you doing?" he said, his face crimson color. "Kathy works for me. I'm getting sick and tired of you always assuming things which aren't there."

"Me too," I said and walked toward the car to wait while he paid the bill.

He drove home in a silent fury, dropped me off and left. I climbed into bed, numb. At three in the morning I woke up, walked out to the kitchen to get something to drink and heard the garage door go up.

Minutes later Don walked into the kitchen. "Can't you sleep either?" he said, this master of pretense. He kissed my forehead and the smell of liquor did not obliterate the distinct scent of White Linen cologne. I couldn't cry and was not even sure I had the energy for anger. My emotional bank had been in overdraft for months.

Don walked down the hall to the bedroom. Too agitated to sleep, I busied myself with laundry. His clothes smelled better coming out of the hamper than out of the dryer; it was a foreign scent which carried the full story of his infidelity.

Examining each shirt as I put it in the washer, I pulled off handfuls of animal hair. I removed the shirts from the washer and laid them on top of his desk in the den, pet hair up, and fell asleep on the couch convinced Kathy owned a black cat.

It was late afternoon when he discovered them. "What the hell are these shirts doing on my desk?" he shouted from the den.

I walked in smiling. "Just wanted you to see all that animal hair. Where in the world did it come from?" My voice was a preschool, sing-song cadence I couldn't resist.

"Don't be stupid," he said. "Where do you think it came from or have you forgotten we have a dog?"

I snapped my fingers. "By golly you're right. Here Gnook," I called. Bless his little retriever heart, Gnook dutifully bounded into the den and rubbed up against my leg. I bent down, rolled him over on his back and ran my fingers through his golden fur.

Don grimaced. "What are you doing?"

I stroked the dog calmly. "Looking for black hair."

He stormed out of the den. "You are such a jerk," he yelled. "Are you forgetting Brian and Marty's dog is black and that I'm at their house as much as I'm here? I'm going to the office. I don't have time for your petty little housewife jealousy."

The door closed behind him and the phone rang. It was Lottie, my elderly little neighbor who had been as kind as any neighbor I had ever had. Her West Virginia hospitality had never left her even though she had moved to California many years before. "Could you use some company?" I asked.

"Love it," she said cheerfully. "Haven't seen you for a long time."

I scribbled a quick note to the kids who were still sleeping and walked over to Lottie's. I told her positive family tales to spice up the dull monotony of her days which help to soothe my frazzled mind. We laughed and joked while she fed me every delicious morsel she could find to fatten me up. Pleased with her cookie jar shape, she always thought everyone else was too thin.

"I tried to feed Don when you went back east but he turned me down," she said with sadness in her voice. "Maybe he doesn't like the way I cook."

Cooking had been her life. "Nonsense. He knows what a great cook you are."

She sighed. "He said his sister was staying with him. Can she cook?"

Sister? Did this sister bring her cat? I wondered. "Don't know," I said. "I've always fed her. Victoria has the appetite of a football player."

Lottie's heavily penciled brows arched in disbelief. "That little thing? I think her bikini was a size two or three."

Victoria was almost six feet tall. "Oh?" I twisted my hands in my lap. "You met her?"

"No. Just saw her floating on a raft in your pool one day when you were away. Now I wasn't being nosey, mind you, I was just watering my roses. I called hello over the wall but I guess she didn't hear me."

"Hope she had on a bathing cap," I said. "The pool filter gets clogged every time her blond hair hits the water. She sheds more than Gnook.

Lottie's eyes widened. "Blond?" She rubbed her eyes. "My eyes must be going along with the rest of me. I could have sworn her hair was black."

CHAPTER 23

March 1985

At about six o'clock one evening, Stephanie started vomiting. I was frying chicken when Bridget raced into the kitchen, her long blondish pigtails zigzagging across her mouth as she ran. "Better come quick, Mom," she shouted. "Steph is really sick. She threw up all over her bed."

Her urgency was contagious. I dropped the tongs into the sink and raced down the hall to the bathroom. Stephie was lying on the cold ceramic tile floor by the base of the toilet, her body coiled in a semi-fetal position.

I gently sat her up, carried her into my bedroom and laid her on the side of the bed closest to the bathroom. For a lanky kid who would turn fifteen in April, she was heavy, her body alarmingly warm and limp. I took her temperature; one hundred and three. I put in a call to the pediatrician and his service promised to try and reach him.

Stephie's dainty porcelain face was flushed, her little mouth painted red by fever and she moaned as I sponged her down. "Mom?" she whispered. "Something's burning."

Dinner! I quickly draped a fresh cloth across her forehead and left Bridget to stand watch. As I dashed down the hall to the kitchen, I could see smoke billowing up from the frying pan, like something had crash landed into the stove top. I pulled the smoldering pans from the burner, dumped them into the sink and turned on the water. I scraped what was left of the beans and rice in another burnt pan into the garbage disposal and was tossing pieces of barely recognizable chicken into the trash when the phone rang.

"Hello?" I said, panting.

"This is Dr. Johnson. I understand Stephanie is sick." His voice was relaxed, reassuring and using basic physician brevity; he explained the symptoms of a twenty-four hour intestinal flu making the rounds. "I'll order Compazine suppositories and have the pharmacy deliver them." He cautioned me to watch her for signs of dehydration and instructed me to give her small sips of water or Coke.

I was hanging up the phone when Don stalked into the kitchen, his tie sloppily lowered to the middle of his chest, a suit jacket irritably flung over his shoulder. "What the hell's burning?" Before I had time to answer, he tossed his briefcase on the dining room table and walked down the hall. I raced to catch him before he got to our bedroom but was too late.

"What is she doing in my bed?" he said like a modern day Red Riding Hood wolf. He acted like Stephie was a stranger and did not so much as glance at her. "Well?" he yelled, his arms flailing. "Do I get a damn answer or what?"

The tension between us had reached an atomic stage and this made things worse. "Will you please calm down? Stephie is very sick."

"Calm down?" he said. "Damn. I have worked myself into oblivion to provide the best for this damn family and finally get home after a twelve hour day and can't even use my own bed. With over thirty-six hundred square feet in this house, surely you can find some place for her besides my bed." He tore at the buttons of his white dress shirt, pulled it off and dropped it on the floor.

The urge to deck him was overwhelming. "Stephie has been vomiting heavily, Don. Yelling isn't going to help. She vomited all over her bed. So just calm down and have a little respect for a sick child."

His eyebrows arched, his face contorted. "Would you quit your mommy-whining bullshit? I don't care what's wrong with her at the moment. That's your job. What I do care about is having my room to myself!"

He sat down on the edge of the bed and kicked off his shoes. Suddenly he stood up and advanced on me. Using his index finger as a poker, he began jabbing my shoulder with each syllable spoken. "I want that kid out of my bed, out of my room, now." He slapped some change on top of his dresser and walked into the closet to finish undressing.

Stephanie's face winced. Tears beaded on her eyelashes as she slithered under the covers. Bridget cowered in the corner next to the bed, her eyes widening with each word. I walked over to the bed and whispered, "Don't be afraid. I'll handle him." Seeing their frightened faces drew me back to the past; it had been so long since he had behaved this way. But one thing had not changed. They were depending on me to protect them. To protect myself.

I walked over to the closet and stood in the doorway. "We need to go out into the hall. Now. We've had a bad day too. Stephanie started vomiting an hour ago." I paused and we locked glances. I placed my hand on his arm and continued. "I haven't had a chance to change her bed. Be patient. She's a child."

He pulled on some jeans and a shirt, walked out of the closet, grabbed my arm and pushed me into the hall.

"Get your damn hand off of me," I growled softly. NOW!"

He met my plea with an unflinching stare and backed me up against the wall. Placing his hands firmly on the wall above my head, he pushed his face into mine. "Have you forgotten Victoria is coming for dinner?"

I winced. It was like talking to a gin bottle.

"Are you listening to me?" he said.

"Call her and cancel," I said and pushed him away. "I have more important things to do than cook. Stephie is dehydrating. I need to get fluids into her."

Wriggling free from his arms, I ran down the hall to the kitchen looking for Coke before I remembered I had put them in the refrigerator in the garage. I walked through the laundry room which separated the kitchen from the garage, opened the door, jumped off the top step to the garage floor. My path was blocked. Don had pulled his car in so far the bumper was kissing the back wall, another sign he was drunk. I climbed over the hood of his car to get to the refrigerator, grabbed a few cokes and finally using common sense, walked around the back of his car.

As I reached for the handle of the laundry room door, Don suddenly snapped the door open from the other side and shoved me back into the garage.

Standing on the top step, he loomed over me with a savage look. "What in God's name are you doing? That sick kid can take care of herself. They don't need you smothering them with attention like you did when they were babies. Get your butt in here and get dinner started. Victoria will be here any minute."

"Grow up," I yelled and moved toward the door. With his arms braced against the door jam, he stood rigid.

"Don, get the hell out of my way."

"You stupid bitch," he growled. He lunged forward and slapped my face with such force it threw me off balance and I fell to the garage floor, coke cans rolling in every direction as my head hit the side of his car. "Get that kid out of my bed," he roared. "NOW!"

I struggled to my feet, backed up against an exposed stud in the garage wall, and fumbled for my hiding place. "You insufferable bastard," I shouted. As he raised his arm back to swing, I pulled the gun from around my back and aimed. "Get out!"

A cataclysmic look spread over his face. "Where the hell did you get that thing?" He pointed at the gun but his hand was shaking so badly he had to pull his hand back to steady his inebriated body. "Put it down it down before we're both hurt!"

I pulled the hammer back. "Final warning, Don!"

He started laughing. "You piece of garbage. You don't know the first thing about guns." He started toward me.

"That's not what Tom told me during our lessons."

"You're bluffing," he yelled, putting out his hand. "Give me the damn gun."

My palms were sweaty. "Don't take another step." I pointed the gun at his chest and he dove for the floor. "Stop waving that thing around," he said. "It could go off."

"Get out," I said, "or I'll do more than wave it around."

He stood up and pressed the button for the garage door. "Just let me pass, you crazy bitch."

"You'll need car keys," I said.

They're here." He reached into his pocket and held them up. They were mine. Just car keys.

My house keys were on a separate ring.

I motioned with the gun for him to move forward.

"You're nuts," he yelled as he cautiously moved past me. "I'm going to call the police as soon as I get out of here."

"I'll call them right now if you don't get out of here. Want to spend time in a jail cell?"

I curbed the temptation to lower the door on top of him, watched him get into his car and back it out of the drive with a wild abandon then closed the garage door. Putting the gun in my pocket, I quickly removed the cover from the garage door control panel and changed the code. Then picking up a few Cokes from the floor, I ran inside and checked every door to make sure all entrances were locked. I was just checking the last one when the phone rang.

"Yes?" I said

"Pen?" It was Don.

"What?"

"I can't believe you almost killed me."

"Likewise," I said.

"What has happened to you?"

"You. You can only come back to pick up your clothes. But that will be by prearrangement only. You can't stay here. If you violate any of these rules, I will get an order of protection against you."

"You're kidding," he shouted.

"Did it look like I was kidding?" I hung up and ran into the bathroom. My hair was matted with blood and my cheek was cut. I quickly washed my face and combed the blood out of my hair. The kids had heard enough. They didn't need any visual assistance. I poured a glass of Coke and raced back to the bedroom. Stephie had vomited again. Her limp head bobbed over the toilet bowl while Bridget held her hair back like the reins of a horse. Both were crying. I washed Stephie up and put her back to bed. "Take a few sips, sweetheart."

Stephie was crying too hard to drink. "Mom, how long are you gonna let Dad do that to you?

I sat down on the edge of the bed and cradled her head in my left arm, then wrapped my right arm around Bridget. "Never again," I promised. "Never."

It was after midnight before the Compazine quelled her nausea and she fell asleep. I fed Bridget and sat on her bed smoothing her hair until she was asleep.

I walked back through the house for a final door check then stopped cold. There was a noise coming from the den. Like someone sobbing. I moved slowly toward the door, took a deep breath and turned on the light. "Victoria?" I stammered. "What are you doing here?"

She was curled up in an overstuffed chair, her arms wrapped tightly around her legs. She raised her head and wisps of hair clung to her tear soaked cheeks. "Are you okay?" she asked, her words slurred with emotion.

I sat down on the coffee table in front of her and stroked her hair. "Sure, Vic. I'm fine. How long have you been here?"

"Since the fight in the garage. When I pulled into the driveway, I heard Don yelling so I left and parked my car on a back street, walked back and hid by the pool until he left." She stopped to catch her breath. "I used my key to get in the side door."

"I'm so sorry you had to be here for this."

"He's just like my father was," she sobbed. Her body heaved as I put my arms around her and her body fell against mine.

She put her head in her hands. "I always knew, Pen, and I felt guilty for a long time, not telling anyone. But I don't anymore. Counseling helped."

I made us both a cup of tea and carried it back to the den. "I need to get home," she said. "I have finals tomorrow. Sure you'll be okay?"

I hugged her tightly. "Of course. Will you?"

"Yes, in time."

Mommy doesn't break promises, I thought when I called my parents. The next morning they wired me money for the lawyer's retainer.

"I wish you had listened to us," she said.

"I do too, Mom. You were right," I told her. "You always were."

I hung up and called the American Bar Association in Los Angeles. They gave me five names but I didn't have time to comparison shop so I called the first name on the list and made an appointment for the next morning at ten then paced the house allowing the children to sleep in.

They woke just before noon. Stephie was weak but improved and neither one asked about their father as I tucked blankets around them in the den so they could watch television.

I was in the kitchen making them something to eat when the doorbell rang. I looked outside. A van was parked in our drive. I could see the word Florist painted in colorful letters across the side. The delivery boy stood on the porch cradling a bouquet of roses.

"Hi," I said, and without asking, plucked the card out of the arrangement. In an unfamiliar scrawl was written, *'Honey. Am so sorry about last night. Please forgive me. I love you. Don.'*

FTD, I thought. Forgive the destruction? "Please take them back," I said and closed the door.

The next morning I awakened to the scent of fresh flowers in the bedroom. I rolled over on my side and felt my body convulse. The same bouquet I had rejected yesterday was now on the nightstand.

I closed my eyes and willed myself to stay calm. Don was in the house and today I had to meet the lawyer; a meeting I wanted kept secret until the papers were filed. I quietly slipped out of bed, gathered makeup, clothes and shoes and stuffed them into a gym bag. I opened the window over our bed, unlatched the screen and dropped the bag into the flowerbed, put on a robe and walked out to the kitchen feigning that just-woke-up look.

Don was seated at the table, freshly showered, and dressed in jeans and a T-shirt.

"Good morning," he said sweetly. "Just made some coffee. Pour you a cup?"

Damn you! I thought. *How the hell can you just sit there like nothing had happened, trying to pave over torment with contrived normality.* I stared beyond him and his charade and refused to fall prey to this scenario again where nothing was ever resolved. Nor could I allow the damage of yesterday to slide into a mental Bermuda triangle. I didn't speak or attempt eye contact. Pretending he wasn't there, I walked down the hall and awakened the children. Stephie was feeling much better and wanted to go to school, which, under the circumstances, was the best place for her to be. "I can hear him," she whispered.

"Don't worry," I whispered back. "He's sober and being nice."

Bridget was awake and I could tell by the bags under her eyes that she had probably been thinking for hours.

"Why is Dad here?" she asked softly.

I kissed her and whispered, "Just acting like nothing happened. But don't worry. If you hurry up and dress, brush your teeth, we'll go to McDonald's for breakfast. Deal?"

"Deal," she said smiling.

I pulled on jeans and a tee shirt, went to start my car while the girls gathered their books, then cautiously opened the side gate and grabbed my gym bag, put it in the trunk and went back inside. While Don was in the bathroom, I quickly ushered the girls out the door and we left.

After our McDonald's breakfast stop, I dropped the children off at school and drove to Marty's house to get dressed. "Sorry I didn't call first," I said, and briefly related the events.

"Did you get that job you applied for?" she asked, as I stood in her bathroom putting on makeup.

"Yes. I start next month thanks to your referral."

"Wish you could have found something sooner," she said sadly. "Maybe you could have avoided that hell last night."

I smiled. "It's okay, Marty. I also found a place to live, four minutes from our house so the girls won't have to change schools. But first the house has to be sold."

She frowned. "You can keep the house, you know."

"I don't want it," I said. "I couldn't afford the upkeep. Besides, I need the money. It won't be much but I'll have about fifteen thousand if it sells at even the lowest listing price."

"Do you have a real estate agent?"

"Yup. But I have to run." I gathered up my belongings, checked the mirror one last time and followed her to the front door.

"Hope you remembered to bring the tax returns and his pay stubs."

I kissed her cheek. "Thanks to you, my business savvy friend, I have it all!"

She gave me a strong hug. "I'm really proud of you, girl. And I had Brian check the law firm you chose. Top of the line. You'll do just fine."

"I'm proud of you," she shouted as I left. And I was proud of me too.

Mr. Griffin sat formally behind a desk stacked with papers. Plaques covered the richly papered walls of his office. He looked quite distinguished and there was a peaceful ambience about him. Dressed in a dark blue suit, maroon silk tie and matching pocket square arranged in too many peaks, Griffin appeared to be in his early forties, a stocky build and sun bronzed face. *Business must be good,* I thought.

"Please have a seat." He gestured to a leather chair in front of his desk. Not knowing what to expect, I fiddled with the large manila file in my lap, and caressed the edges with my fingers.

"To begin," he said, "I need to ask you some questions to get the process started." He smiled and said, "and try to relax. I'll be right there with you through the entire thing."

"For free, of course," I joked.

He laughed then rambled through the basics. Number of children, length of marriage and so on. When it came to finances, he was more specific. I had been collecting data for several months and handed him the applicable paperwork. "I believe you will find everything there. But I need to talk about something more important at the moment."

Griffin put his pen down and leaned back in his chair. "Certainly. Go ahead."

"There has been a great deal of physical abuse in this marriage," I began. "I will need a restraining order as soon as possible."

He jotted something in his folder, and asked me several questions. "Our firm is here to protect our clients. I will get that filed today. But knowing how to protect you is always necessary."

"There's one more issue," I said and related the story of the night before and the gun, fearful Don's lawyer would use it in court."

Griffin was concerned. "I understand your need for protection, Penne, but guns don't solve anything. How and where did you get it?"

I cleared my throat. "Toys R Us."

Griffin's eyebrows arched in shock before he laughed. "Clever, however, you were lucky. If the bluff had failed, he could have killed you." He shifted in his chair and continued. "Domestic violence is a felony, thanks to President Reagan's Administration." He readjusted his glasses before continuing. "You know, Penne, there was a time in this country when it was considered okay for a man to beat his wife or any woman. And there are still people out there who continue to harbor that misconception. If you are not already aware of it, there are numerous organizations which will help you and your children through this and get you back on your feet. Safely. Contact the National Domestic Violence Hotline. They can help you immensely."

"Thank you," I said. "I do want to see a good counselor and one for the children as well. I'm certain they feel as bitter and frightened as I do.

He nodded. "My office will provide you with a list."

"On the issue of child and spousal support, we will base it on his current income. I will also petition the court for him to provide medical insurance for the children until they turn eighteen." He paused then asked, "Have you listed your house yet?"

"No. I meet with the agent tomorrow; however, I know it will be difficult to get him to sign the agreement. As the financial documents show, neither he nor I can afford to keep the house."

He rubbed his chin. "I will need to review all your documents before I can advise you on that one."

The clock was ticking. Billable hours were accumulating so I pushed forward. "Now, about the divorce. Do I file on grounds of abuse?"

"No. California is a no grounds state. The dissolution of marriage will be filed under irreconcilable differences."

"Such an innocuous banner," I said, "considering the truth is that our irreconcilable differences were that he wanted me dead and I wanted to live."

"One more thing before you leaves. Make certain you have other adults in the house when he comes to pick up his belongings. That date will be set by the court. He will not be permitted to come at will, nor can he remove anything beyond the list approved by the judge."

I shook my head. "He already has. He's taken the best years of my life."

"Not really," he said as he stood up. "I think you'll find the best years of your life are yet to come."

When the paperwork was completed, I stood up and shook his hand. "Thank you, Mr. Griffin."

CHAPTER 24

I left the attorney's office in a dead run. It was not the day to be late picking up the children from school. But I had told them just to wait for me in front of the school in the event that happened and made certain they understood they were not to walk home.

"You look nice," Stephanie said as she jumped in the car. "I like you in a suit."

"Thank you, sweetheart. How do you feel?"

"Much better. I even ate the lunch you packed and felt fine. Sure better than yesterday." She was silent for a moment then asked, "Is Dad still home?"

"Don't know, baby. I left when you did. We'll see soon enough," I said.

When I pulled up to get Bridget, I started shaking on the inside and willed myself to settle down. "Hi sweetie," I said as she climbed in the back seat. "How was school?"

"Great. Got lots of A's." She paused and I knew what she was going to ask. "Is he still home, Mom?"

"Don't know, baby. But just stay calm. This will all be over very soon."

Don was in the front yard fixing sprinkler heads in his impeccably groomed lawn. He saw us pull in and immediately stopped working. His shirt was soaked in sweat and a handkerchief was tied around his forehead like he was filming Rambo. A cigarette dangled from his lips as he walked in an angry gait toward the drive. I quickly got out of the car. "Go inside kids," I said. "I'll be in shortly."

He charged toward the drive. "Where in the hell have you been?" he snarled, and stomped his cigarette on the drive. "You've been gone all day. And what's with the goddamn suit?"

I stood face to face. "It's over," I said. "I filed for divorce this morning." I watched his mouth drop open like a baby bird. "And if you don't want to incur further problems with the law, I suggest you pack and leave."

Relieved but quivering, I walked into the house and busied myself by cleaning up the kitchen still dressed in the suit. He had obviously fixed a big breakfast for himself and cleaning up was not part of his executive nature unless he was trying to impress guests. Toast crumbs were scattered across the counters like ants. Uncooked egg yolks coated the stove top.

Suddenly I heard the side door slam. Don charged into the kitchen. "What kind of garbage are you pulling?" The veins in his head pulsated and his forehead was etched in crinkle-cut wrinkles. Without warning, he grabbed a knife off the counter and came toward me.

An almost mystical calm shrouded my body. I didn't cry or cower. I didn't scream. I just stood there unflinchingly, fearless, my arms folded in defiance, playing Russian roulette with my life.

Don's hand began trembling and he backed up slowly. He tossed the knife to the floor and stomped down the hall to the bedroom and slammed the door.

An hour later he walked out, showered, dressed in a suit, with a garment bag flung over his shoulder. His eyes were red, swollen. He passed me in the kitchen then took a step backward. "You're an ass. You'll never make it without me. And I can guarantee you'll never get the kids!" He paused, then added, I have no intention of paying you one nickel. You're going to be the sorriest woman who ever walked the face of this earth."

"Been there, done that," I said softly.

I listened for his car to pull out and went back to the bedroom. Shredded flowers littered the carpet like pastel ashes. And his wedding ring, which he hadn't worn in years, was firmly anchored to my pillow by the blade point of his old Army knife.

I leaned against the bedroom door. I was standing on the edge of the unknown now and would have to trust the fact that the changes I had cowered from for so long would bring with it the opportunity for new and challenging adventures not yet visible. The measure of sadness I felt was not because it was over, but because it should never had lasted so long.

June 1985

When the house sold, Don showed up the day escrow closed. We stood at the front door as he was not permitted entry. "I'm going to pick up the check," he said. "We can sit down and decide the amount each of us will get."

I laughed. "There is nothing to discuss. The remaining funds were split 50/50."

He slammed his hand against the wall. "That's not what I wanted," he said.

I shook my head. "This was not about what you wanted, Don. It was a court order."

"You won't see one dime of those proceeds," he snapped. "I'm depositing the entire sum in my account. You'll just have to wait for whatever portion I decide to give you, if I give you anything at all."

I laughed out loud. "Too late. I already deposited my half."

"You forged my name to a check? Guess who's going to be in trouble with the law."

"Oh, let me guess. Could it be you? I endorsed the back of the check made payable only to me. Yours is still at the escrow office," I said with a smile.

"If you saw it, Penelope, who was it made payable to?"

I tapped my index finger on my chin in thought. "I believe it said 'Payable to An unrepentant husband and father.' Now if you'll excuse me, I have a lot of packing to do. Isn't moving wonderful?"

He stormed down the walk to his car. I heard his tires screech as he left the drive for what I knew would be the last time.

CHAPTER 25

$\mathcal{T}$he children and I shoe-horned our furnishings into a two bedroom townhouse. It wasn't the luxury we had had before, but luxury with fear was emotional poverty anyway. Awarded custodial custody of the children and sharing financial responsibilities for their care, I was relieved that Stephanie and Bridget were finally free to live in the peace they had always deserved; we all deserved.

Money realized from the sale of the house was enough to keep us going until I moved up in my job. The construction company I worked for was promising and my duties at that moment were clerical. But I could see room for me at the top and I focused on getting there. Soon.

June 1988

The grant deed for our new home was framed and hung on the wall in my bedroom. Title to the house was held by me, an unmarried woman. Although it was half the size of the larger home, it was ours. We had a good sized kitchen and dining room which always seemed to be filled with the girl's friends. There were three bedrooms and two and a half baths. It needed work but as an officer of the company now, the repairs were not too difficult or costly to arrange.

We still lived in the same part of town, the addresses of each residence so close I was able to keep the same telephone number we had had since we moved to California. How strange, I thought, as I sat at my kitchen table and looked out at the front yard, to have moved down from the pricey hills to a townhouse, and then to buy a house which was on the way back up the hill again. *Progress,* I thought. *Wasn't it wonderful?*

February 1989

I was sitting up in bed reading one night when Stephanie walked into my room glowing. She walked over to the bed and held out her left hand. A small diamond glittered under my lamp.

"You're engaged?" Of course I cried. It was a surprise. She had dated so many guys I was never certain the same one would return for another date. We hugged and I had to bite my tongue. "You're sure?" I asked her. "You're only going to be nineteen. And college? Are you sure you don't want to continue?"

She smiled. "I'm sure, Mom. I know what I want. He loves me and I love him. We want a happy, loving family. And that will happen with him. We have a mutual respect for each other."

May 1989

"I'm so impressed with what you have accomplished in a few years," Dad said.

"Me too," I answered as I finished clearing the dinner dishes from the table. "I'm really elated you and Mom could fly out for Stephie's wedding. It means so much to her."

Dad stood next to me, dried the last dish and put it away. "I should warn you," he said, while Mom was in the bathroom. "Your mother is going to try and push you into moving back east."

I reached up and took his face in my hands. "I knew she would. But I understand. I just hope she will understand that I have made a new life for myself and moving would be the last thing I would consider, at least for now."

He had mellowed so much and I noticed that his mind was not as clear as it used to be. He had also become very anxious whenever my mother left the room. Mom had privately told me he could not walk Stephie down the aisle as he had become too disoriented. Perhaps it was retirement, I thought. But I knew better. I had to accept that the aging process would always create changes.

He hugged me gently. "You'll always be my Pennycat."

Stephanie's wedding day bloomed bright and beautiful and a azure blue sky put a heavenly dome over the spring lushness of California as if God had been on the decorating committee for her big day. When that all too familiar sound of the Wedding March filled the church, I was standing by my daughter, ready to walk her down the aisle. I had asked her if she wanted her father to give her away but she declined saying, "He gave me away once. He doesn't get a second chance."

Bridget led the procession, proudly leading her sister down the aisle as her maid of honor. She was almost six feet tall and held her head high. A senior in high school, she had become an elegant young woman of character.

The flowing swirl of pastel greens and blues of her gown enhanced Bridget's golden skin.

Stephie was a princess in white who had grown into a beautiful, intelligent woman with purpose, despite all the reasons she had had, not to.

We reached the altar and light tears dripped down my cheeks. I squeezed Stephie's hand as she moved to stand beside her groom.

Parenting was still a matter of deep love and pride. And this time, it was all mine.

After a dizzying day of wedding festivities, Mom, Dad and I sat in my dining room relaxing with tea and cake.

"Why wasn't Victoria at the wedding?" Mom asked. "Don't you talk to her anymore?

I put my fork down. "Sometimes. But she's grappling with some difficult things right now. Don is still her brother. We didn't want to put her in a position of choosing sides. She knew Don was not invited."

"Do you hear from him?" she asked.

"Only by check," I giggled. "He married his right hand girl Kathy shortly after our divorce. They have a child and he has a new life."

"Do the girls see him?"

"They did when they were younger. But not so often anymore. He only contacts them when he can blow his own horn. But the girls have adjusted, perhaps better than I did."

Mom shook her head. "I can see Stephanie has. But Bridget is so quiet I worry about her and what she's feeling."

"Wait here a minute," I said and left the table. I returned quickly and placed a letter in front of Mom. Dad scooted his chair around so he could read along with her.

"Bridget wrote this just after the divorce when Don had phoned her to tell her about his latest promotion and marriage and she was apparently rude to him on the phone. I was at work when it happened." I paused, and then added, "I wasn't sure my power of positive thinking had worked with Bridget until I read her letter."

"And you didn't mail it?" Dad asked.

I laughed. "Of course I did. This is just a copy."

Dear Dad:

This is not a letter of apology because I have nothing to apologize for. Congratulations. I hope you are happy with your new promotion, but more important, I do hope in time you will open your head and heart to the reason you lost three of the best people you will ever have the blessing to have had as your own.

When I was little I used to stay awake listening to you and Mom fighting, wishing, praying, it was just a bad dream. But when I would wake up the next morning to find my mother covered in bruises, beaten by a man whom I am supposed to love, it made me sick.

You have made me cry myself to sleep for too long. The day that my mother divorced you was the best day of my life. She deserves better than you; she deserves to have the world handed to her for what she put up with for so long.

I only wish that you were man enough to apologize for the hell that you put all of us through, but I must accept the fact that you never will. I think you know now why I never want to see you again or your new wife, which I hope you learn to treat with love. Please Dad, I beg of you, make a good life for yourself and don't screw it up as you did with us.

The reason I am writing this letter is in the hope that you can learn from your unforgivable mistakes in the past. Learn to care for your new wife and baby and be sure to tell the new ones you love, that you do love them, not just in words but actions. After all of this you must realize how much I loathe you. But for some strange reason, I love you very much as well and hope you will seek help for the sickness inside you. Make this one count, Dad. After writing this letter to you, even though you destroyed my childhood, I realize at thirteen, I am a bigger person than you have been or ever will be. Bridget.

"Bless her heart," my father said. "And he doesn't contact them now?"

"Only on rare occasions. With him, parenting is still a matter of convenience. His."

Mother pushed her chair back from the table, stood and walked over behind my chair and kissed my cheek. "And how about you, honey? How are you dealing with the anger, grief?"

I closed one eye and looked at her to see if she was ready for my announcement. "Very well, actually. I'm working on a book based on the diary I kept on spousal abuse. I want to help others."

I watched Mom roll her eyes at Dad. "Oh dear, I'm afraid of how that might affect the children, all of us, airing dirty laundry like that."

She put her hands in her lap and began twisting the ends of a lace handkerchief. I saw the same furrowed brow on her face which was reminiscent of the past. *My little white-haired mom,* I thought. I couldn't let her suffer anymore.

I stood up, walked behind her chair and draped my arms gently around her neck. "Don't worry, Mom. Concentrate on the fact that there are abused and battered women all over the world. I want to help them through this book. The story is true but I changed all the names."

I paused for a moment then asked her, "What would you like your name to be?"

---The End---

EPILOGUE

We have come a long way in dealing with
domestic violence. Millions of women around the world
have been abused. But anyone trapped in such a
relationship has the power within to reach out and seek
help. It is there for the asking. Don't delay.
You deserve to live in peace

CONTACTS

National Domestic Violence Hotline

Email: www.ndvh.org

Toll Free Number: 1-800-799-SAFE

National Council on Child Abuse and Family Violence

Email: www.info@nccafv.org

Phone No: 1-202-429-6695

PLEASE CHECK YOUR STATE SERVICES.
THEY ARE THERE TO HELP YOU.

ACKNOWLEDGEMENTS:

Special thanks to: Valerie Pledger, who spent hours editing the manuscript; Susan Montenegro who has encouraged me for over twenty years; to my brothers and sisters who were always there for me and my children who have been my inspiration for so very long. Bless you all for your love and support.

Made in the USA
Charleston, SC
24 January 2015